The American Imagination

The American Imagination

Imagination

A Critical Survey
of the Arts
from
The Times Literary Supplement

WITH A FOREWORD BY
ALAN PRYCE-JONES

New York ATHENEUM *Publishers*

1960

© The Times Publishing Company Limited, 1959
First published in *The Times Literary Supplement*, 1959
Foreword © Alan Pryce-Jones 1960

First published in this edition 1960

Printed in Great Britain by
Cox & Wyman Limited, London, Fakenham and Reading

FOREWORD
BY
ALAN PRYCE-JONES

The American Imagination

Some years ago *The Times Literary Supplement* published a special number on American writing. This was conceived with a two-fold purpose. On the one hand, American writing has had so deep an influence on European letters during the last half-century that it seemed time to pay American writers due tribute as innovators and stimulants; on the other, it may be necessary to explain to British readers some of the misconceptions which arise from the fact that our two nations speak the same language—on the surface.

Both these objects are full of pitfalls. I remember the first time I spent any length of time in the United States being struck by the wide divisions which lie beneath an apparently identical language as written on either side of the Atlantic. Even the later style of Henry James— which in England is heavily parenthetical and slowed down almost to stopping-point by a kind of convoluted and agonized precision— sounds very much easier in New York: it is the rhythm of a great many elderly Americans telling a story. In the same way, an English voice, which at the worst has an Oxford edge to it at home, suddenly becomes of an extreme apparent affectation in Chicago. And these are only two examples of the simplest mechanics of literature: a written and a spoken style have a totally different effect on their readers and hearers simply through a geographical change of environment. How much worse, then, are the subtleties of language. Can we ever be sure that what we see in Scott Fitzgerald or Hemingway, what our American friends see in Evelyn Waugh and Edith Sitwell, is what those writers intended? I found, by experience, that it was essential for both parties to give their contemporary literatures an explanatory setting before they became fully understandable.

This time, we have trailed our coat still farther. For it became clear that to isolate books from other expressions of the American—or any other—imagination was to narrow the examination too closely. So, by extending our plan to cover the subject entire, we expose ourselves to added dangers. A national imagination is a fundamental thing. It lies in immediate contact with the heart and the mind of a people; and in the case of America it is not anything as close-knit as the imagination of an European civilization. What makes the spectacle of America so rich is that every aspect of American life has at least two faces: it is both American and—in its origin or its destination—something else: Polish, perhaps, or Jewish or Italian. Where, for instance, does someone like Berenson ultimately belong? To his native Lithuania, or to New England which moulded his youth, or to Florence which cherished his old age? He is only one of many. Round Eliot and Auden, round Balanchine and Menotti, the same arguments can be raised. And in every case, beside the second element, they will be found at some point profoundly American. The term 'English' is commonly used to cover a fairly small range of possibilities, of which true Englishness is among the rarest. It means a mixture of England, Wales, Scotland, Ireland: and almost certainly some Continental strain—be it only Norman or Jute—as well. But into the American continent a whole world has been poured, and the miracle is that such multifarious ancestors so regularly lead towards the same family pattern.

Trying to discern an American imagination at work is therefore a dangerous enterprise. For it is both easy and logical to dismiss most of its workings as not typically American. Yet the true genius of America has only come to fruition since the age of large-scale immigration. The more extravagantly fresh comers have grafted their own cultures on to old settler stock the more the American imagination has blossomed, and the more vividly American it has become. This paradox has prompted the articles which are here united into a book; and if someone objects that it might have been better to choose quite other aspects of the subject, our retort must be that we are dealing with a theme as wide as the world itself; and that we have had to select and condense the body of our evidence in the light of a single—and not perhaps the only possible—idea of what American culture has created since the beginning of the century.

A positive claim to define and analyse so vast a subject would be presumptuous; but in spite of limitations of scale due to the fact that these articles were originally conceived as a supplement to a weekly paper, a good deal that is positive can be extracted from them. Above all, I think, the vitality of the American imagination is established. In whatever field it asserts itself it is never acquiescent, never merely respectful. As soon as the danger-signal goes up, some irreverent talent always springs to life in mockery of what might threaten to be an Establishment. In painting, in music, in writing alike, the practitioners have to keep on their toes or perish: it is one practical advantage of the American quality of being easily bored.

We have not paid the American imagination the false compliment of withholding criticism. On balance, however, there is far more to praise than to blame, to envy than to regret, in the American world of the humanities. Perhaps we have given too much space to subjects which complement our own skills: to the Beatniks, for instance, who have no wide scope or aim, but appear from a distance all the more sympathetic for the despairing protests they have raised against flaws in society which can be recognized throughout the Western world but which are too easily accepted as an inevitable part of the pattern of things. The American imagination uses one great outlet which, for the rest of us, carries less and less traffic in each generation: a keen sense of irony. Americans are much better than most people at laughing at themselves. And so, wherever we have perceived it we have called attention to this sardonic vein in the hope that it may act as a stimulus here at home. I need only lay side by side copies of *Punch* and *The New Yorker* for this particular divergence in our national imaginations to be perfectly plain.

I had not anticipated that this symposium would one day attain to the dignity of a book. Well, it has done so; and I, and those who contribute to it must feel that at least we have raised a cheer for a good cause. And be proud of that.

Alan Pryce-Jones

Contents

CONTENTS

Taking Stock

'The American Imagination' is a bold phrase, and it is a hardy man who tries to define it. The noun is perplexing and the adjective anomalous. There must be an imagination: Coleridge has said so! but what psychologist would be impressed? The psychologist himself discusses it seldom, and then with caution. The students of the behavioural sciences in general, sober men, write little about it. Beneath their feet they glimpse the depths of Freud and Jung; the prospect, if not dismaying, is thought-provoking. Modern writers about literature and the arts prove almost as wary. Only the fact that they have less information than the behavioural scientist induces them to speculate more. And even that is not much. How little they have to tell us is hard to realize until we contrast the mutterings of to-day with the tumult of talk in Coleridge's time. To-day's philosophers, lastly, have spoken more often than the literary critics, and their approach has been more systematic. Notwithstanding, the result has been much the same.

The idea of an 'American' imagination has received still less notice. However, the general belief in national characteristics—in things American or Spanish or French—has always been strong. Though racialists and propagandists have often used the belief for their own bad purposes, the idea is innocent enough. It has been found in the past in some very good historical writing and continues to be found to-day. If it does not appear there as a formally stated theory, it is evident as a working premise.

In addition to enduring among historians, the idea is quietly coming back into the thinking of certain important, if at times ponderous, social scientists. As one of them has noted, 'Rorschach series from different societies reveal different norms for such series as wholes.' The most interesting study of national character published since the war is *People of Plenty*, by the American historian David Potter, who happens to be far from ponderous. He has not only synthesized the previous writing on the subject but has brilliantly analysed one element, economic abundance, to show how it has helped to form the American character.

Anyone who has known more than one country can testify that national characteristics exist. Of course all Italians are not mercurial; all Englishmen are not reserved. But differences abound. Eat a meal in a Roman restaurant and then dine out in London: the two experiences are indeed unlike. Life in a *pensione* varies from life in a New England farmhouse. Whether it is environment or heredity, or both, that makes the variation no one knows; it need not be argued here. The point is that, regardless of what creates them, national differences flourish; and it is surely not illogical to argue that those differences also are to be found in the imagination. This means, then, that there is an American imagination as distinct from, say, the Italian imagination or the French or even the English imagination. Once granted that it does exist, what is it like? In particular, what is it like now? Any answer is bound to be suspect; any generalization will invite dissent. Nevertheless, experience can be interpreted, and some suggestions can be made.

The better to see the American imagination, we might look first at those elements in the American experience which appear closest to it.

The land itself is the most massive fact and the best one to begin with. A map of the United States tells as much, in some ways, as a book about its history. Anyone who has not crossed the ocean should be reminded of the sheer size and variety of the American land. There is nearly enough desert, complete with cactus and sandstorm, to make a country as large as England. There are more than enough mountain ranges to do the same thing. And especially in the Middle West there is enough rich black soil to arouse the envy of all the farmers from Cornwall to Cumberland. Nowadays you can fly quickly enough over those three million square miles of plain, mountain and desert, but it still takes a long time to drive through them. And all this land has, at one time or another in the short span of American history, been there for the taking. There have always been more acres than persons to live on them.

2

Take this rich and various terrain, and add the many kinds of immigrants who have peopled it. They would be as varied as the land itself: gentlemen and bond-servants, Calvinists and Quakers, burghers and criminals. But there would be some common denominators. Among those, obviously, would be the general determination of the immigrants to better their lot by leaving their homeland instead of quietly enduring conditions there, and—though this is impossible to prove— probably a restlessness that made it easier for them to move across the ocean. Add enough hardship, when America was reached, so that activity was stimulated and resourcefulness required. And then add a shortage of man-power and a need to conserve it; and the main ingredients are present for an American vitality which few observers have denied.

Of course the individual thrived. He was needed and his importance was recognized. It did not take the rulers of Massachusetts Bay very long to ignore such British law as prescribed the maiming of a man. Similarly, capital punishment became far rarer in New England than in Old. There were dozens of other ways as well in which the individual realized his self-respect. And if the newcomer did not feel satisfied with New England, for instance, he could always move farther west. He could go to the frontier, take up free land there, and grow with the country. He could grow as America was growing. Land would normally appreciate, trade would increase, and his own status improve. The rewards for energy were, as a rule, greater here than in any other country in the western world. America was a favoured nation; no wonder its vigour was manifest.

This happy climate for American vitality continued until the twentieth century. America had its wars and its depressions, but not until 1929 did individual enterprise suffer a severe blow. After that, however, the country had ten years in which to learn that progress was a myth, that business did not inevitably become bigger and better, that hard work would not always bring success. And the country did learn something. Then the Second World War taught a few new lessons; so did the stalemated Korean war; and so did the Russian earth satellite. Yet in spite of these checks, the American tradition of ambition and aggressiveness remains. And there lies a great problem. Most Americans are still affected by the expectation, still imbedded in the folk feeling, that progress is not only possible but proper and that they should compete against their fellows and surpass their elders. By now, in actuality, they cannot. The conditions of land and culture that favoured their fathers and grandfathers have disappeared. In their place are different ones, often kindly enough but not what America has always expected. Out of this drive for a success which seldom can be achieved has grown a good deal of American pessimism, disillusion, and insecurity. As one American psychiatrist has said of many of his patients, they 'are driven by a relentless competitiveness in any given field and are at the same time afraid and wearied by this strenuous life of race and struggle'.

Here, then, is one of the great contradictions in the American experience. And its results will often be found in American arts and letters. Side by side with vigour will be morbidity; action will be matched with frustration; death will deny life. This will surely be true at both the conscious and the subconscious levels of the American experience and will be similarly evidenced in both levels of the American imagination. It is to the most important manifestations of this imagination that we come now.

American architecture is a particularly good place to start. In his lively book of a few months ago, *Architecture USA*, Ian McCallum maintains that three conditions for great architecture are to be found at their best in the United States. As he phrases it, these are 'a prosperous and lively building industry, creative freedom, and a conspicuous expenditure'; but they are also, surely, forms of the American abundance, energy, and variety which we have spoken of before. Suppose we look at just one type of building, the single-family dwelling. True, many an American suburb has its rows of brick or wooden boxes, all alike and all built by the same callous promoter. But there is likewise a multitude of houses in different styles. Half a dozen great architects, native or immigrant, have put the impress of their thought on the American home. Wright, Neutra, Paul Rudolph, and Gropius are outstanding. Their houses spread or soar, lie in long planes or stand high. But the one characteristic they have in common is that they invite the outside in. The big picture window is so nearly universal that it is easy to deride. But its openness, its willingness to dispense with privacy, puts it at the opposite extreme from the English house with its walls within walls and its front door without a door knob.

Within, as well, the space is apt to be free-flowing. The living-room and dining-room may be the two legs of an L, instead of separate compartments. The interior walls may be lattices or fences, and the space they enclose only partly private. In the bedrooms alone will the English home-owner find the seclusion he has always insisted on. And even when the English architect attempts to plan a modern dwelling, his client is apt to interfere, while the local council raises its clenched hand against novelty. One of the clearest illustrations of a difference in cultures is provided by the houses going up in America now as compared with those being erected here. The same thing is true for other kinds of building. The variety and splendour of New York's latest skyscrapers amaze the visitor; they are in sharp contrast to the great brick squares which are going up in the West End of London.

The outburst of American abstract art is an almost equally clear result of the current cultural environment. Some of this art is so extreme, so experimental, as to be either lunatic or a stunt. But when the painters who paint with their elbows have been eliminated, there remain a number of American experimenters who have genuinely extended the range of paint on canvas. Jackson Pollock has been the most prominent. Easy to caricature as he dripped his house paint on long pieces of cloth, he still provokes the conservative critics either to outrage or amusement. A serious evaluation of his work, however, such as the Whitechapel show allowed last winter, is all in his favour. His light, elegant swirls of colour, in their repeated designs, have warmth and dignity. They are not a representation nor do they have the expected centripetal pattern; but they are pleasing enough to justify a permanent place in the art collections and in the history of American art. At the moment his canvases are certainly the most influential of any American's. His mark can be seen on paintings as different as those by Sam Francis and Bradley Tomlin.

In his own way Clyfford Still is as indicative as Pollock. He represents the frustrations of American life as well as the individualism pushed to such an extreme that the artist no longer cares to communicate. 'Demands for communication', Still says, 'are both presumptuous and irrelevant.' Yet his canvases, with their huge, apparently random patches of colour, have a good deal to tell. They are works of art in their own right. His *Number 2*, for instance, looks at first simply like splotches of maroon and black on a red background. But study will show a satisfying balance in the composition and in its strong colours. And there is an American amplitude, not merely in the size of the painting but also in the design. For the frame does not contain the picture. The colours and pattern lead the eye up and down the wall, and across it on either side. The wall is itself engaged and dominated by the painting. Nearly all earlier painting has been centripetal in its pattern; *Number 2* is powerfully centrifugal (Pollock's paintings are neither). In its way it, too, is a sign of energy, abundance and creative originality.

American music is neither as brilliant nor as original as American art. Except in its most famous form: jazz. Descended from the music brought by slaves from Africa, it still stands for the dark side of the American experience. It has known many changes and none more significant than those of this century. In two American cities, New Orleans first, and then the Chicago of the 1930s, it found itself and became the music now played throughout much of the world. Its driving rhythms attest to American vitality; its free-wheeling instrumental solos to American individualism. But the key for jazz is minor rather than major. Its wailing strains, its feverishness, its cellar atmosphere are all the heritage of denial. The Negro has long known the frustration which the white American to-day is feeling; jazz is perhaps its main artistic expression.

The merits of serious American music are, on the whole, of the same kind as those of American art, but they are not so pronounced. The works of Aaron Copland and Charles Ives have a place in the music of the world though they are performed less often than one might wish. Among the younger composers Samuel Barber is probably the most popular; his 'Medea's Meditation and Dance of Vengeance' was played in the season of 1956-7, for instance, by ten out of the thirty-one American symphony orchestras performing then. William Schuman, with his 'New England Triptych', came second only to Barber in the same season. These men are notable, serious composers. For sheer virtuosity and range, however, they are surpassed by Leonard Bernstein. He has written the music for films, ballets, musical comedies, and for an opera. He has two exceptional symphonies to his credit, 'Jeremiah' and 'The Age of Anxiety'. The second offers an especially good illustration of his experimentalism, since it is written in a jazz idiom and uses the twelve-tone scale.

Some of the happiest of Bernstein's composing has been done for musical comedy. And it is actually this form, with its marriage of melody, book, and movement, which represents the most widely admired American venture into the arts. Bernstein's music for *Candide* matches the mood of the action and indeed often sets it. His versatility is remarkable, though he has been criticized for parodying the music of others and so making *Candide*, in particular, the less original because of it. His is the music, too, for the remarkable *West Side Story*. Yet, good as that music is, it is overshadowed by the strikingly effective dancing, which constitutes in itself another success of the imagination.

Dance as dance and not merely a series of steps has come into its own on the American stage only in the past twenty years. The pioneer was Agnes de Mille. Her ballets for *Oklahoma* set a style that is still not outdated, and nearly every popular musical comedy now has its big ballet number. *West Side Story* is in a sense an extended ballet. In New York gangs dance with a vigour and flexibility without the slightest need for prettiness. The leading creators of musical comedy have been the composer Richard Rodgers and his distinguished librettist Oscar Hammerstein. Their successes, which started with *Oklahoma* and have by no means ended yet, include *South Pacific* and *The King and I*. However, these men are only the leaders in a brilliant company, others of whom are responsible for *My Fair Lady*, *The Pajama Game*, and many more. That the stories on which the comedies are based come from without is often true; but the synthesis is clearly original.

The dark side of the American experience reappears in American drama. The plays of the leading dramatist of to-day, Tennessee Williams, dwell on themes of frustration and despair. Their setting is always the most troubled part of the United States, the South. The most notable of his plays are *The Glass Menagerie* and *A Streetcar Named Desire*. Their techniques are remarkable for originality, for invention. Symbols appear often, and successful liberties are taken with the standard dramatic forms and staging. Williams does not go as far as Samuel Beckett or other writers of the anti-drama, but he continues the habit, started by Eugene O'Neill, of widening the ways to present a play. The other outstanding playwrights, Arthur Miller and William Inge, stay in the tradition of the well-made play; their originality lies in the development of facets of the American character.

Of all that the American imagination has created, American literature is perhaps the most impressive. Both poetry and prose are striking. If we compare the work of contemporary American poets with that of contemporary English poets, there is a contrast almost as strong as in architecture. With this difference, however: contemporary English

7

architecture is weak; but contemporary English poetry is not weak, it is modest. The English poet of this decade writes in a moderate tone, restrains his feelings, and strives for an almost neo-classical effect. He moves his reader by deficiency rather than excess. Philip Larkin is possibly the best English poet now at work, and his verse is characterized by quiet self-depreciation and pensive clarity. He is effective enough to make many an American poet sound hoarse or shrill.

Notwithstanding, an American vitality is to be seen in the lines of a dozen of the best poets in the United States. In many cases the vitality is tense; often its expression is obscure. But the vigour is there. So is the experimentalism. New forms, new combinations of words and emotions frequently appear in the so-called little magazines. The resources of the word are pushed as far as intention can push them. The imagery is often thick and clotted; sometimes after a few pages of it one wishes heartily for Larkin or Ted Hughes. The most respected American poets make their own sense, however, and time has already seen it appreciated. The early poems of Karl Shapiro and Robert Lowell, the recent ones of Theodore Roethke and Stanley Kunitz, have an organic form and inner logic. Sometimes they demand a fresh approach by the reader; though it may be given reluctantly, its results are often good.

The obscurity of much American verse is significant. It stands not only for the fact that words cannot bear all the meaning one would like to give them. It also represents the isolation of the individual, the man so far away from society that he no longer cares to talk with his fellows. This is the recoil against American openness and neighbourliness. More than one American poet would agree with Clyfford Still that communication was not important. The result is a loss to both sides, and the blame for it must be shared by most Americans because of their indifference to poetry. The English poet is better off. One of the reasons, no doubt, that he speaks clearly is that he feels that readers are waiting to understand. Many an American poet feels that he is writing in a wilderness with himself as his only audience.

But all this has its exceptions, and for American poetry the noblest is in the poems of Robert Frost. Abounding energy, long-continued, characterizes his work; but the energy is not feverish, it is almost classic in its control. The idiom is strictly his own. It is New England speech but raised beyond any geographical bounds. His view of life is Olympian in its wisdom and yet is marked both by sympathy and a sense of sin and evil. The sympathy is there often—in 'The Death of the Hired Man', for example—but sin appears seldom. Yet sin and evil have their place and are the stuff out of which such a baleful little poem as 'Design' is made.

It might well be argued that Frost is now the greatest poet writing in English. The greatest novelist, though this is more debatable, is possibly William Faulkner. They both explore the range of American character but their emphases are exactly opposite. For Faulkner, unlike Frost, stresses the morbid, the isolated, the lurid. But his work, too, has an American variety. The range of his novels is considerable. The summertime sadness and clarity of plot in *Sartoris* are far removed from the powerful, intricate fiction of *Absalom, Absalom!* The story of Bayard Sartoris is told in a straight line, while Quentin Compson's discovery of the meaning of the past in *Absalom* is effected through the interweaving of three different points of view and the frequent use of a complicated interior monologue. Tone and temper, too, vary in the novels of Faulkner; nevertheless, the stamp is always his own. His vitality is reflected not only in his quarter-century of sustained writing but in his creation of a whole county—much more than a microcosm—in Mississippi for his characters to live in. Yoknapatawpha County is William Faulkner's just as much as if he had homesteaded there and proved his claim.

Among the remaining novelists of importance, Hemingway is still the first. After him come several others, all writing books with vitality to them. In most cases the vitality is accompanied by a sombreness of subject, for the characteristic American fiction of to-day is dark. The frustration and insecurity mentioned before are stronger stuff for the novelist than the brighter side of life; and often his own rebellion is reflected in his books. The novelist who has gone farthest in repudiating the traditional, and now unrealistic, American scale of values is Jack Kerouac. To him progress, hard work, and morality are in their various ways nonsense. He detests the top of American life and prefers to be at the bottom, looking up. His characters live a life of negation, and are positive about it. *On the Road* is his best novel so far. It is the essence of this negativity which the twentieth century has developed. But the book also has as one of its major themes the restlessness Tocqueville remarked in Americans a century and a quarter ago. Kerouac's Dean Moriarty is always driving headlong from one side of the country to the other. His search for what he calls his kicks sends him on to the highways. He pushes his automobiles to a steady 110, never really sure of his destination.

The group of San Francisco writers, of whom Kerouac is by far the best, have attracted a good deal of attention. Some of it has been undeserved. However, they are entitled to a place, if a limited one, in any study of the American imagination of to-day.

And that imagination has its deficiencies, without doubt. It is sometimes grotesque, often naïve. But it is never pale, never passive. It has the vigour, the variety, and the creativity to justify anyone's attention.

Jumbo Fish-tails

Just as the Scaliger fish-tails fret the battlements of North Italian buildings with the symbolic tooth-marks of one particular family biting magnificently at the Lombard sky, so in contemporary America a fish-tail of different shape has come to symbolize, in recent years, a particular and characteristic yearning. This American fish-tail is most readily seen in the shape of those great rudder fins, larger every year, which sprout from the sterns of Cadillacs to support ever more monstrous red rear-lamps. In London, you may study them in and around Grosvenor Square. In the United States they leap backwards from taxicabs and super-automobiles with impartial splendour. They are useless, absurd, vaguely attractive. Most Americans laugh at them. Every American finds them on his new car, whether he wants them or not. They are great slabs of 'extra', semi-humorous tributes to the spirit of 'Jumbo'. It would be as futile to search for a new American car without fish-tails as it would be to seek out an American shrimp that was not Jumbo-sized.

With a rumbustious good nature so characteristic of American life, the Jumbo embodiment of the Jumbo imagination quickly becomes commonplace—and common property. The rich do not try to prevent you and me from wagging our own fish-tails on our more modestly priced (but equally magnificent-looking) Plymouths and Chevrolets. They simply make their fish-tails larger still, until some new gimmick comes along to replace them. Within a couple of years there will be some new differential. What will it be? Pink tyres? Shirts with diagonal stripes? Calorie-free champagne? Whatever it is, it will in turn, like the rarest products of higher education, soon become regrettably commonplace—and, magnificently, common property.

Meanwhile, it is still the hey-day of the Jumbo fish-tail. Even more striking than those elongated triangles stuck on the backs of cars are the great triangular road-signs sprouting in happy arrogance along the highways, each one the banner for a new example of that splendid American invention, the motel. A few years ago, motels flaunted their variously shaped signals in happy disarray. Then somebody discovered that a remarkable impression of grandeur was achieved by jabbing into the ground a large sign shaped like a carpenter's T-square standing upon its sharpest point. The inner rectangle suggests solid worth: flat sensible top, fine upstanding spine. The sloping side just out over the road in mannered dignity, suggesting all sorts of proud surges: a war-horse, a swan, the prow of a cruiser.

One could hardly find a better symbol for the genial taken-for-granted extravagance of American imagination than the modern motel. Originally conceived as an economical one-night-perch for motor tourists who required only a single cabin, a quick shower, and space for the car, the motel has been blossoming, in tune with the prosperous imagination of post-war America, into a very luxurious perch indeed. In their present glory the motels, laid out invitingly be-hind their Jumbo fish-tail road-signs, are symbols of the mobility, the competition, the comfort and the unease that together make American living so puzzling and so exhilarating. In these days when Fulbright visitors and budget-minded American tourists have taught us that not all Americans are millionaires in sober fact, the motel and all that it represents may well stand as a reminder that the old well-worn theme of size, of broad vision, of boundless possibility, is still the one inescap-able clue to the imagination—and hence the literature—of the United States, to-day as in the days of our grandparents.

All the way down the Atlantic sea-board of Florida, flanking the tail-end of the great highway U.S. One as it rushes on towards Key West, the motor courts grow thicker every hour. The final crescendo of number and magnificence is achieved in and between that string of holiday resorts and ostentatiously 'secluded' homes for the retired rich that culminate in the stupefying Babylon of Miami Beach. The fish-tails outside these palazzi are Jumbo indeed. The jutting pride they embody and the creature comforts they promise tap an even richer vein of suggestion: the *Queen Elizabeth,* the Taj Mahal, Bucentaur.... But, indeed, one need not search for names. The names are already there, blazoned on the fish-tails or winking feebly in neon lights against the

Floridian sun. Some carry the romance of the native American Dream:
Golden Nugget, Sun Ranch, Thunderbird, Colonial Inn, Blue Grass.
Some flaunt names born of the tutelary deities of Florida itself:
Sunaqua, Neptune, Bonaire, Golden Strand. Still others re-create the
splendours of that even more potent American Dream, the gorgeous
Hollywood fabrication of exotic lands and those ultimate goals of the
travel-sated: Bali, Aztec, Safari.

Behind their fish-tails, the entrance halls of these Valhallas blaze out
through walls of glass—each one a match for the Lion and Unicorn
pavilion of the Festival of Britain. Driving past, you may glimpse
other motorists who have at last succumbed to the awful dictates of
choice—for to select one entrancing façade from the rest is to brave
that agony of greed, hope and indecision that will keep a farm-yard
hen in a state of demented bliss when you throw down before her a
repeated cascade of maize: can the next grain possibly be even more
succulent than this one she has almost—but not quite—pecked up?
If you should slow down while quizzing one of these strangely Scandi-
navian pleasure-domes you may catch sight of mural designs representing the title on the heraldic fish-tail: pyramids, mermaids, temples,
a bestiary of fabled creatures. A far cry, all this, from those modest
log-cabins which used to offer the pre-war tourist a haven where he
could unroll his sleeping-bag upon a wire pallet, find water in which
to wash his shirt and a frying-pan in which to cook his frankfurter
sausages. Yet even in these, the collective apotheosis of the motel, you
will find chief among the luxury attractions a curiously abrupt sign
labelled 'Efficiencies', by which token you will learn that your expensive quarters are furnished with reality: reality in the shape of an up-
to-date kitchenette. Inside the 'efficiency', when you have unloaded
your alligator-skin baggage from the hold of your hyacinthine star-
studded land-cruiser, you may (for the outlay of only a few more
dollars) indulge the pleasing fancy that, like your pioneering great-
grandparents, you are still energetically 'roughing it'.

All these wondrous motels, washed up in a glittering silt against the
conurbation of Miami by the stream of traffic flowing down the eastern
seaboard of the United States, prepare the traveller for those more
elaborate palaces still ahead of him. Their curious blending of fragility
and substance, monstrousness and impermanence, attune the mind to
Miami Beach. The motels, to be sure, are only a little way beyond the
sensible. Their glass, their dainty new furniture, their pastel drapes

and interior flood-lighting may add up to a sizeable catalogue of un-reality, especially at night when the moon itself, shining down on these festive courts, seems only another advertising lantern. Yet the people who stay in the motels look real enough. They may be wearing pine-apple shirts and salmon-pink shorts, they may sit about in the cocktail lounges exchanging jokes from the ready-made anthology printed on their paper napkins which are labelled 'You can't beat fun'—but one knows that the wives will soon be busy in the 'efficiencies' and they are all still wearing, in spite of their colourful clothes and their new sun-tan, the purposeful expressions of the northern states. Even the 'You-can't-beat-fun' napkins were printed, one observes, by Beach Products Inc, of Kalamazoo, Michigan.

From Palm Beach southwards, past the modern fables of Lake Worth, Delray Beach, Fort Lauderdale and Golden Beach, the proportion of unreality to reality seems to increase every mile. The transition is tactful and fortifying. Farther north, the marvels are still assimilable. It may be a little odd to see at Juno Beach a formation of some score of pelicans winging across the sands. Mildly disturbing, perhaps, when the pelicans are followed, a moment later, by a jet aircraft skimming the Atlantic breakers. Still more disturbing to know that from a point near Cocoa Beach guided missiles are being shot off down-range over the Caribbean Islands towards Ascension. But pelicans, though un-familiar, are real; and jet bombers are real; and even Ascension Island is known to exist. Between a sky and an ocean so blue, so dreamily yet naturally blue, anything at all may be expected to whizz—and if it should turn out to be a space ship, it is pretty certain that such hard-headed bodies as Pan-American Airways or the Radio Corporation of America will have been popping them off.

Along a road fringed with Nature's astonishing palms and man's astonishing motels, it is perhaps to be expected that the speeding cars, another daily index of the American imagination, should be powder-blue, heliotrope, tan and cream. If, bowling along the same road, one can accept *La Traviata* swirling in from the New York Metropolitan *via* the car radio with as little surprise as the hot breeze from the win-dows, it would surely be pernickety to express shock at a wayside café menu as large as a newspaper, offering green turtle chowder and Jumbo platters of sea-food: Canaveral shrimps, Cape scallops, Balti-more oysters, fingers of red snapper, broiled Florida lobster tails and steamed Maryland soft-shell crabs with garlic butter. The fishy

Atlantic is real enough, even in its holiday dress of blue and green and gold; and so is the sea-food from the Gulf of Mexico on the other side of the peninsula. Florida's marvels are anchored, if only by some wispy platinum chain, in recognizable reality. The motel 'efficiencies' contain ice-boxes; the golden-pile magic carpet is this year's Oldsmobile; the 'planked pompano almondine' was fished out of the Gulf.

It is on the threshold of Miami Beach that reality sickens and all but gives up the struggle. Fantasy takes over. Like yourself, the other visitors have passed at last beyond the clutch of the real world. There they are, sitting on stoeps of gigantic splendour before the pink, pale blue or lime green walls of fairy palaces, but it is idle to pretend that they are real people. Real people do not wear mink stoles on subtropical evenings. These are not motels at all. They are dreams. They have been created by a djinn from the *Arabian Nights*. And yet. . . . Yes, something at last gives the show away. Some familiar shape or movement will wake you up and you will rub your eyes and recognize above a mink stole the face of undeceived America. No doubt about it: the lady's pink plastic sun-glasses guard her eyes not only from the real Florida sun but also from the night glare of Miami Beach— equally real. It is those pink sun-glasses, after all, that give the show away: for at the top of the frame there are two shrimp-coloured fish-tails. Fish-tails! The dream *is* a reality, and the symbol of a dream realized is there to prove it.

What has happened? Where does dream end and reality begin? These mammoth motels: what are they? Is it all just an upsurge of catastrophic ugliness saved only from the absurd by its size, and from despair by its impermanence? Is it the Great Good Place? The American Dream? The American Hell? Hateful? Irresistible? A modern version of tall Brighton as viewed from the Downs on a sunny June afternoon? Is the appropriate cry of recognition: 'Lost! Lost!' Or is it: 'Hurrah!'? Is that man in the rocking-chair a sultan sitting before his palace, or is he a silly old fuddy-duddy who has more money than he knows what to do with? Are the builders of all this just plain crazy, or battening on stupid appetites, or are they designing a world in which man may at last take no thought for the morrow and by imitating Solomon in all his glory become in the end like the true lilies of the field?

Miami Beach, enshrining the reality within the American dream, is

15

all these things—and none of them singly. For it is in effect the ultimate creation (to date) of the world of American advertising. That world is both real and unreal, humane and fraudulent. It starts by inventing a need, then satisfying it—more or less—until the need itself has become real and people find themselves unable to do without something they once knew only in dreams. The unreal, based on dreams that disturb the uneasy slumbers of people who have a restless temperament and an over-full stomach, has been embodied, frozen into actuality. For around and beneath the created, invented realities of the Floridian dream-world lie the original realities of Florida itself— and these, the 'hard facts' of Florida, as of any other state of the Union, can indeed boast elements even stranger than the frozen dreams. One can grow *blasé* about man-made wonders in a natural setting where pink flamingoes stand improbably in the water. A sign inviting the tourist to watch alligators wrestling is quickly taken for granted once the tourist has grown accustomed to the presence of alligators anyway, whether wrestling or not.

So within the mammoth nursery of Florida (chosen as representative of the American dream-world) a visitor must—contradicting St. Paul—put off adult things. It is rude to judge a nursery by non-childish standards. As soon as the traveller has thrown his workaday notions out of the car window, then he may find both good and bad in the dream-world—a dream-world in which genuine articles have been embedded. Alongside Indian River Creek the dream-houses overlook dream-yachts, but also a very utilitarian tanker. Along the preposterous sidewalks of Babylon stand homely hitch-hikers in pale blue jeans. Floating over the neatly tailored lagoon is a dream-balloon, but it advertises Goodyear tyres. As for the spendid MacArthur Causeway linking Miami Beach with its parent city, it is difficult to decide whether the bridge itself or the name it bears enshrines the reality or the dream: the bridge is real, and so is General MacArthur, but once again the collocation takes on a curiously mythical quality. Back along the road near Palm Beach there is the Norton Art Gallery; across on the Gulf coast there is the vast Ringling Museum at Sarasota: in both places the visitor wavers between acceptance and rejection. Had they, these latter-day art saints, come so exhausted upon the field that in their efforts to sweep together something of everything they could find only poor works by good artists or good works by poor artists? Outside, in the sunlight, there is little wit and no malice.

Must one have a flavour of both qualities before Babylon graduates from conurbation to city?

Most instructive of all is the 'placing' of Babylon against its hinterland, the preposterous dream against the preposterous reality. Here, as in a convex mirror, is reflected an essential factor in American culture: the Jumbo imagination sprouting somehow from the Jumbo actual. Across the Everglades the motor road unrolls magnificently over swamps. The finger of metropolitan know-how has reached out to place concrete picnic-tables on the canal banks, where tourists from parked cars may join Seminole Indians fishing idly in the shade of palm trees. Road signs along this strange profusion of vegetable sparsity point ahead to new records, new achievements of enterprise in a world of dreams. 'The world's largest shell factory' awaits your dollars near Fort Myers on the Gulf coast; and when you arrive you will find that American zest, even in the Florida climate, has scooped up shells not only from Florida's beaches but also from all the world's coasts, so that you may admire local industry and still waddle back to your car, like those other dream-land shoppers who bask in the advertisement pages of the *New Yorker,* with convoluted tributes from the shores of China and Peru. Spin the wheel once more, and along the road through Kissimmee and across the waist of Florida you are back again in the exotic actual, where orange groves evoke Andrew Marvell and the very cattle, cropping the prosaic luxuriance of grass, are White Brahmins from India.

Just as the state of Florida makes violent assault upon its visitors, so the comparable physical shocks of the American Union find a parallel in the staggering impact of American confidence—which is as much as to say 'the American imagination'. To-day, one's throat may be choked by an upsurge of: 'Vulgar!' and 'Fake!' and 'Crass!' To-morrow, a group of old wooden fishing-boats in the Caloosahatchee estuary will compose along the Gulf shore so ancient a memory that one speeds across the mile-long bridge, named after Thomas Alva Edison, feeling that American men and American nature have come to wonderful terms. No extravagance of Thomas Wolfe, no symphonies in the Hollywood Bowl, no team of scholars joining hands to edit Milton seems any longer remarkable. Calmed by the knowledge that Floridian egrets are nesting near by, you may forget to sniff at a notice advertising rides in a glades-buggy ('automobiles specially equipped', interprets the guide-book, 'to lumber through

17

the Everglades swamps') and come instead to the conclusion that the men who built a road across this morass and found amusing ways of skimming over its surface are neither fools nor vulgarians.

And there is, in conclusion, one by-product of this Jack-and-the-bean-stalk *donnée* of the American imagination which brings its sprawling fecundity back into a manageable focus for European eyes. By going to all the trouble of making his sham dreams real, the energetic American has made it possible for his more speculative countryman to reap a full harvest of disillusion and thus to prepare himself for a more spare and sinewy way of life. Through the dream-maze runs the sharp ironic thread of a 'minority culture' in America, an intelligence seemingly helpless in the Madison Avenue flood and yet for ever conscious of problems still to solve. When we Europeans carry our unsound romantic self-indulgence to Venice (Italy) we may run the risk of overlooking the Venetian substance in the authentic Venetian surface, and thus leaving our shoddier dreams intact. But when a sensitive American takes his dreams to Miami Beach, then he should be cured for ever.

More Than Enough There

Although it is too early to tell for certain, it is possible that the recent increase in the number of English university posts in American literature—from two to four—augurs a change in the general English attitude towards this subject. At any rate, it is in the belief that the time is now ripe for a reconsideration of the place and nature of American literature that the following notes are offered.

Time, and the critical revaluation of the past two decades, have quite altered our perspective. Books such as Charles Feidelson Jnr's *Symbolism and American Literature* and R. W. B. Lewis's *The American Adam*, by intelligently applying and extending the ideas of Perry Miller and F. O. Matthiessen, have confirmed the intensity of the American experiment and the high seriousness of the major American writers. But these are relatively late-flowering plants and would not have been possible without that intensive cultivation of the ground which has been going on in the American universities and critical journals since the 1930s. Yet although some of the books in question have been reviewed in this country, the English public seems curiously unaware of the weight of evidence now assembled. The fact that Richard Chase's *The American Novel and its Tradition*—which made use of and carried to an extreme a generally accepted body of ideas about the American novel—should have been received in this country as a pioneering work is some indication of our general reluctance to concede the fact that after 300 years American literature has its own traditions and its own distinct and remarkable traits.

There is little point at this stage in going very deeply into the reasons for this reluctance, or in berating ourselves for not seeing before now what the Americans themselves have seen only comparatively recently. Whatever the reason, it might generally be agreed that up to now the Englishman has not seen American literature as a sufficiently distinctive thing for him to devote himself to it as a separate area of study. For one thing, it is written in English. What more natural, therefore, than to consider such American writers as recommend themselves to him as part of English literature? Nothing more natural except that they are Americans and that to annex them, as we have occasionally found it convenient to do, is a discourtesy about which we ourselves no doubt—were we in their place—would have been much more vociferous than the Americans. American literature exists because Americans write it. However, if this were the only reason for recommending the general acceptance of American literature as a separate 'subject' it might not be expected to carry a great deal of weight. It has to be proven, to the Englishman at least, first that there is enough there and secondly, that there is something to be gained by considering American writers all of a piece.

One has in mind adequate critical demonstration. There are sufficient books available now, from the monumental, standard *Literary History of the United States* edited by Professor Spiller and others to the latest Ph.D. thesis from the latest University Press, to make it quite clear that from the point of view of sheer weight of material there is indeed 'enough there'. However, the Englishman sometimes has the feeling that Americans tend towards a somewhat uncritical acceptance of their own writers. Whether this is true or not it is the quality more than the quantity of American literature which must be established if it is to be accepted in England as a literature in its own right. Who, the Englishman might ask, for example, are the great American writers?

This is still to some extent a matter of opinion, and since opinion, if it is to be widely accepted, must be supported by illustration and argument brief answers cannot but be unsatisfactory. However, for the purpose of this short piece perhaps the reader might accept little more than names, if only to provide a talking-point. One or two names come to mind immediately, first those of Melville and Mark Twain. For *Moby Dick* alone Melville might be reckoned to have the stature of greatness, although there may still be found Englishmen to maintain that it is not 'a proper novel'. In the light of the development of the novel during the past hundred years it is proper enough, however, being an exploratory, a symbolist novel before Symbolism and, for all its melodramatic passages, a work of delight as well as of profound seriousness. The same may be said of *Huckleberry Finn,* on the subject of which one might almost be prepared to go as far as Mr. Eliot when he says: 'So we come to see Huck himself in the end as one of the permanent symbolic figures of fiction, not unworthy to take a place with Ulysses, Faust, Don Quixote, Don Juan, Hamlet, and other great discoveries that man has made about himself.'

Whitman and James are also indisputable world-figures, and in the twentieth century Faulkner, Hemingway, Pound, Eliot and—as time probably will show—Wallace Stevens. Eight or nine names, then, one can feel confident about, four of them in the nineteenth century. Over Hawthorne there might be more debate, although at the very least it might be agreed that he is a literary artist of importance and is coming to seem more so in the light of recent critical revaluation. In half a dozen of his short stories and in one novel. *The Scarlet Letter,* Hawthorne—another symbolist—achieved perfection, and gave an example to Henry James. In his concept of the "poetic" novel, of the novel as an art form rather than as an unambiguous story or a document of life Hawthorne not only influenced later American novelists but also anticipated the preoccupations of those twentieth-century novelists—Virginia Woolf is one example—who have paid such attention to word and texture.

There are also indications that we may seriously have underestimated the importance of Edgar Allan Poe. It has been the habit to stress his vulgarity and the 'meretriciousness' of his poetry and to marvel at what we have taken to be an uncritical acceptance of his work by the uncomprehending French. However, it was Poe's use of musical sounds, his anti-didacticism and initiation of a form of symbolism, and his declaration in the *Philosophy of Composition* that poetry ought to be subject to no laws but its own, which inspired a not inconsiderable movement in modern literature. Poe's recognition of the importance of the irrational in life and art, his exploration of the dark side of the human mind, would alone give him an important place in the later development of Romanticism and of that movement which led through *les fauves* to Surrealism and the work of Hart Crane and Dylan Thomas. But perhaps his greatest achievement was in his short novel *The Narrative of Arthur Gordon Pym* and in his short stories, which are memorable beyond mere excitement. They are the work

of an artist, and it is as an artist that he writes in his review of Hawthorne's *Twice-Told Tales,* suggesting precepts which, in the light of
the subsequent development of the short story, have proved very
much to the point.

Another figure who is coming to seem much more interesting is
Fenimore Cooper, who, although obviously not of the stature of
Melville or James, has a quality of his own which is not at all defined
by calling him 'the American Scott'. That he was trying to do something very different from Scott the 'Leather-stocking Tales' clearly
show. For too long he has lived in the shadow of realism, his qualities
largely unappreciated because of the tendency to compare him un-
favourably with the nineteenth-century English novelists, as if their
preoccupations were the norm by which all novels should be judged.

In considering the major, if not the very greatest figures of American
literature, Emerson and Thoreau must not be forgotten, nor indeed
Emily Dickinson, William Dean Howells, Henry Adams, Edith
Wharton, Stephen Crane, Theodore Dreiser, Robert Frost, Sherwood
Anderson, Willa Cather, Sinclair Lewis, Marianne Moore, John Crowe
Ransom, E. E. Cummings, Scott Fitzgerald, John Dos Passos, Hart
Crane, Thomas Wolfe and John Steinbeck. Yet such a list is a very
small one compared with the total number of American authors and
does not by any means cover all those to whose writings it is worth
devoting some attention. In the Colonial Period, for example, the
Puritan poets are not entirely pietistic or didactic bores. Edward
Taylor, as Miss Helen Gardner has acknowledged, is a not uninteresting
minor poet. Out of the mass of historical, diary and, above all, theological material of the American seventeenth century the works of
Bradford, Winthrop, Sewall, Mather and Byrd stand out; in the
eighteenth century loom the polar figures of Jonathan Edwards and
Benjamin Franklin; in the nineteenth century there are the almost
forgotten but still very readable works of Irving, Bryant, Longfellow,
Whittier, Holmes, Lowell, Bret Harte, Ambrose Bierce, Hamlin
Garland and O. Henry; and in the twentieth century there is a pro-
fusion of talents as yet unmentioned, among them Edwin Arlington
Robinson, Carl Sandburg, William Carlos Williams, Ring Lardner,
Robinson Jeffers, Katherine Anne Porter, James Thurber, Allen Tate,
Robert Penn Warren, J. D. Salinger, Robert Lowell and Richard
Wilbur. There is, in fact, quite enough to get through, quite enough to
justify our regarding American literature as a 'subject' in its own right.

But even so, it might be asked, what would be gained by considering American literature separately? Might not this give the impression that it had developed entirely on its own, without relation to English literature? If it did, of course, it would be a bad thing. But there seems to be little danger of this impression gaining much currency —certainly not in Great Britain. One does not receive formal instruction in American literature, much less teach it, without first being thoroughly grounded in English literature and in the process becoming well aware of the obvious and natural dependency of American literature on the English until the nineteenth century, and after that of the constant cross-fertilization that has occurred. It is, in fact, precisely because we are all so well aware of the dominance and superiority of English literature that it needs to be established that American literature did slowly develop its own traditions and characteristics.

It happened because Americans are not Englishmen, have a different background and do not live on a small temperate island. England was a seed-bed of several different strains and when one of these strains was transplanted to another, wilder land with a different climate one could hardly expect the flowers to have the same characteristics as those in the original bed. What is gained therefore by considering American literature separately is an understanding of American literature, and unless it is considered in terms of its own development—for its own development it has certainly had in spite of the influence of English books—it cannot be properly understood.

The English colonists who went to America naturally did not think of themselves as writing something called 'American literature', any more than the Anglo-Saxons thought of *Beowulf* or *The Seafarer* as material for the opening chapter of histories of English literature. Nevertheless, just as we may see in the writings of the Anglo-Saxons the earliest beginnings of that language and spirit which was to be the glory of England in the late sixteenth and seventeenth centuries, so in the writings of the American colonists we may see the beginnings of that language and spirit which was to flower in America during the nineteenth century. It is not so much a matter of conscious difference— although that, too, did develop and became a problem in itself. It is a matter of a certain type of Englishman living in an alien land and not only developing over a period of time different emphases in the language and subject he shared with Great Britain but also working out a new idiom and choosing different subjects (and objects). Hawthorne,

as American consul in Liverpool, fell to wondering what subtle influences had, over two hundred years, changed the Englishman in
America from the red-faced phlegmatic types he saw on his wanderings
to the sallow, nervous, dyspeptic Yankee of legend. We, too, may
wonder what influences made the work of Hawthorne and Melville so
different from that of Dickens and Thackeray. But if this must to some
extent always remain in the realm of speculation, there are other areas
of investigation in which we may be more precise. First, we may
examine American literature closely from the seventeenth to the
twentieth centuries and note what American writers have in common.
Second, we may compare American with English literature. By so
doing it is possible to identify the distinguishing characteristics of
American literature and to chart their growth and development over
three hundred years. Looking backwards, indeed, it is possible to see
how the very narrowness and peculiar preoccupations of the American
colonists directly foreshadow the troubled conscience and symbolic
imagination of the 'New England renaissance'.

From the very beginning, even, American literature exhibited
characteristics which marked it off, slightly but noticeably, from the
English. For example, compared with the poetry of England in the
seventeenth century the poetry of the Colonies is all of a piece. On
one level, of course, there is no comparison at all. America has no
Donnes, no Miltons, no Drydens. A few thousand fanatical, hard-
pressed colonists can hardly be expected to put up much of a showing
against the mature and eclectic might of the nation from which they
sprang. But one would surely not wish to compare on this rather
childish basis. What one is concerned with is a certain homogeneity
of tone in the limited output of the New Englanders, which may be
illustrated by comparing Edward Taylor's 'Huswifery' with the
nearest one can find to it in seventeenth-century English literature.
Since Taylor's poem may not be widely known it perhaps ought to
be quoted in full:

> Make me, O Lord, thy Spinning Wheele compleat;
> Thy Holy Worde my Distaff make for mee.
> Make mine Affections thy Swift Flyers neate,
> And make my Soule thy holy Spoole to bee.
> My Conversation make to be thy Reele,
> And reel the yarn thereon spun of thy Wheele.

> Make me thy Loom then, knit therein this Twine:
>   And make thy Holy Spirit, Lord, winde quills:
> Then weave the Web thyselfe. The yarn is fine.
>   Thine Ordinances make my Fulling Mills.
>   Then dy the same in Heavenly Colours choice,
>   All pinkt with Varnish't Flowers of Paradise.
> Then cloath therewith mine Understanding, Will,
>   Affections, Judgement, Conscience, Memory;
> My Words and Actions, that their shine may fill
>   My wayes with glory and thee glorify.
>   Then mine apparell shall display before yee
>   That I am Cloathd in Holy robes for glory.

Perhaps the most remarkable thing about this poem is the way in which the domestic images of spinning and weaving are made to serve a pietistic purpose. Technically, perhaps, one would have to consider the extended metaphor a conceit, but it is a conceit which is vastly different from the extreme and sophisticated conceits of Donne and his school. The tone is one of sincerity and naturalness. The poet's thoughts slip as easily into the analogy as his words slip into a form which conveys the very effect of spinning and weaving. AB/AB runs the monotonous wheel, then CC the process is brought to a temporary halt, only to start up again. This naturalness of analogy and homeliness of imagery is a strain which runs through American literature.

Taylor's contemporaries in England were Dryden and Matthew Prior, but since there was always a time-lag in the Colonies and Taylor is obviously still living in the poetic age of the late Metaphysicals, Herbert seems the fairest comparison and 'The Pulley' the most apt and convenient example. The tone is quite different. Instead of the fusion of domesticity and unforced piety with naturalness of manner and analogy we hear in Herbert the note of worldly wisdom. Herbert, who lives in an altogether larger, richer, subtler, more difficult world, is forced to come to terms with human nature:

> Let him be rich and weary, that at least,
> If goodness lead him not, yet weariness
>   May toss him to my breast.

Taylor, on the other hand, is not concerned with such problems. His poem merely reflects the force of his conviction, which is the community-conviction of his people. One has the feeling that in the last resort he would claim eternal bliss, the final folding into Abraham's bosom, as his inalienable right. At any rate he ignores the vagaries of human nature. His world is a world of blacks and whites. Herbert's admits in-between shades, and there is a touch of cynicism about his conclusion, which a dedicated and pious member of the Commonwealth of Massachusetts (also a clergyman, but of quite a different strain) could never permit himself.

At the beginning, then, one remarks in American literature, along with the crudeness and dullness of much of the verse, a certain felicity of tone which arises from the homely imagery and the forthright attitude of mind. From Anne Bradstreet and Edward Taylor to Emily Dickinson and Robert Frost this strain continues, but by the nineteenth century it is not by any means dominant. It is, in fact, found rather in eddies and side-channels where something of the strength of the old Calvinist way of life has remained, rather than in the main stream where Puritanism lapsed into the 'genteel tradition'.

One sees, therefore, from the time of Bryant onwards, a second strain, which draws on the high moral tone of Puritanism but which, over 200 years, has lost its earthiness. 'Thanatopsis' is a good early example. Its tone is remote, its style thin. If we compare Bryant with Wordsworth, of whom—with a certain admixture of Blair—he occasionally reminds us, we notice how warm and personal the Englishman is by comparison. Bryant is curiously detached; there seems to be something between him and the reader. It is the characteristic note of a people who, lacking their forefathers' ardent faith in the next world, have nevertheless retained something of their attitude towards this one.

These two paradoxical qualities, the one of earthiness and naturalness, the other of thinness and a high moral tone, afford something of a key to the understanding of American literature. They are in fact its two constant and intermingling 'traditions'.

Much has been made, in recent years, of the symbolistic tradition of American literature, as if that were the only preoccupation that one finds there. It is, certainly, remarkably strong, but scarcely less strong is the tradition of realism, later becoming naturalism. These two literary strains which combine in different proportions in different writers, are nothing more nor less than the residual elements of those twin halves of the Puritan soul, so neatly represented in the eighteenth century by Jonathan Edwards and Benjamin Franklin. It would, of course, be foolish to equate nineteenth-century American symbolism exactly with the high moral tone of seventeenth-century New England theocracy. However, that they are associated, the one developing from the other, seems reasonably clear. Similarly, American realism derives from the practical and lusty side of Puritanism, which never disappeared in spite of the seeming dominance of symbolism and the genteel tradition in the first half of the nineteenth century. The so-called 'rise of realism' after the Civil War, therefore, is merely the re-appearance of a strain which was present all along.

Because they have approached them from different points of view, the different critics who have noticed the two basic traditions in American literature have given them different names and emphases. Philip Rahv's 'paleface' and 'redskin' traditions are witty labels for the symbolist or genteel tradition on the one hand and the realist on the other. Other critics have used the term 'vernacular' to describe the kind of writing which emerged after the Civil War and made that their term of contrast with the 'genteel' tradition. This is to approach the dichotomy from the point of view of style rather than of tone or emphasis. It is a useful distinction, but the most convenient and self-explanatory terms for these former attributes of the Puritan whole man crystallized into nineteenth-century literary modes seem to be the 'symbolic' and the 'realistic'.

Like those other two famous strains, classicism and romanticism, however, they exist not merely as the dominant tendencies of certain periods but also as 'moments of the human spirit', present, and con-flicting, in individual writers. At the time of the New England 'renaissance'—in the work of Hawthorne and Melville, for example—symbolism seems dominant; then, for a period after the Civil War—Twain and Howells are examples—it is realism which appears to triumph. Yet even in these two classic periods no one writer is com-pletely either realistic or symbolic and the more we approach the twentieth century the more do we find these elements mixed in pro-portion to the heat of the creative talent which fuses them. Let us take the work of Ernest Hemingway as an example.

Hemingway's work seems, on first reading, that of a particularly brutal realist. One discerns the saving graces of honesty and of a rather peculiar code of honour, but what strikes one immediately is the narrowness of the human experience described. His characters do not act like any human beings we have ever met; they are flatter, more

stoical, they seem to live on a purely physical plane. One's first conclusion, therefore—after having conceded that the man writes an exciting story—is that Hemingway has been vastly overrated. When one
looks more closely at his work, however, one notices that for all its in-
articulateness the style is very fine and careful.

The opening of *A Farewell to Arms* is a good example of the sensiti-
vity of this so-called 'dumb-ox'. Not only the descriptive passages
but the by now famous laconic dialogue is the work of a master, and
a master whose purpose is much more than that of telling a good story.
No doubt he learnt something from Chekhov, and from Conrad, of
whom he once said that if by grinding Mr. Eliot's bones into fine
powder and sprinkling it on Conrad's grave he could bring the old
gentleman to life he would leave at once for London with a sausage-
grinder. But it is only after reading him in company with his fellow-
Americans, in particular Hawthorne and Mark Twain, that one realizes
that for all his expatriatism he is American to the core, and that it is the
sense in his blood of what is represented by these two writers which
makes him what he is.

In the first place his work is shot through with symbolism, although
since he is a twentieth-century writer it is a far subtler kind of symbolism than Hawthorne's; it is so buried sometimes that one can easily
fail to notice it. In the second place his style is an artful literary manipulation of the American vernacular, that mode of writing which was
first used in a great way by Mark Twain, admiration of whose achievement made Hemingway say in his characteristically extreme way:
'All modern American literature comes from one book by Mark
Twain called *Huckleberry Finn*.' The more one reads Hemingway's
work the more one realizes that, far from being a mere realist, he is a
romantic moralist in the great, if narrow, American tradition, and is in
fact in his own way, in his attention to words and impressions and the
careful moulding of his work, as 'poetic' as Hawthorne himself. The
understated realism and the translated vernacular are merely the
skeleton fabric into which he weaves the thread either of moral teaching or of symbolism.

To read American literature from beginning to end in terms of its
own development is to realize that the subtle pressures which beset all
writers in all places have been rather different in America than in England, and to know, by an examination of the evidence, what these
particular pressures have been is to understand American works far

better than if one tried to force them into an English context. The American knows these things by a process of spiritual osmosis; he is aware in his blood of a different cultural climate and the only way for the foreigner to be possessed of this awareness is for him to immerse himself in the currents of American literature, to see the parallel between Hawthorne and Hemingway and between Whitman and Wallace Stevens. The work of even so 'English' an American as Mr. Eliot is not completely understandable until one realizes that he has felt these same pressures and that his very emancipation, his act of conscious revolt, has made his work different from that of any English poet one has ever encountered.

When one lifts an American out of his context, as Dr. Lewis did in the case of Henry James, merely because, like most Americans, he is a moralist and, among a dozen other writers, paid close attention to George Eliot, it is to half-comprehend him. The oddness of the procedure will perhaps be apparent if one contemplates putting W. H. Auden in the 'great tradition' of American literature. Affected by America he no doubt has been, but one can hardly understand his work if one does not take into account the gritty Englishness of the early verse. A writer is not born in a vacuum and he does not live in one. To understand the work of these Anglo-Americans and American-Englishmen one needs to take into account the traditions and preoccupations of both English and American literature, but where they are clearly more in the one than in the other stream in terms of that one they ought, initially, to be considered. Nor does it matter that many American writers have read English books. English writers read American books. French writers read English books. Does that make them Americans or Englishmen?

The study of American literature needs to be insisted on in this country for the sake of that literature, and for its sake alone. Politics should not enter into the picture, and even when it does that does not justify the indulgence of emotional prejudice. American writers are not politicians and on the whole their politicians neither understand them nor agree with them when they do. But to know American literature is to understand the soul of America in a way that all the speeches of all the politicians could never convey.

The Characteristic Form

Like Great Britain, America has suffered from the disappearance of its literary magazines, but Americans can still grow excited over their short stories. Anyone who was in the United States when J. D. Salinger's 'Franny' appeared in the *New Yorker* will remember the discussion it created. One group held that Franny was pregnant, another that she wasn't. A third, one of whose members had the honour of corresponding with the author, announced that Mr. Salinger disclaimed all intention of making his heroine pregnant, but a fourth, with access to the magazine itself, quoted the retort of one of its staff that, 'of course Franny was pregnant but Mr. Salinger didn't know it'. Pregnancy apart, this is how the great novelists were discussed in Victorian England, and, though the popularity of a work of art is no indication of its merit, it is part of the greatness of the form itself, since it provides the atmosphere of intellectual enthusiasm in which great works can be produced. Partly at least, it explains why the short story is the characteristic American art form, and why any anthology of modern short stories would almost necessarily be dominated by Ernest Hemingway and William Saroyan, Katherine Anne Porter and Eudora Welty, J. F. Powers and Wallace Stegner, and a full score of other writers who have done their best work in the form.

In some way it would appear as though the development of the short story were bound up with periods of acute national self-consciousness, for already there are signs that it is becoming the favourite form of writers from India and the West Indies. As Russians felt round the middle of the nineteenth century, and Irishmen in the second decade of the twentieth, Americans would seem to have begun to feel about 1910. By 1912 Greenwich Village was beginning to attract young writers and painters with the old dream of the artists' homeland, and its importance can be seen in the early stories of Willa Cather. It is both the strength and the weakness of the short story that it is a highly self-conscious form which, on the one hand, runs to intense individuality, and on the other, degenerates into mere mannerism. Of all the great modern American writers Mr. William Faulkner, for all the rugged individuality of his style, is perhaps closest in spirit to the Victorians, and so finds no great difficulty in ending a story with what Americans call a 'gimmick'. 'Lonnie never did use his paddle, he even kept the skiff tied to the same tree his trot-line was fastened to, and the paddle stayed in his house. . . . But the paddle was in the skiff when that boy found it.' An old-fashioned editor would not hesitate to print the final line in italics in order to emphasize the shock we may be supposed to feel. How differently, in 'The Downward Path to Wisdom' Miss Porter ends her story of the little boy who has at last reached 'the desolation of reality!' 'I hate Papa, I hate Mama, I hate Grandma, I hate Uncle David, I hate Old Janet, I hate Marjory, I hate Papa, I hate Mama. . . .'

As Mr. Faulkner derives from Mark Twain and the frontiersmen with their tall tales, so one feels, Miss Porter must derive from Sherwood Anderson's *Winesburg, Ohio*. To the young American Anderson's book of stories is as important as one assumes *Dubliners* to be to the young Irishman, and for the same reason. It is the first voice of the new America that was seeking companionship in the cold-water flats of Greenwich Village; a piercing cry of anguish at the emptiness and solitude and conformity of American provincial life. In memory of Chekhov, both books might have been called 'To Moscow!' and one guesses that in the years to come there will be many 'to Moscows!' in the work of Indian and West Indian story-tellers. *Winesburg, Ohio*, lacks the high degree of formal organization that makes *Dubliners* so imposing, but the self-consciousness is of a less arbitrary kind. We may have our doubts about the 'paralysis' that afflicts Joyce's characters; we have no doubts about the paralysis against which Anderson revolted. Anderson was part of it as Joyce never was. And the awareness was not Anderson's alone, though he expressed it more vividly than any other American writer of his day; it can be found in an even gloomier, more poignant, less organized form in Willa Cather's *Youth and the Bright Medusa*. Both announce America's rejoining of the human race.

In almost every writer of the time we can see how the American self-consciousness has added intensity to the short story. Scott Fitzgerald's 'Babylon Revisited' would be a remarkable story, whoever wrote it, but it is remarkable in more ways than one. It is the story of an alcoholic American widower seeking to regain the custody of his daughter from his dead wife's relatives in Paris, but what gives it another dimension is the realization that Charlie (with 'the Irish mobility of his face sobered by a deep wrinkle between his eyes'—a phrase characteristic of Fitzgerald, who rarely wrote without studying himself in the mirror) is himself a victim of the reunion with Europe. 'His first feeling was one of awe that he had actually, in his mature years, stolen a tricycle and pedalled Lorraine all over the Etoile between the small hours and dawn.' This is no mere alcoholic remembering his own follies; it is a whole people looking at itself and wondering at its own behaviour.

But finely as Fitzgerald's story is told, it is not in his work that we find the story reaching the high degree of formal organization that seems to be its distinguishing mark as an art. It would appear that the story-teller's problem was not to dispense altogether with the elaborate organization of material imposed on the serious novelist, but to reduce this to its appropriate scale in a miniature art. The simplest form of this reorganization can be seen in the use of dialect, as in the stories of Ring Lardner, Damon Runyon and Eudora Welty—indeed, for critical purposes many of Hemingway's own stories are written in dialect. In a story like Miss Welty's 'Why I live at the P.O.' the use of dialect leads directly to the dramatization of the narrator, simplifies the form by the extrusion of a mass of detail that would simply not be visible to the narrator, and gives the writer all the freedom of dramatic irony he would have in writing for the stage.

In the early Hemingway and Saroyan the reorganization is both stylistic and formal. 'In the fall the war was always there, but we did not go to it any more.' The opening sentence of a famous Hemingway story at once shows his preoccupation with problems of style and his debt to Joyce and Gertrude Stein; and the monotonous dead-pan dialogue ('Two more brandies, he said'), clumsily inked in over a seething background of melodrama and hysteria, is one of the most remarkable achievements of twentieth-century story-telling. Since then the technical seriousness may have degenerated into mannerism and the intellectual gravity into portentousness—it is the danger of any form as self-conscious as the short story—but the achievement remains.

Perhaps under the influence of Harold Ross and the *New Yorker* later story-tellers have more carefully masked the solution of their technical problems, and in a story like Elizabeth Parsons's 'The Nightingales Sing' scarcely a ripple stirs the surface from the deep feeling below. At the same time Mr. Salinger's extraordinary creation of a whole Jewish-Irish family of abnormal sensitiveness—with footnotes blandly referring us to members of it we have not yet met, like the brother who is a Carthusian monk—is a formal achievement as remarkable as that of Mr. Hemingway, and the intellectual gravity is of the same order. Mr. Salinger's stories seem to be a series of variations on a theme from *Hamlet*—'whether 'tis better in the mind to suffer'; and if one brother, Seymour, is lost ('A Perfect Day for Banana Fish') another may, it seems, be saved by the intervention of a pert little English girl ('For Esme With Love and Squalor'). The sensitive plant is a dangerous subject, as one can see by comparing Mr. Salinger's 'Uncle Wiggily in Connecticut' with James Joyce's treatment of the same theme in 'The Dead'. Joyce goes the roundabout way to the core of romance in his heroine, but Mr. Salinger makes her seek help from the gin-bottle, and though there is no doubt which story is the more vivid, we may be permitted to wonder whether anything as commonplace as a love-match would have saved so sensitive a soul from the gin.

Pending the arrival of the Carthusian we are driven back on Mr. J. F. Powers, whose characters are also God-obsessed, though they seek salvation in the Roman Catholic Church rather than in Zen Buddhism. But Mr. Powers's church is saturated with the vulgarity of American commercialism from which his characters are trying to escape, and even he sometimes seems to wonder where truth lies, or if truth lies here at all. If in 'Prince of Darkness' he builds up a tremendous indictment of a worldly priest, in 'The Presence of Grace' it is the old worldly priest who is right and the young energetic one who is wrong.

The quality that makes the short-story writer great is not so much his power to keep his stories short as his power to keep them neither shorter nor longer than the material requires. One thing that all these American story-tellers have in common is that in each of their best stories the length is an essential part of the form. Indeed, one might say that the form *is* the length, and that this is dictated not by editorial considerations but by the demands of the material. The material of the novel is man's life, and this one may conventionalize at any length one pleases, but the more limited and specialized material of a story like

'The Downward Path to Wisdom' is far more difficult to conventionalize, and, for that reason the author must adhere more closely to it.
The story is over only when the last clouds of glory have dispersed,
when the last protective angel of the little boy's magical universe has
revealed itself as merely another dreary egotist, and he can finally sing
his tragic little song of experience—'I hate Papa, I hate Mama. . . .'

And we may as well admit that for Americans the form has certain
obvious advantages. The American writer turned novelist is very often
garrulous. Whether it is because the practice of the short story, with its
close attention to detail, induces a sort of myopia in him, or because the
self-consciousness that makes him such an extremely perceptive story-
teller robs him of the inner security from which the great novelist can
contemplate life as a whole, he does tend to imitate his own engineers,
and think of the novel in terms of the Empire State Building or the
George Washington Bridge, on a scale other than that of everyday life.

The American way of life, so much praised by its propagandists,
does not seem to appeal to the American way of thought. There is certainly a profound conflict, almost unintelligible to most Europeans,
between the average educated American and his background and
family. A visiting professor once asked a member of his class 'Why do
all my students imitate Joyce and Kafka?' and received the reply—
given without irony: 'So that their fathers won't understand them.' It
takes some time for the foreigner to adjust himself to such an attitude
and realize that it is part of the self-consciousness that has left the
American short story supreme in modern literature. These are the
young people who later turn into the Eudora Weltys and J. D. Salin-
gers, and while that self-conscious, critical attitude remains it is the
short story rather than the novel that will represent to Europeans what
is most significant in American life.

The Limits of the Possible

I t would, of course, be absurd to attempt to sum up a great
literature in a single generalization, and that American literature
is a great literature needs no arguing now. But compared with
English it is, for obvious reasons, sparse in bulk, and its fiction, at any
rate during the nineteenth century, consists of a number of towering
works flanked by little minor work of importance; Mount Melville,
Mount Hawthorne, Mount Twain, Mount James seem now to rise
sheer from a prairie-like flatness. A novelist like Howells, worthy as he
is, does not really stand comparison with a secondary English novelist
like Gissing; and even Cooper, for all his historical importance, his
status as the founding father of American fiction, cannot compare in
literary merit with the founding father he derived from—Scott—or
from other founding fathers like Lermontov or Manzoni; his importance, which is enormous, is historical; fascinating to read about, he
remains a bore to read. His significance is that he established the
themes that seem to have preoccupied American novelists constantly
since his day. They consist for the most part in contrasted pairs that
have become familiar in the criticism of the American novel, and Mr.
Marius Bewley has recently rehearsed them all. They may be summed
up very roughly in the polarity between the idea of America—'O my
America, my new-found-land!' with its promises of the infinitely
expanding frontier, of the human being infinitely unrestrained—and
what it is opposed to, the classically American notion of Europe that is
its corollary, Europe depraved and beguiling, the ever-to-be-fled and
the eternally alluring, the Great Good Place, in the end, both of Gil-
bert Osmund and Lambert Strether.

These great themes have as their accompaniment an especial tone, the voice as it were of a national experience that is the voice also of the American novelist himself. Two tremendous lines, it might be said, reverberate down the corridors of the American novel from its earliest days until the present: Melville's 'Call me Ishmael' and Whitman's 'I was the man, I suffer'd, I was there'. Along with the themes, they suggest the quality and feel that distinguish American fiction certainly from our own and probably also from the other great bodies of fiction.

Our own fiction, more than we ever realize until we set it against American, is rooted deeply in society; man for the English novelists is social man—and this is so even for Lawrence, who is as much obsessed with class as with sex—man as he exists in the context of a very old, exceedingly complex, hierarchical society; and though the society may be criticized or rebelled against, it remains inescapable. It is part of the English novelist's essential data, part almost of his Englishness, and that this is so is seen in the fact that there is only one major English novel that cannot be construed in some sense as a social novel, *Wuthering Heights*, which F. R. Leavis, unable to assimilate it into his 'great tradition', has called a 'sport'.

This is not to say, as some recent critics have seemed almost to suggest, that the hero of the American novel exists in a social void. One of the most obvious features of American fiction for at least the past half-century has been density of specification, specification carried at times to absurd lengths, so that it seems sometimes that the novelist is unconvinced that he can persuade us of the genuineness of his hero unless he can persuade us first of the genuineness of his hero's suit and shirt, which he does by quoting price-tags and makers' labels. Society is there, in the American novel, but the role it plays is essentially different from its role in English fiction. Take for example the novels of James Gould Cozzens. A book published earlier this year, which did not escape criticism, was called *The Young Rebel in American Literature*: from the outside American fiction frequently seems nothing if not a rebel fiction, a fiction of protest whose authors are writing against the society in which they find themselves, dissociating themselves from it, sometimes in the sharpest possible way by not writing about it at all. When did Hemingway last set the scene of a novel or story in the United States? Now it is plain that Cozzens is not at all a rebel. His values are deeply conservative, almost reactionary indeed. For him man is thoroughly implicated in society, conditioned, inhibited, thwarted, in the end created by it; the pressures of society, and of the smaller societies that are vocational or professional groups, upon the individual human being compose his main theme. If ever there was one, Cozzens is the novelist of man in society.

Even so, there seems an obvious difference between the attitude towards society implicit in Cozzens's novels and that in almost any English novelist's. In Cozzens society is something which the individual must wrestle with and come to terms with, possibly reluctantly; it is something hard and recalcitrant, like the New England winter, something to adapt oneself to since it cannot be tamed. Certainly it is not something the Cozzens hero can take for granted, as, for example, the central characters of C. P. Snow's *Strangers and Brothers* series and Anthony Powell's *The Music of Time* sequence can.

Among American novelists, Cozzens is the supreme anti-romantic. In the end, most American war novels, for example, whether of the last war or the one before, strike European readers as agonized wails of protest that in armies some must be officers and some men. That one should be placed above another to exact from him unquestioning obedience is the intolerable thing. How coolly, by comparison, Cozzens in *Guard of Honour* analyses the nature and necessity of military discipline!

In this as in his other major fiction, he seems to be saying to his readers: 'Do not kid yourselves. Protest as you may, this is what being a man implies.' His novels may be construed as calls to his readers to accept the reality of the human situation, which involves men in living together, hierarchy (in practice if not in theory), obedience. But— could it not be maintained that, historically, the North American colonies and the United States came into being precisely as a result of the refusal to accept this view of the reality of the human situation? And perhaps, if a man is to be an American, or if to be an American is to mean anything distinctive at all, he must continue in his refusal to accept it. Perhaps, indeed, as Crèvecoeur proclaimed so eloquently 175 years ago and as the South African novelist Dan Jacobson was arguing only the other day in his most interesting *No Further West*, the American is a new type of man.

If this can be seriously maintained, then those who hold the view will be right to regard Cozzens as a black reactionary; and certainly much more in the main tradition of American fiction will seem such a novelist as J. D. Salinger, whose *The Catcher in the Rye* captures and sums up its period and stands in the same relation to it as *Appointment in Samarra* did to the 1930s and *The Great Gatsby* to the 1920s. Of these novels,

Fitzgerald's, now almost thirty-five years old, is already of classic stature, but what all have in common is extreme disquiet about the relationship between the individual and society that Cozzens would have us accept. *The Great Gatsby* is permanently fascinating as an evaluation of American experience at a specific point in American history, and what Fitzgerald was up to the last paragraphs of his novel make abundantly clear. Gatsby is, as it were, an ideal figure whose odyssey captures, in Nick Carroway's eyes, that 'transitory enchanted moment when man must first have held his breath in the presence of this continent, compelled into an aesthetic contemplation he neither understood nor desired, face to face for the last time in history with something commensurate to his capacity for wonder.' *Appointment in Samarra* is a lesser work; its chief interest now is probably sociological —it remains, for the European at any rate, the best introduction to the mysteries of the class structure of American society that we have; but it is because there is nothing in the world of Gibbsville, Pennsylvania, commensurate with his capacity for wonder that Julian English is finally undone. The weakness of the novel is that Julian English is never quite adequate as the tragic hero, but throughout the novel there is the sense that somehow American society has gone subtly wrong and has gone wrong precisely because it has become complex, at least as compared with that simpler society, so much closer to the values of the frontier, of which Julian's father, Dr. English, is the acceptable and adequate hero.

At present *The Catcher in the Rye* seems the better novel and may well be of classic stature. Professor Arthur Mizener, talking in the Third Programme, said not so many months ago of *Huckleberry Finn* that it 'is really a lyric elegy for Mark Twain's lost youth, and it is perennially fascinating to all varieties of Americans, from business men to T. S. Eliot, because it is the nearly perfect American lament for all lost youth.' It seems that for nine years now the intelligent young in the United States have seen Salinger's novel, which they regard as speaking to them and for them, in similar terms. It is indeed a work of almost magical charm, though charm is not a quality its hero-narrator, Holden Caulfield, would approve of. Almost certainly he would find it 'phoney', to use the word which is for ever on his lips as his capacity for wonder is unsatisfied. *The Catcher in the Rye*, like *Huckleberry Finn*, is a triumph of the vernacular. Holden is a year or two older than Huck but, like him, is a conscious Ishmael who dreams, though we know the dream is even more hopeless now than it was a century ago, of 'lighting out for the Territory', and for similar reasons, because his experience of the grown-up world falls so far short of his expectations of it.

It is this that relates Holden Caulfield to Jay Gatsby and Julian English—and also, as with them, to the doomed heroines of James. It is as though for the American novelist his characters' most dearly cherished possession is a highly burnished innocence that eternally re-creates itself but is destined to be destroyed because of the corruption of society, and society is seen as corrupt precisely because its nature is such that it must destroy innocence. It is the knowledge of this that makes the American hero an Ishmael.

But there is something else. The American heroes that we think of as characteristic—Natty Bumppo, Melville's Ishmael, Huck, Isabel Archer, Milly Theale, Gatsby, English, Holden—seem to have an especial quality that sets them apart from the creations of any English novelist. It is obviously not a question of convincingness or vividness of delineation in any simple sense. It is rather that they are myth-figures as the characters of no English novelists are, myth-figures in that they recapitulate within themselves deep and apparently abiding national experience, and that they are conceived by their authors with a lyrical intensity that seems to confer on them a more than naturalistic stature. They can *stand* for more than characters in English fiction are called upon to do.

It is here that Whitman's great line, 'I was the man, I suffer'd, I was there', resounds through American fiction, in the lyrical intensity which makes it possible for a novelist to express a whole national experience. Whitman, too, is one of the founding fathers of American fiction, perhaps in a double way, one lesser, one greater. All the attempts to write The Great American Novel, Dreiser's, Dos Passos's and Thomas Wolfe's alike, come out of Whitman, out of his own heroic attempt to encompass all American experience. But in a less direct way, Whitman helped to make the American novel simply by being Whitman. Whitman, in fact, remains the great exemplar of the American artist: *Song of Myself* is the song of America because somehow myself and America are identical. The interesting thing is that the attempts to write The Great American Novel have largely failed. Success has lain with those novelists, like Twain, Fitzgerald and Salinger, who have eschewed the vast panoramic vision and rendered the American situation in the intensely narrow focus of an apparently personal situation. But if this were all, a nagging doubt might well remain in the critic's mind, in spite of the manifest achievements of American fiction. It is a matter of observable fact that society and the individual, even in his deepest aspirations, are not always and necessarily in opposition. It is a matter of observable fact also that it is possible to play the part of Natty Bumppo altogether too successfully, as Hemingway has done. To say that the strength and weakness of much of the finest American fiction are those of the acutely personal lyric would not be quite true, since, as we have seen, so often the lyric becomes myth. It may be, though, that the national experience the myth recapitulates now needs critical examination, or that the lyric utterance is no longer enough, or that the highly subjective lyric view is not the best foundation for fiction.

At any rate, it is here that the real importance and greatness of William Faulkner become apparent. To have created the fictitious country of Yoknapatawpha County in such solid detail and proliferation of characters would be much in itself. But Faulkner has gone beyond this: Yoknapatawpha County has a significance beyond that of Barsetshire or even of Hardy's Wessex. The critical point is what Faulkner has used his fictitious county in Mississippi for; and he has used it, in the sequence of novels and stories that relate its story, in order to examine in depth, over the passage of a century, an idea of the South. In these novels, society and individual human beings are not in automatic opposition, for, as Faulkner shows, society, whether good or bad, is made by individuals who become part of what they have made. The idea—or the ideal—of the South is there all the time, constant, yet continually restating itself according to the pressures of history. It is not something static. In the end, what impresses in Faulkner is what impresses in all the very great novelists, his superior grasp of reality. He knows that it is exceedingly complex and that it takes in tragedy and comedy alike.

Faulkner may be used to illustrate all the stock generalizations about the nature of the American novel; the recurring themes, the sets of opposites, that so many critics have discovered in it are all there in his fiction; and as much as any novelist who ever wrote he can be placed by the literary historians within a definable tradition, a succession of influences. But he transcends all this. In him the contradictions and oppositions are resolved. It is this, his international status apart, that makes him the greatest American novelist of our century.

Eternal Verities

The time has passed when we could classify the traditions behind modern American poetry as those deriving respectively from Whitman and from Emily Dickinson. Ever since the first impact of Eliot on American poetry nearly forty years ago American poets have been studying new techniques, absorbing new influences, and expanding their horizons, on a scale that makes the modern British poet look positively provincial. In matters of sheer craftsmanship, in the mastery of varieties of technical skill, the American poets, exercised in 'poetry workshops' and broadened by travel grants, are to-day remarkably expert. This cannot be properly demonstrated in a single article, but some features of the contemporary American poetic scene can perhaps be distinguished and explained.

The American poet tends to be romantic by temperament but ironical by conviction. This is very nicely illustrated in Robert Penn Warren's recent distinguished collection of short poems, *Promises**. Many of these are broodingly reminiscent of childhood scenes, with the nostalgia sprinkled with irony (the sprinkling done afterwards, as it were). He can begin:

> Wandering, in autumn, the woods of boyhood,
> Where cedar, black, thick, rode the ridge,
> Heart aimless as rifle, boy-blankness of mood,
> I came where ridge broke, and the great ledge,
> Limestone, set the toe high as treetop by dark edge
> Of a gorge, and water hid, grudging and grumbling ...

* Eyre and Spottiswoode, 1959

But he ends:

> But of course dark came, and I can't recall
> What county it was, for the life of me. . . .

Warren has clarified his poetry considerably since the *Variations on a Theme* published nearly twenty years ago by New Directions. The compulsion to be cerebral and symbolic simultaneously, legacy of the early Eliot, is lifting from modern American poetry. Warren is more himself when brooding on history, memory and places. (Southern American writers in general find a fascination in history which Northern writers lack: they feel conditioned by their past, and in an odd way by topography as well as history. This can be seen in the novelists too: geography for the Southern writer is real, it is *placed* in both time and space, as Faulkner's Yoknapatawpha County is; whereas, for example, the Africa of Saul Bellow's *Henderson the Rain King* is a purely symbolic country belonging to no specific time or place; its significance is moral and psychological but not at all historical. When Englishmen say that the Americans are an unhistorical people they mean the Northerners: Southerners are haunted by history.)

A sense of ancestry is not the same as a sense of history; ancestry is something immediate and personal, and many contemporary American poets are trying to find themselves by relating themselves to fathers or grandfathers:

> They were human, they suffered, wore
> long black coat and gold watch chain.
> They stare from daguerreotype with severe reprehension. . . .

This is Robert Penn Warren again, and here he is voicing not a specifically Southern but a general American preoccupation. We can compare John Malcolm Brinnin's 'Rowing in Lincoln Park' (*The Sorrows of Cold Stone*, 1951):

> You are, in 1925, my father;
> Straw-hatted, prim, I am your only son:
> Through zebra-light fanwise on the lagoon
> Our rented boat slides on the lucent calm. . . .
> Now I am twenty-one and you are dead,

And late in Lincoln Park the rowers cross
Unfavored in their odysseys, the lake
Not dazzling nor wide, but dark and commonplace.

And in his 'Cradle Song' Brinnin writes:

I seek a father who most need a son.

Robert Lowell has a poem 'Grandparents' (*Life Studies*, Faber, 1959), which begins:

They're altogether otherworldly now;
those adults champing for their ritual Friday spin
to pharmacist and five-and-ten in Brockton.
Back in my throw-away and shaggy span
of adolescence, Grandpa still waves his stick
like a policeman;
Grandmother, like a Mohammedan, still wears her thick
lavender mourning and touring veil. . . .

Modern American poetry has discovered *pietas* as a way to self-knowledge; poets look back to parents, grandparents or ancestors to note, in irony, compassion, nostalgia, or wonder, the differences between the generations. British poets, who are altogether more used to the notion that they belong to one in a series of generations, do not as a rule show this kind of interest in this theme. The poem by Lowell just quoted ends:

Never again
to walk there, chalk our cues,
insist on shooting for us both.
Grandpa! Have me, hold me, cherish me!
Tears smut my fingers. There
half my life-lease later,
I hold an *Illustrated London News*,
disloyal still,
I doodle handlebar
mustaches on the last Russian Czar.

The flippancy at the end is deliberate; it represents the safeguard against parody, against the perils of solemnity, that Robert Penn

Warren recommended in his essay 'Pure and Impure Poetry'. America is a country of public rhetoric, a country whose politicians and business men use the strong language of black-and-white moral contrasts in their formal utterances. The modern American poet, anxious to avoid this kind of innocence or this kind of dishonesty (for American public rhetoric can represent either) adds the shrug, the clowning, the self-kidding, the deliberate anti-climax, to show that he is not fooled. The result is something quite different from the gusty irreverence culti-vated occasionally by some English poets; at its best it yields a genuine double vision. This is of course the very antithesis of the Whitman tradition, or at least of the Whitman tradition as it was interpreted by Whitman's successors, though there is more of this sort of thing in Whitman than is generally realized.

The suspicion of eloquence can also yield a kind of mischievous wit that is not at all Empsonian nor in the least like the wit of the English poet when he is playing the naughty schoolboy or the out-to-shock student. It is well expressed by one of its most accomplished practi-tioners, Delmore Schwartz, in the opening poem of his *Vaudeville for a Princess and Other Poems* (1950). The poem is a comment on Pascal's 'True eloquence mocks eloquence':

> Eloquence laughs at rhetoric,
>   Is ill at ease in Zion.
> Or baa-baas like the lucid lamb,
>   And snickers at the lion.
>
> And smile, being meticulous.
> Because truth is ridiculous.

This is not related to the Yeatsian dictum about rhetoric arising out of a quarrel with others, poetry out of a quarrel with oneself. The move-ment from rhetoric to clowning, from elegy to irony, from self-pity to self-mockery—such a common movement in modern American poetry—is related rather to the modern American poet's fear of the solemn and the naïve.

Nevertheless, the American poet is concerned with the eternal verities, not with making casual yet precise observations or capturing the mood or impulse of the moment which is the concern of so many modern English poets. He approaches the eternal verities obliquely, he is liable to laugh wryly at himself for showing this concern, but the concern is there, it is indeed the American poet's reason for existing. The tone is sometimes oracular, but saved from pretentiousness by a quiet control of cadence that derives, perhaps, from the Eliot of 'Journey of the Magi' and 'Marina':

> But sentenced are the seasons that we know.
> The serpent holds and the whirlwind harries
> The last oceans where the drowned pursue
> The daze and fall of fabulous voyages.

That is a stanza from W. S. Merwin's 'Anabasis' (*A Mask for Janus*, 1952), a poem which has the eloquence of poised suggestiveness rather than of strident profession. When the modern American poet is eloquent, he is likely to be eloquent in this way, organizing a train of quietly grave images which are mysterious enough to raise expectations of profundity and elemental enough ('seasons', 'serpent', 'oceans') to suggest an ultimate simplicity. Robert Fitzgerald is the modern American poet who cultivates this style at its most stately. Here is the concluding stanza from his 'Souls Lake' (in *The Rose of Time*, 1956):

> The heart's planet seemed not so lonely then,
> Seeing what kin it found in that reclining.
> And ah, though sweet the catch of your chorales,
> I heard no singing there among my friends;
> But still were the great waves, the lions shining,
> And infinite still the discourse of the night.

This kind of eloquence, with its suggestions of mystery and of archetypal echoes, can incorporate almost colloquial references to American place-names without loss: indeed, it is the combination of the sense of history, a sense of the disturbingly elemental, and a feeling for American place-names that gives Robert Lowell's 'Quaker Graveyard in Nantucket' its special flavour:

> All you recovered from Poseidon died
> With you, my cousin, and the harrowed brine
> Is fruitless on the blue beard of the god,
> Stretching beyond us to the castles in Spain,
> Nantucket's westward haven. To Cape Cod
> Guns, cradled on the tide,
> Blast the eelgrass about a waterclock
> Of bilge and backwash. . . .

'Poseidon' here reminds us that the modern American poet has discovered the classics and classical mythology. The discovery is real, for the Latin and Greek classics are not in modern America an existing but slowly dying part of national education, as they are in this country, but something which has been largely lost and is being consciously and excitedly recovered. The best verse translations of Greek tragedy are now coming from America: Richmond Lattimore and Dudley Fitts, to name only two, have done admirable work on Pindar and Greek tragedy respectively. The modern American poet can often use classical references with a freshness denied to us on this side of the Atlantic: his readers find the references as difficult and challenging as the obscurer references in Eliot or Joyce. There is, of course, a paradox involved here. The loss of a common background of knowledge between writer and reader is a very real loss to a poet—and equally a loss to his readers, as anyone who has discussed Milton with American students can testify—yet an age which expects the poet to provide his readers with the challenge of teasing and provocative allusions which have to be worked at to be fully grasped but which, once grasped, are seen as exciting and illuminating is lucky to have rediscovered the Greek classics for this purpose. Here are the concluding lines from Stanley Kunitz's 'The Approach to Thebes' (*Selected Poems*, Dent, 1959):

> Blinded and old, exiled, diseased, and scorned—
> The verdict's bitten on the brazen gates,
> For the gods grant each of us his lot, his term.
> Hail to the King of Thebes!—my self, ordained
> To satisfy the impulse of the worm,
> Bemummied in those famous incestuous sheets,
> The bloodiest flags of nations of the curse,
> To be hung from the balcony outside the room
> Where I encounter my most flagrant source.
> Children, grandchildren, my long posterity,
> To whom I bequeath the spiders of my dust,
> Believe me, whatever sordid tales you hear,
> Told by physicians or mendacious scribes,
> Of beardless folly, consanguineous lust,
> Fomenting pestilence, rebellion, war,
> I come prepared, unwanting what I see,
> But tied to life. On the royal road to Thebes

I had my luck, I met a lovely monster,
And the story's this: I made the monster me.

John Frederick Nims has a poem 'Penny Arcade' (*The Iron Pastoral*, 1947), set in Chicago, which begins with a description of 'This pale and dusty palace under the El' and proceeds to expand the implications with Biblical and classical references:

> Some for a penny in the slot of love
> Fondle the bosom of aluminum whores,
> Through hollow eye of lenses dryly suck
> Beatitudes of blondes and fallen drawers.
> For this Clithaeron wailed and Tempe sighed,
> David was doomed, and young Actaeon died.

The Bible, too, is often treated as a new book, a fresh and stimulating source of imagery and allusion, by the contemporary American poet. Here is the conclusion of one of Richard Wilbur's craftsmanlike lyrics:

> Thinking of Noah childheart, try to forget
> How for so many bedlam hours his saw
> Soured the song of birds with its wheezy gnaw,
> And the slam of his hammer all the day beset
> The people's ears. Forget that he could bear
> To see the towns like coral under the keel,
> And the fields so dismal deep. Try rather to feel
> How high and weary it was, on the waters where
> He rocked his only world, and everyone's.
> Forgive the hero, you who would have died
> Gladly with all you knew; he rode that tide
> To Ararat; all men are Noah's sons.

We have passed the period of aggressive nativeness in American poetry, the sort of thing illustrated so determinedly (and for the British reader often so bewilderingly) in the poetry of William Carlos Williams. The contemporary American poet is almost too much at home in European culture from Sophocles to Yeats, and he has got his awareness not only from books but also from travel. We are in the midst of another great age of travel for American poets, in many ways a more fruitful one than that which Henry James chronicled (and in

James's day it was not often the young poets who travelled). The great American foundations send promising young writers to Italy, France, Greece—wherever they want to go. Italy seems to be the present capital of expatriate American culture, and Italian imagery, history and culture pulse through much recent American poetry, often used for purposes of commenting on and giving meaning to the poet's American experiences. The result is that the contemporary American poet is much less insular than his British counterpart. He is now so assuredly American that he does not have to be strident about it and proclaim of his country that 'I like it here'; he can expand to influences of other times and places in the confident awareness of his own American personality.

As for what Delmore Schwartz has called the Howlers of San Francisco, in spite of their protestations and manifestos they do not at their best really represent anything basically different from what is going on elsewhere in American poetry. Their leader, or sometime leader, Kenneth Rexroth, was an able poet long before the Beatniks arose and his work is not really motivated at all by generalized rebellion. He is, indeed, one of the most learned of modern American poets, and his collection of poems *The Signature of All Things* (published in the late 1940s but not dated) contains the note that 'much of this book was done on a Guggenheim Fellowship, an honour and an aid of which the author is sensible'—which is not the voice of a Howler. The book contains verse translations from Greek, Chinese and Italian, and restrained, reminiscent poems, one of which begins:

California rolls into
Sleepy summer, and the air
Is full of the bitter sweet
Smoke of the grass fires burning
On the San Francisco hills.
Flesh burns so, and the pyramids
Likewise, and the burning stars.

But the best American West Coast poet is till Yvor Winters, whose distilled combinations of speculation and emotion represent something at the opposite remove from the programme of the Howlers. The studied leanness of style, the careful sharpness and concentration of expression, suggest what some of the younger English poets are seeking

48

after, and it is significant that Thom Gunn went from England to California to go to school to Mr. Winters. It is perhaps a paradox that it is at the farthest point west that we find an American poet whose work seems in some senses most English. But then modern American poetry is full of paradoxes: that is part of its excitement.

The Reflecting Mirror

On Beacon Hill, in February, 1838, under the shadow of Boston State House, Henry Adams was born. 'Had he been born in Jerusalem under the shadow of the Temple and circumcised in the Synagogue by his uncle the high priest, under the name of Israel Cohen, he would scarcely have been more distinctly branded, and not much more heavily handicapped in the races of the coming century, in running for such stakes as the century was to offer': that is what he says of himself in the opening chapter of his autobiography. And any consideration of the American character as it shows itself through autobiographical writing must start from that point.

The Education of Henry Adams was not written until 1905, yet even after nearly seventy years of experience the writer remained uneasily fixed in mind and feeling somewhere between America and Europe, and the extreme fascination of his book lies in the painful effort reflected on every page to combine, as it were, both root and flower in the same plant. The root belonged to New England, and Adams would not have transplanted it anywhere else. On the other hand, he hardly seems to have expected much blossom to survive the rigorous climate of the Eastern seaboard. Henry James—a rather bolder gardener—might have agreed with him; Edith Wharton no less. Europe, beastly and irresistible, was the continent in which things happened—if by 'things' were meant such events as the writing of good books, the painting of good pictures, the fertilization of new ideas. In the second half of his life Adams crossed the ocean with Rudyard Kipling, and he tells how Kipling

dashed over the passengers his exuberant fountain of gaiety and wit—as

though playing a garden hose on a thirsty and faded begonia . . . yet . . .
one felt the old conundrum repeat itself. Somehow, somewhere, Kipling
and the American were not one, but two, and could not be glued together.
The American felt that the defect, if defect it were, was in himself; he had
felt it when he was with Swinburne, and, again, with Robert Louis Stevenson, even under the palms of Vailima; but he did not carry self-abasement
to the point of thinking himself singular. . . . All through life, one had seen
the American on his literary knees to the European; and all through many
lives back for some two centuries, one had seen the European snub or
patronize the American; not always intentionally, but effectually. It was in
the nature of things.

But of course it was nothing of the kind. Kipling was no Bostonian,
but he was partly an American by marriage and election. The sensation which troubled Henry Adams through five hundred pages of self-
analysis was less that of the American suffering a sense of exclusion
from the Old World than of an upper-class New Englander who felt
himself, by the mere fact of existing, a being apart from every world
but his own. The sensation was heady, and not altogether disagreeable
—after all, even the Cabots had God to speak to; but the assignment of
standing up as the mouthpiece of Boston civilization was a heavy one,
since it had to be squared somehow with a number of American ideas
which were not precisely Bostonian: ideas of democracy, of thrust and
resource in the creation of new wealth, of the equality of all men before
Heaven. Some of this could be given an unqualified blessing as an act
of dedication—unostentatious, of course—to the good of the State, and
so of all mankind; but it was hard not to feel a twinge when brought
face to face with Europeans who possessed the maddening faculty of
not worrying, not even searching their own hearts, and so, by the fact
of taking daily life in their stride, called implicitly in question the grave
debate in which the thoughtful New Englander strove life-long with his
conscience.

It is hard not to believe that the mark of the American character during the nineteenth century was a tang rather than a sustained flavour.
This may partly explain the still unvarying popularity of Westerns.
They fire a universal imagination because there is nothing idiosyncratic about them. No time need be wasted in introspection, in deciding between fine shades of character. A way of life is established,
and those who touch that way are roughly cast for the good or the evil
part. Something of this self-explanatory division of the majority into

E

sheep and goats seems early to have been imposed upon the American people by the caprice of History. Even the Civil War—the historical turning-point between an old and a new testament—throws up events, however grim, in a series of primary colours. It wore few of the subtle shades of horror which have marked civil wars elsewhere.

If we look back to the second half of the century, then, we find that there is a bright colour-wash laid across the growing fact of American prosperity and independence, yet that the kind of individual who writes an autobiography is extremely rare except in a limited sector of society. The eye rests on a whole gallery of picturesque figures: pushing out to California and Texas, orating like Brigham Young, transforming hunches into dollars or bankruptcy, performing text-book feats of valour in the process of turning an angry colony into a deafening assertion of empire. But nobody seems to have found time to sit back and think about the first person singular. It would be like sitting down to meditate in an express train gathering speed. And the very fact that Henry Adams—one of the rare exceptions to this general concentration on the present tense—put his autobiography into the third person is itself important. It made an extra profession of objectivity; it denied, as far as it might, the possibility of carrying out the egoistic exercise of sitting back and talking, in favour of setting up a mirror and pretending that the gesticulations recorded there belonged to someone else.

There is an exasperating factor in family life which drives some men to say, before they have been asked to do anything in particular, 'Very well then, leave it to me; I suppose I shall have to do it in the end; I might as well take it off your hands straight away.' This factor seems to have operated strongly in New England. It is as though the very name had taken possession of the inhabitants. Very well, then; they would have to represent the thought of the United States; if it was a burden it was also a duty; they might as well take up their place without waiting to be invited. Were they not the bond between the two seaboards of the Atlantic? Such thoughts are barely compatible with writing about one's self; for they spring from a didactic attitude to others which finds little time for mere recollection. The poems of Emily Dickinson, the notebooks of Hawthorne and Thoreau, the essays of Emerson, take what autobiographical matter is needed and turn it to other uses; because to write straight autobiography presupposes a settled readership of like-minded individuals. A world in flux, where the self-conscious are in a tiny and shifting minority, is no place for re-fashioning the past.

So while the United States as we know them to-day were establishing their own tone, it is not surprising that the individual whose education had disposed him to value—perhaps over-value—that past, kept his gaze fixed on Europe. The palazzos of Florence and Rome, the Paris apartments and the little Mayfair houses which recur in the annals of Americans abroad have set a most misleading stamp on the world's assessment of American character. The Berensons and the Howellses and the Storys, the Sturgises and the Irvings, set the tone for a sequence of generalizations which have very little to do with the real America still finding its feet in the world. They no more resembled their countrymen at home than the expatriate Englishmen of the same period, among whom they moved, represented the Victorian majority in Man-chester or Glasgow. Their collections underlined the fiction that all Americans are rich; their essays and novels suggested a morbid pre-occupation—quite foreign to the true American at home—with the *qu'en dira-t-on* of intellectuals abroad. And even when more rapid means of transport were added to ever-mounting prosperity for those who counted their income in dollars a greater familiarity with Europe did not quickly cure the Adams complex. Books like *King Lehr and the Golden Age* or the autobiography of Madame Balsan are still an uneasy witness to the hampering effect of European imagination. Europe and America could still not be, as Adams said, 'glued together' except by the power of money.

The change, when it came, was abrupt. It has reached its full force in the past twenty years, hastened by the war; but from the time of Scott Fitzgerald onward the premonitory signs were clear enough. From one decade to the next, the American character became self-sufficient; and to-day it would be unthinkable for an American writer to be conscious of his literary knees on meeting a European colleague, however eminent; the sense of awe would be more likely to work in reverse.

This change can be linked, in part, to the growth of American auto-biography written from the point of view of bearing witness. The history of the world since 1939 has made all social groupings much more self-conscious than they used to be. Pride or guilt or hope or anxiety have fastened, as dominant emotions, on different parts of the world, and the echoes of passionate feeling have been especially felt in countries, like the United States, which enfold dominant parcels of immigrants among a dwindling autochthonous minority. In a sense, there is no such thing as a North American of the United States except among the Indian remnants; in another sense, there is no nationality in the world so tightly embracing as that of the Union. No wonder, then, that, as the pulse of the country quickens with a growing knowledge of power and responsibility, the different elements which have fused so miraculously into a single civilization wish to leave some record of special experience. Mr. Alfred Kazin's *A Walker in the City* can stand as the exemplar of a whole range of autobiographical writing.

But there is another strand in the autobiographical skein which is even more typically American. The process of binding together so vast a continent, of making so many disparate elements into a single culture, has only been perfected by sacrificing, more often than not, the individual to the community. You can cover hundreds of miles—as you cannot in Europe—and arrive at a town exactly like the town you have just left. You can find a general pattern and rhythm of life fitted to the surface of local conditions so carefully that the very minimum of surprises will be sprung on an inquirer. But when it comes, the reaction to this uniformity is all the sharper. A Thomas Wolfe, a Jack Kerouac hammers away at the even crust of living, in order to force a furious dent on the surface. The optimism of ordinary existence is balanced, at the same time, by moments of corroding pessimism. This is the atmosphere in which a writer like Henry Miller flourishes. He builds himself into a personal assertion against the whole conforming world. And so, in a general climate of assent, a general will to be as inconspicuous as possible, there are recurrent figures embodying a need of protest. They fly in the face of their fellows and enlarge to the maximum their conviction of a separate identity in order to maintain a freedom which they feel both to be an essential part of the American character and also an easy victim of the accepted conventions of 'normal' living.

In other words, the individual who in Europe might feel satisfied by asserting in small gestures his right to be different from his neighbours may well feel, in the United States, that his independence has something heroic about it, far transcending any gesture. Nobody thinks it odd for a Lawrence to live at Zennor, or a John Cowper Powys to shut himself off from the outside world in North Wales. Big Sur, however, is another matter altogether. For it is part of the enlargement which marks everything about North America that an act not particularly noticeable elsewhere may take on hieratic significance when it has to be performed against the background of an upsurging, practical and matter-of-fact way of national welfare.

This enlargement closely affects the tragic sense of life—a perception normally missing from the gamut of North American reactions, but tending to hypertrophy when it is there at all. It may be thought exaggerated to insist that the best autobiographies in all languages have been written against a background of pessimism: that they have been built as a stay against the onset of dark thoughts about mortality. But a moment's thought about any introspective European from Rousseau to Sir Osbert Sitwell—and the span is a wide one indeed—will show that the characters who write best about themselves are seldom euphoric for long at a time. Yet it is an ordinary tenet of social belief in the United States that happiness is not always within reach but must, as a duty, be garnered and displayed. Those who react against this duty are thus likely to be at odds with the world around them, unless they describe their own fate in the brilliant colours of a copy-writer, using their experience as an example of the gospel of optimism applied for profit. American autobiography often consists of such works: the conquest of obstacles is a theme which has never lost its power to exert a vaguely improving influence on others ever since Mary Baker Eddy brought health and wealth so spectacularly together.

What strikes the foreigner, however, is the amount of assured self-analysis which is purely American in tone. The volumes may be signed Chotzinoff or Behrman; they may have as their theme the discovery of the United States by a first or second generation American. But they have by now the total assurance of an established literature. Papers like the *New Yorker* continue this work. It seems almost unthinkable that within this century Henry Adams was not alone in writing of American literature as a derivative of some elder branch. For the final test of a living tradition has by now been passed. Writers who once might have hesitated to claim their place except as novelists, or poets, or historians, now feel the authority of a tradition behind them. In the last twenty years the American writer has acquired a fresh sense of his own past: he can at last write of himself in his own way and nobody else's. It is the final sign of having grown up.

The Community of the Campus

'The Campus'—the word has a resonance, a weight that its English equivalents lack. 'Varsity', 'College', 'Court', 'Quad' do not evoke even among the graduates of Oxbridge or Redbrick the nostalgia, loyalty and, still less, the generosity that the memory of 'Bright College Years' does even in the alumni of less favoured institutions than Yale. It matters not that the most famous American campus is the Harvard 'Yard', the most beautiful the 'Lawn' of the University of Virginia. The Campus is central to the ambitions, experience and emotional background of many millions of Americans in a way that has no parallel among us. For with us the university is still a hidden obscure institution, known at first-hand to only a small minority of the population. The Boat Race apart, it impinges, as an institution, as a way of life, hardly at all on the masses of the people for whom Oxford may suggest cars as much as scholars, Cambridge proximity to Newmarket as much as the Cavendish. Redbrick is in a worse position, for although local loyalty is growing, the university is not central to the life of the city or the region. Even in Scotland, with an old and democratic university tradition, in Glasgow and Edinburgh at any rate, if not in St. Andrews and Aberdeen, the university, so often so vulgarly called 'the Uni', is just one among the civic institutions of which the average citizen is more or less vaguely aware. (When Glasgow celebrated its fifth centenary there was criticism of the *Glasgow Herald* for devoting so much space to the academic ceremonies at the expense of an agricultural show.)

In the United States we are in another world. There are nearly three million college students; soon there will be five million. University and college teachers are not numbered in thousands but in hundreds of thousands. The exclusive audience that goes to Twicken-ham or Lord's is replaced by millions of rooters. Rose Bowls and Cotton Bowls are great regional events. The heroes of football and, more recently, of basketball are figures of a stature not attained by the most distinguished university performers with us and the old *cri de coeur*: 'I'd die for dear old Rutgers' is repeated with only half an ironical intonation on hundreds of stadiums.

Confronted with this historically unprecedented phenomenon, the European observer is either swept off his feet in uncritical admiration at this extension of democratic opportunity (such admirers are reported on more often than they are heard), or the whole apparatus of higher education in America is dismissed as being, except for a few favoured institutions of which Harvard is easily first, an expensive and rather ludicrous substitute for a good secondary school system. College sports are believed to be adequately dealt with in movies like that lost masterpiece *Rackety Rax* and the formally educational aspect of the system is treated as just above the margin of contempt. A Frenchman, contemplating the undemocratic character of the educational system of his own country with regret, may yet shudder when faced with the results of so open a system as the American, as a passionate English preacher of the comprehensive secondary school may turn away in disgust from the majorettes of Podunk High.

Yet if the American system is to be understood, if its role in Ameri-can life is to be assessed justly, we shall have to abandon many or most of our prepossessions. We must begin, for instance, by abandoning any notion of an easily classified and rated system. Harvard is a 'university'; so are church colleges set out on the lone prairie or among the cotton fields that it would be absurdly kind to class as *studia generalia*. An American college student may be exposed to batteries of world-famous scholars, have made available to him libraries, labora-tories, the physical means of study on a scale unknown to any other country or to any other age in history. He may go to a college con-trolled by the teachings of Mary Baker Eddy or of Joseph Smith, to a college for which the six days of Genesis are days and no bones about it, to a college in which the old rabbinical schools of Poland and Russia have their traditions and biases preserved. All that can be said of the system at this level is that 'going to college' is accepted by most Americans as a good thing, an enviable thing and by many as a natural right.

Each year sees the threshold of expectation made lower; more and more millions assume that they will go to college and it is a rare week in which the simple financial advantages of going to college are not stressed, in which the lifetime earnings of the graduate are not compared very favourably with those of the less fortunate or less ambitious who never tried to pass or, at any rate, did not succeed in passing four years in what Miss Mary McCarthy calls 'the groves of Academe'.

To most Europeans and to many Americans this insistence on the cash values of a college education is distasteful. Forgetful of the economic rewards of classical studies as set out in a famous Oxford dictum, they dismiss the rush for a college education as a mere childish infatuation with a meaningless status symbol, or a prostitution of the noble idea of pure scholarship to the idols of the market-place. A cynic may suggest that a constitutional amendment making all American citizens A.B.s at birth would meet the case. Others distinguish, with pharisaical strictness, between college and college. They admit in many cases only the graduates of that small group of eastern colleges, christened by a sports writer of genius, 'the Ivy League'. Others, not even exempting the Ivy League from their strictures, point with hostile intent at the Harvard Business School and the Yale secret societies as different examples of what is wrong with higher education in America.

The criticisms are not new. It is long enough now since Thorstein Veblen laid down, in his ponderously ironical style, the contrast between the university as he asserted he conceived it, and the reality of the American college, a school for not very forward boys, and the American university, ruled and moulded by the business man. Veblen's ideal has not, indeed, many defenders or exemplars to-day. 'This highly sterilized, germ-proof system of knowledge, kept in a cool dry place, commands the affection of modern civilized man no less unconditionally, with no more after-thought of an extraneous sanction, than once did the highly personalized and mythological and philosophical constructions and interpretation that had the vogue in the days of the schoolmen.' Veblen knew and asserted that the higher education of the Middle Ages was often utilitarian enough and, so far as he was not merely salting the wounds of new institutions like the University of Chicago, he was indulging in what is still a common pastime among American academics, exhibiting a longing for another academic world where professors are treated seriously and paid respectably, not hailed as 'Prof' and reduced in economic status to the level of less fortunate truck drivers. So the late Morris Cohen hankered after the career of a *Professor Ordinarius* in pre-Hitler Germany; so Santayana took off for Oxford, Cambridge, Avila and Rome.

Standing with his plastic tray in the cafeteria chow line in the expensive Gothic or Georgian hall of his university, another type of academic may remember, with anguished pleasure, the amenities and food of the high tables of Cambridge and even of Oxford. Reposing in an armchair in the Athenaeum, he may feel for a brief moment as much at ease in Zion as an oversea bishop at tea in Lambeth. But the cold dawn will, must come. He puts away the dream of an air-conditioned ivory tower (even the Institute of Advanced Studies at Princeton does not quite meet the bill, nor does the 'think tank', the Centre for Behavioral Sciences at Palo Alto). The drab realities of life, trustees, graduate students, faculty meetings, grading of papers, above all the visible and sensible fact that the economic status of the academic profession has declined disastrously in the past generation, float before his inward eye and the day-dream ends, leaving him frustrated and angry.

In a sense it is an old story. The new college that took the name of its first benefactor never quite reconstructed on the banks of the Charles the life of the Cambridge on the banks of the Cam. Harvard fairly quickly went its own way, not merely because of comparative poverty as between the Trinity of Bentley and the Harvard of the Mathers, but because the needs of the new society had to be met. What indignant critics used to see as the great weakness of the American system, the domination of the universities and colleges by lay trustees, was a Harvard innovation. The 'Fellows' of Harvard are very different from the Fellows of Trinity and the American professor, in his dark moments, will refer to himself as an employee and envy either the dons of Oxbridge who are their own employers or the Professors of the Sorbonne who are the employees of the French State, not of a group of business men and lawyers. True, this view simplifies American academic history. The rule by president and trustees was more or less effective. When Dr. Angell came to Yale after the First World War he was scandalized at the slackness of the reins that controlled the academic officers and the faculty. But the pattern in general was set. The final decisions in all important matters were in the hands of an often autocratic president, supported or thwarted by lay trustees—most of them, as befitted a business society, business men.

The problem is a real one. The authors of a very remarkable investigation of the inner life of American universities (*The Academic Market Place,* by Theodore Caplow and Reece J. McGee) have aptly quoted Adam Smith on the advantages and disadvantages of internal and external government as, no doubt, Professor Smith had observed them not only in his torpid Balliol, but in the far from torpid and autonomous College of Glasgow and the far from torpid but not autonomous 'Town's College' of Edinburgh. Yet in spite of the pessimism of Veblen and the precedent-forming reigns of 'King Charles' Eliot at Harvard and William Rainey Harper at Chicago, the drift in modern times has been toward more and more faculty consultation and even effective authority, a drift most vigorously attacked by Messrs. Ruml and Morrison in their highly controversial *Memo to a College Trustee.* The professoriate, as far as it has any consolation for its economic decline, has found it in its increasing control of its own business, notably its control of the curriculum. It is hard, to-day, to think that there could be a revolt against the academic organization like the campaign against the 'old, fortifying curriculum' that nearly wrecked teaching at Yale just after the First World War. If not quite a university of masters like Paris or Oxford, the American university has been becoming more and more like it in the past generation. 'The gild', as some Americans are fond of calling the academic profession, is more autonomous, more capable of self-defence, more able to determine its own duties than it has ever been in American history. And yet, and yet, it can hardly be said that the American academic community is a 'happy ship'.

The old autocratic president, like the old fire-breathing public school headmaster, is a thing of the past. The trustess are themselves now almost always alumni full of piety and even of docility. But the great outside world suddenly turned hostile and the whole academic community is only now emerging from the shock of the assault on the academies that was one of the most sinister results of 'McCarthyism'. It is possible, even likely, that the disastrous effects of the assault on truth conducted by the late junior Senator from Wisconsin have been exaggerated. It is certain that the academic community itself has not been willing to admit how much it played into its enemies' hands by its gullibility in face of the realities of Soviet power. But the spectacle of the harassing of the teachers, of the battles of the books, of the imposition of special oaths, of the usurpation of authority by demagogues, tolerated by graduates of even the most eminent universities, like the late Senator Taft of Yale College and the Harvard Law School, combined with other causes of alarm and despondency to make the American academic ready to see himself as a martyr and his country as hostile to the life of the mind. A resignation to the domination of public life by fools and knaves, a conviction of one's own virtue and intelligence so smug and unrealistic as to be worthy of Alain or M. Benda, spread among the learned. There were enough follies and crimes to justify anger; there was Senator McCarran as well as Senator McCarthy. There was passport nonsense from the State Department and 'procès de tendance' from the administrators of Fulbright grants.

But compared with some of the purges that marked the First World War and its aftermath, the McCarthy terror was the mark of an ebb, not the wave of a conformist future. The assaults of Mr. Buckley on Yale and of Father Halton on Princeton did no harm to the institutions attacked, and provoked speculation as to the role of such intransigent Catholic critics at Protestant or formally neutral institutions. More serious was the shock to the simple faith in the good will of 'the People'. As Professor Holstadter has pointed out, the old, agrarian, radical tradition was not notably friendly to the things of the mind. William Jennings Bryan was more representative than Clarence Darrow. The original 'Wisconsin idea' of Charles McCarthy was parodied by the later Wisconsin idea of Senator Joseph McCarthy and it was in the great, private, rich, snobbish 'Ivy League' institutions that academic freedom was best preserved (a truth that knowledge of the Laski case at Lawrence Lowell's Harvard in 1919 should have made no novelty). But even in the world of state universities the worst seems to be over, although in at least one institution, an *affaire des moeurs* is being investigated not by the university but by the zealous *missi dominici* of the sovereign people in the form of some itinerant legislators. If the idea of academic freedom, in itself not a simple one, has not, perhaps, won genuine acceptance in the minds of the people, the need for the results of academic freedom have been accepted ever since Sputnik I 'flamed in the forehead of the evening sky'. Eggheads and longhairs suddenly acquired national importance and American business was for a moment caught at a disadvantage, as it was realized that a Compton or a Fermi is harder to come by than a Wilson or a Humphrey. Men who never met a payroll have suddenly become as valuable as those who have.

This sudden and panic-stricken appearance of a seller's market for some kinds of academic talent has, of course, brought its own problems. Even in the days when the 'service' idea was most preached in the state universities, the Professor of Butchering Practice or of Physical Education was often ill at ease in the presence of such formal equals as the Professor of German, not to talk of the Professor of Fluid Mechanics. Now a new pecking order has been established in which all eggheads are superior and equal and some are more equal and superior than others. The engineers, long the academic darlings of the men who got things done, have recently been complaining of the *de haut en bas* attitude of the pure physicists and the younger physicists talk with kindly pity of their elders whose best work *has* been, *must* have been done.

If the new Prometheuses of Berkeley and Chicago are regarded with something like superstitious awe, the whole academic world has gained by the discovery that there are things good for the nation that are unknown to General Motors or the Marcus A. Hanna Company. It is easy to exaggerate the character of the revolution, because it has been easy, in the recent past, to ignore the steady rise in the content and competence of the public instruction given in the colleges. This rise has been hidden, especially from long-suffering instructors, by the flooding of the colleges with the great semi-literate masses often, naturally enough, ill-taught in any intellectual sense by the flooded high schools, often ill-prepared for more than life adjustment by some of the more foolish products of the more foolish Schools of Education. Faced with semi-literacy, a great state university like Illinois has firmly announced that it will *not* any longer give instruction in 'remedial English'. Students will be expected to be able to read and write before they get to college. The universities and colleges have had to do much work that in other countries is done by the secondary schools, a state of affairs which has led Dean Jacques Barzun, of Columbia, to give them, in his best-selling *House of Intellect*, somewhat acid praise.

This is not to say that the best liberal arts colleges do not achieve remarkable results as remedial institutions. In four years they often manage to re-awaken the high school graduate narcotized by the special dullness of the eleventh and twelfth grades.

It is easy for an Oxbridge teacher, assuming more or less consciously that Eton and Manchester, St. Paul's and Birmingham will send him their best boys, to laugh as well as commiserate with his American colleagues—as he secretly commiserates with his colleagues exiled to Redbrick or even to Scotland. But the social decision has been made in America and not all its consequences are bad. If it is correct, as it well may be, that Mr. Vance Packard is right and that the great dividing line in present and future American society, the divison between *noblesse* and *roture*, is the college diploma, then social peace is helped by an absurdly generous policy of admission to the higher learning. Whatever the future of a 'meritocracy' in England, it would be a revolutionary change of the temper of American life. For good or ill and for both, the American educational system must be even more wasteful than our own, promoting to colleges boys and girls we should condemn to Secondary Modern schools. The 'parity of esteem' between a minor state university or an under-endowed and possibly declining denominational college and Harvard may be as fictitious as the parity of esteem between Eton and its Secondary Modern neighbours in the Slough district. But all great States that have a healthy political life live by fiction; and the American fiction is more plausible than ours.

Nor are all the results disastrous, except for those English spectators of the American academic scene who can think of nothing superior to our system or have no doubts about the applying of the basic principles of the honours system of Whewell's Cambridge and Whateley's Oxford to our new society. We all know of the evils of the absurdly 'tailored' courses designed to make the illiterate feel at home on the campus, even if only by giving them, slowly and expensively, a training they could have got more cheaply, better and more quickly at a trade school or on the job. As long as too much of the resources of the colleges, in men and money, are not wasted in that way, the dollars that might go to the advanced study of nutrition not wasted on Home Economics, no great harm is done. And less harm *is* done than the outsider thinks; if here is a diversion of funds it is often from the allegedly useful arts to the more austere fields of study and in at least one great state university the new Home Economics building provides some needed extra classrooms for what the Americans call 'the Humanities' and we, the Faculty of Arts.

More serious, or so it is alleged, is the multiplication of courses, the feeding of the young on a diet of *hors d'œuvres* with never a main course to the meal. The survey course, the introduction, *can* be overdone. Many a young man or woman leaves college with a conceit bred of smatterings that are possibly worse than ignorance. But it is un-realistic not to look at our system, which may be admirably designed for the very able who, only studying one narrow field, can yet be trusted to broaden themselves (this is often an illusion, as C. P. Snow has testified and as much high table conversation reveals). But we do not sufficiently consider the case of the mediocre boy who specializes early at school and who continues to specialize in the university and finally emerges as a 'Master of Arts' with a flaccid grasp on one limited field of study. An American of the same capacity would emerge knowing as little about more—which is an improvement.

A more considerable advantage of the American system is that the bright boy or girl need not be 'loyal to his subject', as an Oxford don once put it. He can change his mind, start Greek or biochemistry at an elementary stage, and emerge, a little late and a little breathless, as a serious student. For this reason (and because of a corollary of the American way, a fluid system of examinations), it is much easier to open a new field of study, to get recruits for Russian or Chinese than it is with us. The United States may produce few elegant scholars of the Etonian type, but it produces plenty of competent scholars in dozens of fields that are only formally studied among us. There is a bad side to the fact that nothing is alien to the American academy; there is a good side which we neglect either to notice or admire.

The proof of the pudding is in the eating and in spite of all the lamen-tations from the sidelines and from the press of battle, there are fewer examples in the United States of what Mencken called 'the Sahara of the Bozart' than there used to be. The paperback revolution is at work everywhere, but especially in college towns and in college book-stores. It may not be a mark of progress that you can get, in many col-lege drugstores, the selected works of the Marquis de Sade, now under such severe condemnation in Paris or *Lady Chatterley's Lover*, which you cannot buy in Lawrence's Nottingham or Dr. Leavis's Cambridge. It may not be a total advantage that modern abstract art has conquered the art schools of most colleges and that, while President Eisenhower is protesting against the trend of modern American art as exemplified in the exhibit recently sent to Moscow, Jackson Pollock, Henry Moore and their peers and imitators are welcome in small college towns in Indiana and Tennessee. There may be an element of bogusness in all this, but as is revealed in *Pictures from an Institution*, even the sceptical can be won over. We may not know what the new artists are saying and yet be willing to believe that they are saying something. If the American people are so willing, it is at least as much the work of the colleges as of *Time* magazine.

In another way, the colleges are playing an important role in the sustaining of a serious culture in the United States. As Mr. William Sloane, director of Rutgers University Press, has recently pointed out, the economics of serious book publishing in America have made the lot of the scholar harder and harder. A few firms may nobly publish, for prestige reasons, works of pure scholarship, but few of them pay (although it is reported that the first of Professor Burrows's books on the Dead Sea Scrolls, published as a gesture to scholarship, became a best-seller, to the gratified surprise of both author and publisher). In such a world the role of the university presses is of the first importance. On their enterprise (and Mr. Sloane's own press is one of the most enterprising) depends the future of 'serious' publishing in America. And if there is any rival in the modern history of the South to the role of the University of North Carolina as a lighthouse, it is the university press that has made the imprint 'Chapel Hill' a call to light and wisdom and sometimes to battle.

The universities are not only patrons of learning in a world not over friendly to pure scholarship, they are patrons of the arts, not only the visual arts, but of music and literature. It is easy to poke fun at the institutional Maecenas, the university or the foundation. It is easier to poke fun at resident poets and creative writers, still easier to poke fun at conferences and courses designed to foster 'creative writing' in only too many of the young. Some of the sharpest finger-nails in America have been employed in this pastime. But the poets need to eat and they can't all live in Paris or Rome. It is easy to attack the puritanical rigours of the 'New Criticism'. (Even Dr. Cleanth Brooks has recently relented a little—at a Georgetown University conference on criticism.) It is possible that too much has been read into James and Melville and that 'American studies' have been pursued in too parochial, intense and esoteric a sense. (Some American critics can dive as deep and come up as muddy as any German.) But the academies are being not only academic but boldly so, and in the war with the Beatniks it is not necessarily the dons who have the worst of it.

As the Americans are so much more self-critical than the English, there is no danger that the flies in the ointment will be ignored. There is the problem to which Messrs. Ruml and Morrison have directed themselves, the salvation of the liberal arts college. Gone are the days when it was a matter of Mark Hopkins at one end of a log and a student at the other. To-day the college that can hope to survive and deserves to survive is to the old college what the Mark Hopkins in San Francisco is to the Wayside Inn. But the small and not so small college can only survive if it reforms itself and if, as is daringly suggested, the trustees decide not what shall be taught but how much of the basic subjects shall be taught and by how many people.

To suggest that the university teachers have too much power even over the curriculum is heresy indeed, but it has been done. And the reward for cutting down on the number of courses offered and the number of teachers employed is the doubling of the salaries of the survivors! This may be more than heresy; it may be taking the academic leaders up to the top of the mountain and tempting them, but the case is plausible and, in advocating it, Messrs. Ruml and Morrison recall the style of Cornford. The much touted tutorial method provokes them to note that 'it is not a cheap method, no matter how immature and badly paid the tutors may be', and even academic committee meetings do not escape criticism. 'Discussion of a committee report on a complex problem provides irresistible opportunity for critical minds.'

The suggestion that academics do more teaching, above all that senior academics condescend to teach undergraduates and even freshmen, will evoke bitter resistance, but the need for some alteration in the sacred 10:1 pupil-teacher ratio will be imposed not only by money but by numbers. For if the old 'ideal' ratio is preserved or attained, the United States will soon need half a million college teachers. It is highly unlikely and, indeed, highly undesirable that so many people of presumably first-class abilities can be seduced from the life of action. The community can afford the money better than it can afford the men.

There are other problems. Messrs. Brukaber and Rudy in their excessively complacent account of *The Higher Education in America* assert that the 'numerous and excellent opportunities for women to secure higher education in the United States never cease to amaze visitors from abroad'. That is as it may be; what more certainly amazes them is the small opportunity given to women in America to enter the academic profession and to rise in it, the spectacle, in an allegedly feminist country, of women's colleges with male heads and largely male staffs. They are likely to take more seriously the judgment of Messrs. Caplow and McGee, who state that 'women scholars are not taken seriously and cannot look forward to a normal professional career'. They may even recall the anecdote of the young English woman scholar who was appointed, unseen, to the staff of a great State university and who learned on arrival that owing to the ambiguity of her 'given name', she had been taken for a man and would not have been appointed had her sex been known.

To-day, not only do academic women have limited entry to the best jobs (this is a common thing in American life) but marrying early, they abandon their own careers and work to keep their husbands through the long years of academic apprenticeship. Here is waste.

Although there is less of the circus in American academic life than there was when Woodrow Wilson complained of the abandonment of the main tent for the sideshows, there is still a great deal of it, although the rise of professional football has been a blessing in providing post-graduate employment for many gridiron heroes. The fetish of the Ph.D. has been carried to absurd lengths; the naïve imitation of 'science' has produced some odd dissertations, even bred some odd departments.

Yet the universities are among the grounds for hope in the American situation. More and more they send young men and women into the public service as H. G. Wells hoped and believed that they would do. Most of the presidential possibles in this year are college graduates and Governor Rockefeller of New York was, among other things, a distinguished soccer player at Dartmouth. Even making all allowances for a tax system that puts a great part of alumni generosity on to the shoulders of the other tax-payers, the loyalty that the colleges evoke is admirable and in startling contrast to the indifference of our own graduates.

If there are weak segments of the American academic scene, there are also dark segments. How much is known of the two hundred odd Roman Catholic colleges among the administrators of the other colleges and universities? It is obvious that given the resources of American Catholics, or the use that they are willing to put those resources to, the rulers of Catholic America have spread their butter very thin indeed. No Catholic institution, not the Catholic University, not Fordham, not Notre Dame, has the financial resources of scores of not very well known 'Protestant' colleges. The religious Orders, even the prudent Society of Jesus, are curiously bold in expanding in area instead of deepening the foundations, and if the level of Catholic scholarship is much higher than it was, there is still no Institut Catholique, no Louvain, no Fribourg in America.

The Southern universities and colleges are wrestling with the problem of segregation, opening the door just a little to the advancing Negro. There are too few medical schools and possibly too many law schools. So it goes. But in the three hundred and more years since the founders of the Massachusetts Bay colony set up their little tabernacle of learning in the wilderness and called it by the name of John Harvard of Emmanuel, what elms have grown from that early planting!

Call Me Madam

The biggest woman in the United States of America, and the most important one, is made of cast iron and stands 307 feet high on Liberty Island, in New York harbour. She is the world's largest instance of the usefulness of the female of *homo sapiens* as a symbol, an image for some aspiration or concept which the male, with his far stronger powers of imagination, wishes to represent as both enduring and endearing. Over scores of pedestals and porticos in London one can see examples of the adaptability of the female form to this intellectual need. The idea-to-be-symbolized can easily be specified by what she wears on her head or carries in her arms. A halo can be paraphrased as bronze spikes representing light-rays; for a child one can substitute a book, a torch, or a sheaf of corn. But in any case the choice of a woman as the model makes it clearer at first glance that the artist's object has not been to portray a real human being but to symbolize something. And for sheer bulk and constructive courage, there is no more striking illustration of this particular usefulness of women than the statue which was the gift of the third Republic of France, to her older sister-Republic across the sea.

The Fathers of the American Constitution were, predominantly, Freemasons of high degree: people who looked with immense respect upon respectable women—and most vigilantly barred any female from the intimate comradeship of the Lodge. The Revolution which turned the American colonies into states, the Constitution which legally united these states, and the Civil War which tested that legal action and made it possible for the first time to say 'the United States *is*' (not 'are') doing thus and so—these things happened at a period in history when the substitution of power-driven machinery for manual skill was altering many old assumptions about women's functions in the social system—apart from their biological contributions to the perpetuation of the species. With one thing and another, the voting citizens of the young Republic had more occasion than other countries had to draw a firm and friendly line of demarcation between themselves and women, and to look upon the latter not only as wives and mothers but as potential allegories and symbols.

The European visitor who concludes that American business men 'let their wives look after the cultural and social side' is generalizing far beyond his data, but that familiar criticism only marks his recognition of the relative degree of confidence with which a well-to-do male bread-winner in America sends a female member of his family forth to any committee meeting or lecture or other event in which her presence can symbolize and enact the family's concern for the cultural health of the community. The high incidence of divorce in the United States (where one out of four marriages is likely to be dissolved) may not be unconnected with the fact that live women are not at all efficient as symbols. Sculptures are far more satisfactory. They never open their mouths, they never put on weight and wrinkles, above all, they never try to act like human beings.

A large section of American fiction could be described as what novelists have imagined around the basic situation of a woman's inability or unwillingness to act as the living symbol of some man's ambition or aspiration. Many fictional heroines nowadays are fighting back in that way, but the American ones seem to do it more realistically, as if their problem had focused sharper images in the attentive minds of their authors, male or female. Daisy Miller stands out in European minds as perhaps the most memorable martyr of her line; she came all the way across the Atlantic, and caught her death in the Coliseum through her unwillingness to act the role specially assigned to unmarried young ladies, that of a well-pedestalled living statue of Propriety in Society. Carol Kennicott's inefficiency at conforming to the ideals of Main Street provides the element of detachment in which the *mores* of the community can be examined without pedantry. In the standard plot of the novel about the big industrialist who fought his way to the top there is good material for conflict in the wife who could share the early struggles of her fellow human being, but could not carry off the mink coat which to-day symbolizes prosperity as effectively as any sheaf of corn, or fruity cornucopia, in the arms of a seventeenth-century goddess. It was not an American novelist who invented Mrs. Merdle; but Dickens did not exhaust the fictional possibilities of 'the Bosom', acquired by a rich man as something fit to drape with golden offerings to Mammon. The necklaces flash better when the living jewel-stand is heaving with scorn and rebellion.

The sculptors and painters, in America and elsewhere, are now rapidly abandoning the use of female models as allegories. Liberty will continue to enlighten the world, and the power to imagine her beauty will still be evoked, in philosophers and others, by some proud turn of a handsome young woman's head. But the graphic and plastic artists are no longer trying to represent abstract concepts by concrete young women. It is in the literary arts that Galatea, hopping down from her pedestal, still stimulates and focuses creative imagination.

Hollywood and the Face

What the Tower of London is to England in foreign imagination, so is Hollywood to the United States in those parts of the world which do not fly the Stars and Stripes. The Tower stands as a symbol, giving the impression that beefeaters are still common among us, that our lives are governed by ceremonial and that we spend our time dancing round maypoles on village greens. The last enchantments of the Middle Ages whisper down the wind not only from the spires and towers of Oxford but from every bell throughout a countryside that is one unspoilt meadowland, where there are no by-passes, no Black Country, no subtopia.

The Tower, however, is static, and in that again runs true to symbolic form, but the products of Hollywood go all over the world, flown in jet aircraft and climbing the goat track. They are dynamic, ubiquitous, brash, shameless, persuasive, compelling the cultures of ancient, alien countries to copy their formula and imitate their style. Here is the Voice of America made visible, yet when the serious critic sets out to analyse what that Voice has to say he is met with a babble of childish contradictions which comes to the same thing as a mute and unrewarding silence. It seems that it is the megaphone that matters and not the words—and pictures—that come out of it.

Americans, naturally enough, are never tired of insisting that Hollywood is not America any more than New York is, but what seems an obvious fact to them is not so easily understood abroad. Nor, to be frank, does Hollywood—and here the word may be defined as the American film industry—do much to make it so. American films, on the contrary, go out of their way in insisting that they are representative of American thought and culture, of American institutions, of the

American way of life. How many epics describing American feats of arms have not opened with a proud dedication to the men of the various services and claimed that the story about to be unfolded is founded in history, a proof of the valour of American arms? They further proclaim their debt to various official bodies and organizations, a fact which implies that these, by their collaboration, have given the seal of their approval to the work. A sizeable proportion of Hollywood films, then, are marked not only 'Made in America' but "Made in Official America'.

It is not so easy, then, to shrug off the products of the industry as the irresponsible creations of individual companies out to make money from whatever may be the current fashion: horror, Outer Space, gangsters, or anything else in the line and of the standard of the cheap comic or brash paper-back. These exist everywhere, and it is no more —and no less—proper to look in them for evidence of the trends of American thought than it is to cite our own displeasing variations on the Frankenstein theme as proof that our tastes in everything are ghoulish. It is the prestige film, the film that congratulates itself on its courage and sincerity, on its message, on its patriotism, on its humanity, that should provide the pointer to contemporary American thinking, and here it is that the final full-stop seems to be reached before the first real paragraph has begun.

Chesterton, in his history of England, wrote that when the critic looked round for the hero of the First World War he could point to nothing but a mob; when the critic of the American cinema looks round for the film that can give him his clue to American thought he can point to nothing but a Western. This is an unsatisfactory state of affairs, for more than one reason. The first is that the Western would seem to have nothing to do with present circumstances, with the immediate problems and preoccupations of the time. Westerns were made as soon as the primitive cameras began to turn. They were made in the days when Roosevelt meant Teddy Roosevelt; in the First World War; in the 1920s and the reign of isolationism; in the days of the depression and the New Deal; in the Second World War; before Korea and after it; they are being made now and will go on being made as far into the future as imagination and the inward eye can reach.

And yet this capacity of the Western to survive all kinds of changes and chances, to maintain its individuality from the era of the buggy wagon to that of the man-made satellite, argues the possession of certain characteristics in the nation that makes them, characteristics that resist the wash and erosion of time. The truth would seem to be that America has never really got over the tremendous adventure of its own expanding frontiers, of pushing westward until it reached the sea. What the ocean was to the Elizabethans, so were the vast spaces of the West to the Americans of the last century, and the glamour and wonder of it have never faded. Yet, as the opportunities and responsibilities of America as a nation increased, as she moved out of the era in which she could rely to a great extent on the fact that British naval power was supreme and into that which saw her involved in the affairs of Europe and beyond, and, finally, into the position of the first Power in the world, so did the simplicity with which her films played their game of cowboys and Indians give way to a more complex and introspective approach. At first the only thing Indians could do was to bite the dust and the only good Indian was a dead one. Then the screen began to reflect doubts whether the American treatment of the original inhabitants of the country was, after all, anything to be proud of; the hero was often found to be sympathetic to the Indians and their grievances. Of late the tendency has been for the Indian to fade out of the Western picture and for conflicts between the pioneers themselves to force their way into the foreground. Is it enough, these films seem to be asking their audiences and themselves, that the sheriff should always be satisfied that the problems of his shanty town are settled when in that final sequence he beats the villain to the draw? Might that shot, instead of settling matters, merely begin a new cycle of violence, with all that it entails for the peaceful inhabitants, represented in films by 'extras' perpetually engaged in hurrying indoors and closing windows as the marauders ride in?

Such questions have long been implicit in Westerns, but a few months ago Mr. Henry Fonda was given a part which called for a discussion on them in direct terms. Mr. Fonda represented a sheriff with a reputation as a crack shot and for ability in 'cleaning up' districts terrorized by bad men. But Mr. Fonda was allowed, indeed encouraged, to go a little further into the matter, and, in the course of some stirring events, he finds time to describe himself as the victim of his own myth. At first he is welcomed by law-abiding citizens; then he is feared and resented and begged to move on somewhere else—his is the classic fate that awaits the liberator who comes with a gun in his hand.

While Mr. Fonda was meditating, sensibly if not too profoundly, on this moral dilemma, Mr. Gregory Peck in *The Big Country* was putting forward the case for pacifism in a Western setting and against a Western background. True, he did not altogether practise what he preached—that, the producers of the film may be imagined as deciding, would be to go too far—but, when he fought with bad men he fought with his fists and in secret, as though he were ashamed of tackling ethical difficulties in so crude and unsatisfactory a way. When Mr. Gary Cooper appeared in a film as a Quaker, the period being that of the Civil War, the author of the novel on which the film was based recounted her difficulties in trying to make the director realize what the Quaker philosophy meant, and she did not appear to have been too successful. Mr. Peck in *The Big Country* was not, perhaps, a true pacifist, any more than Mr. Cooper represented a true Quaker, but at least there was a willingness to agree that perhaps, after all, the gun was not the final arbiter and its voice far from being the clinching, unanswerable argument.

If this tendency in the Western to substitute reason for gun-play persists, then perhaps it is not too much to hope that the other products of the Hollywood machine—the 'Dream Factory' as it was called in a most perceptive book which treated the place and its inhabitants from the point of view of the anthropologist—will gradually lose their preoccupation with violence, their conviction, both conscious and subconscious, that all comes down to it, all can be solved by it.

Perhaps there is hope, too, in the fact that the modern American film, determined to fill the screen with corpses in the manner of the last act of *Hamlet*, now sets about reconstructing the atmosphere of the big cities in the time of prohibition. In the recent cinematic biography of Al Capone, the film seems to be going out of its way to emphasize that the horror of the St. Valentine's Day massacre belonged to a past that was farther away than the thirty or so years of actual time—and that may be accounted a virtue in it.

And yet the face Hollywood gives to America and which glares out on the world is still contorted with the grimaces of a kind of idiot ferocity. Watching those fictional reconstructions of war which show the American soldier as a subnormal sex maniac with little idea of discipline and less of self-respect, those crime stories in which the police are no less brutal and only one degree more moral than the criminals themselves, it seems at times as though the whole thing were some

75

gigantic act of sabotage, a conspiracy backed by foreign influence, to parody rather than to reflect the soul and spirit of the nation.

It would indeed be a grim look-out for America and the world if her cinema was as closely knit to the philosophic thought and instinctive life of the country as, for instance, the French cinema was to the thought and life of France in the days immediately before the war. Here Carné's metaphysical confusion of mood allied to what a critic has called 'the black pessimism of Duvivier, the bitter disenchantment of Feyder and Renoir's sensitive, sympathetic understanding of human weakness' spelled out in plain and simple words the story of defeat to come, but the French directors enjoyed a relationship both with the cinema and their country which was far more intimate than any their transatlantic counterparts understand or achieve.

They were the medium which made French thinking at that particular moment articulate; they spoke the thoughts and represented the feelings of the nation and the films those directors and others like them made were real films and not artificial products shaped and planned to fit a world-wide box-office. The film in America is, as a general rule, at the extreme end of the scale away from the 'natural' film, the film made for love and on a shoe-string such as Continental countries from time to time produce, and when an American film of that kind does make an appearance—as it did, for instance, with that small masterpiece *Time Out of War*—the contrast it makes with the normal run of their big commercial productions is breath-taking.

Perhaps Hollywood is too absorbed in technical, material proficiency (and here, perhaps, American characteristics are truly reflected) and in the business, as opposed to the aesthetic side, of film-making to find time to express, even subconsciously, the real American fears, hopes and preoccupations. All film-making countries, of course, borrow freely from their playwrights and novelists, 'baaing'—a word capable of an infinite elasticity—their films on this play or that novel, and certainly whatever is intellectual (and it is precious little) in the American cinema is simply American theatre and novel and television translated into celluloid. Mr. Tennessee Williams and Mr. Faulkner, to take two examples, have put certain aspects of life and feeling in the South under their own highly selective microscopes, and, since some of their work has been reproduced on the screen, it follows that English, and other, audiences have a glimmering of an idea of how some Southerners think and feel. But Hollywood adds nothing and, indeed, takes

something away, smoothing and levelling down the awkward insist-
ences, the inconvenient obsessions.

Sometimes, indeed, the whole point of the original disappears and
what is meant to be an attack becomes, in celluloid, something not far
removed from a defence. A case in point is the film version of the novel
The Last Hurrah. The novel implied that the America of to-day is uneasy about the manner in which its politics are conducted and is as suspicious of the new, smooth television approach as of the old buc-
caneering election methods of those who were out to get into office at
all costs and, when in, to make a good thing of it. The central figure
in *The Last Hurrah* was just such a man, Irish in origin, loyal, indeed,
and generous to his friends, but a pirate at heart, up to every trick, fair
and unfair, in the political game, avid for the money and influence
implicit in coming out at the top of the poll. In the film Mr. Spencer
Tracy stresses the Irish charm and makes him out to be a hero rather
than an enemy of the people. His career is as unblemished as the driven
snow, and, if he has been guilty of an irregularity or two, the motive
has been the benefit of the community.

The defenders of the honesty of Hollywood may point to the fact
that America can be shrewdly critical of herself and her institutions, and
Hollywood has indeed come out with some admirable exercises in self-
satire, but even in the best of them there is a hint of an indulgent consciousness that it and America can well afford to score a point or two
against themselves—the attitude is that of a Test-match batsman, who
with a century to his credit on the board, plays a shot that belongs in
spirit to the village green.

Perhaps in that attitude there is a hint of the real America, just as the
world of Disney, that carefully constructed empire of whimsy and folk-
lore, contains elements of the American character, but it would
seem that only the more superficial elements in the thought and nature
of the country find their way on to the screen. A German book boldly
called itself *From Caligari to Hitler*, thus implying that a study of the
German cinema in the 1930s would make it clear in which direction the
instincts of the German people were moving, while Eisenstein, in making *Alexander Nevsky*, spoke for Russia and issued what was in fact an
official warning to Nazi Germany on what would be the consequences
of invasion.

It is impossible to think of any American film performing that kind
of service for America, however much American war films may boast

of their country's strength. English and Continental people are apt to find American diplomacy tinged with self-righteousness and given to moralizing, and here American films which are often shot against European—and Japanese—backgrounds are faithful in reflecting a national characteristic. The American film hero, finding himself in Rome, Paris or Tokyo, acts in precisely the opposite manner to the Henry James character who is formed and conquered by environment and an older civilization than his own. The American film hero may have a good word to say for St. Peter's or Notre Dame, but by and large he remains unaffected by whatever of beauty or culture surrounds him, regarding the natives with some benevolence, convinced that his own country and its ways are best. In that he is, of course, not unlike the Englishman abroad, or, if it comes to that, the inhabitants of most other nations finding themselves in foreign places, and, indeed, the American film hero often represents the generality of mankind at its dullest and stupidest. He never appears to read anything and has no interest whatsoever in anything that concerns the mind. His conceptions are simple and materialistic to an extreme. He is sentimental and incapable of precise thought and logical expression. His ambitions are puerile and his morals a mess, although he gets them sorted out in conventional order in time for the last reel. He is, however, presented and 'put over' with astonishing technical skill, skill so unfailing and self-confident that it almost amounts to genius. Perhaps it is genius; it is certainly very American.

By the Lights of Times Square

It is more than thirty years since Stephen Vincent Benét sought vainly to discover the American Muse.

> . . . how to see you as you really are,
> . . . how to suck the pure, distillate, stored
> Essence of essence from the hidden star. . . .

So we can search in vain for the spirit of the Broadway theatre, the American theatre. Almost exactly at the time Benét was writing, London audiences were listening to a play called *Broadway*, about bootleggers, show-girls, and what Mr. Phillpott's Thirza Tapper would have described as 'sex challenge'. Crude and tough, but dramatically efficient, this piece, blending 'low comedy, hoofing, and melodrama—the three principal forms of Broadway entertainment', was typical of drama at that time in and around the Main Stem. The American stage had not fully grown up: it would have been useless for a Benét of the theatre, had one existed, to seek for anything that he could point to proudly as 'national' drama.

To-day American drama is either on or off—let us say, based on Broadway or off it. But theatrically a nation must be known, in the final count, by its so-named 'commercial' theatre; and American theatrical historians will turn in future to Broadway just as their British colleagues will turn to Shaftesbury Avenue (with, perhaps, a long, wondering glance at Sloane Square). An American recorder, Edmond Gagey, wrote in 1947 that

contemporary American drama was formed by three great revolutionary drives—the revolution in manners and morals that broke down the restraints and inhibitions of the nineteenth century, the artistic revolution that invested a pedestrian theatre with colour, poetry, and beauty, and the leftist revolution of the thirties that brought missionary fervour and social consciousness in a crusade against war, poverty, and injustice. Some other revolution must come if Broadway is not to return to the 1912 status of escapist show business. . . .

Has that revolution come yet? There are few signs of it, though now and again we hear hopeful cries.

It will not help us much to catalogue every piece in the mosaic of a Broadway season—no more, indeed, than it helps, in a discussion of the London stage, to list the programmes at, say, the Victoria Palace, the Haymarket, the New, and the Prince of Wales's. The Broadway theatre, like that of the West End, can appear to be an unplanned muddle, 'a trendless jumble', as Arthur Miller wrote in 1956. Yet, if we look at it closely, two or three fragments of mosaic do dominate the rest.

Broadway, it has been affirmed, has usually three current dramatists: two living, one dead. It has also various musical plays, one of which is apparently immortal. And it has generally something contentious (possibly *A Raisin in the Sun* qualifies at present) that in some quarters is groomed as a masterpiece. A London critic who observed moodily, not long ago, that every American play seemed to be from the Deep South was being ironical; but we could understand someone who had just experienced in the West End several works by Tennessee Williams, with others by Carson McCullers and William Faulkner. Judged upon their exports only, American dramatists can appear quite remarkably single-minded.

Already in this article we have mentioned the two living writers who speak for the modern American drama: Tennessee Williams and Arthur Miller. The third (and dead) Broadway dramatist is Eugene O'Neill, who has come to posthumous fame. For three decades we had known that O'Neill—angry, striving, rebellious, rushing from mood to mood and style to style—could be a dramatist of high voltage. The trouble was that, too frequently, he confused power in the theatre with violence, and wasted a good deal of time in flexing his muscles like a professional strong man. Suddenly, though his old faults were evident, *Long Day's Journey into Night* re-established him. It was done first in Stockholm. Mrs. O'Neill said in a newspaper interview just before the Broadway première: 'The Swedes did this to O'Neill, not America. America was not a damn bit interested, excuse my language.'

America has been interested enough since then. In 1958 *A Touch of the Poet* arrived, the last complete play of O'Neill's unproduced, and one of a series of nine he had contemplated (but never finished) as a saga of American life from the Pilgrim Fathers to the present day. Still, the theatre cannot exist on a few posthumous works. *Long Day's Journey into Night*, for all its grinding power, did show that O'Neill could be like a melancholy Bellman, bent on saying everything three times. Here his intention was less dramatic than biographical. The characters were inclined to run on like this:

> Out beyond the harbour, where the road runs along the beach, I even lost the feeling of being on land. The fog and the sea seemed part of each other. It was like walking on the bottom of the sea. As if I had drowned long ago. As if I was a ghost belonging to the fog, and the fog was the ghost of the sea. It felt damned peaceful to be nothing more than a ghost within a ghost.

The two American writers who, more than the dark ghost of O'Neill, govern the drama of the period are Tennessee Williams and Arthur Miller. One speaks of them together much as in Britain seven or eight years ago the theatre talked of Eliot and Fry, or as, very much farther back, it would couple Pinero and Jones. The names follow each other on the same breath. Williams, the Southerner, is the more prolific. Indeed, Broadway is usually wondering when Miller will write his next play. Both dramatists brood. Both are resolutely pessimistic. Each likes to be caught thinking, and the atmosphere of the self-conscious drama can get too portentous for comfort. Williams, much the more inventive, has also a sharper sense of the dramatic, even if he can over-write in prose that a rapturous addict has described comically as 'fuelled with human speech, taking off and soaring with a warm, jet-driven roar'. Certainly very heated, very noisy, especially when Williams explains that he is dealing with 'human extremities of emotion'; for the parodist he can sometimes be a target like the side of a house.

Miller is a sterner, more immediately purposeful writer, aware that Ibsen is looking over his shoulder, and with none of Williams's semi-poetic lunges. Each has written an excellent play, Williams's early and gentler *The Glass Menagerie*, Miller's surprising flare in *The Crucible* (where modern 'witch-hunters' can see themselves in the historical looking-glass of the Salem persecutions). But at the moment Williams has grown predictable, and one waits for Miller to break a too long silence, just as British playgoers wait for that very different writer, Christopher Fry, to speak again in a theatre possessed by Mr. Behan, Miss Delaney, and the author of *The World of Paul Slickey*.

Each dramatist has discussed his craft. Arthur Miller has said: 'The common man is as apt a subject for tragedy in its highest sense as kings were.' Tennessee Williams has said emotionally:

> Personal lyricism is the outcry of prisoner to prisoner from the cell in solitary where each is confined for the duration of his life. . . . The fact that I want you to observe what I do for your possible pleasure and to give you knowledge of things that I feel I may know better than you, because my world is different from yours, as different as every man's world is from the world of others, is not enough excuse for a personal lyricism that has not yet mastered its necessary trick of rising above the singular to the plural concern, from personal to general import. But for years and years now . . . I have been trying to learn how to perform this trick and make it truthful, and sometimes I feel that I am able to do it.

Neither of these dramatists has followed Broadway fashion: they have helped to make it. But none of their imitators has progressed very far, and Broadway's difficulty is to find new writers with any hint of permanence.

Such notable figures as Sherwood and Maxwell Anderson have gone. Elmer's Rice's recent *Cue for Passion* is best forgotten. Clifford Odets (it is nearly a quarter of a century since he wrote *Waiting for Lefty*) has had nothing new of late. William Saroyan, capriciously, whimsically, idiosyncratic, has no staying power, though he has expressed himself volubly:

> I cannot mind that I am accused of peopling the plays I write with only myself. I wouldn't know who else to people them with. I also cannot mind that I am accused of not hating the human race. As long as I am willing to go on being a member of that race, it goes against both nature and truth for me to hate it. I cannot mind, further, that the tone of my plays is decent, as charged: that I am *with* it all, and not against it . . . here is drama in my plays because they were written, because I am in them, and because I equal an order of the human race which is not unfamiliar to any other member of it.

William Inge, one of whose most recent works was his family play, *The Dark at the Top of the Stairs*, is a dramatist of growing quality and assured technical craft, who has so far had little impact on the British theatre. Arthur Laurents has written a praised study of a woman's soul, called *A Clearing in the Wood*. A new dramatist, Morton Wishengrad, is author of *The Rope Dancers* (about a child with six fingers) which comes to us in performance as something almost ferociously over-charged. One is forced to believe that self-consciousness is the bane of the Broadway theatre. Dramatists are either too solemn to be true, or else they are relentlessly and determinedly funny. They think too much, and in the theatre such men can be dangerous.

Writers swarm; Broadway waits. The plays ribbon out, psychiatric studies, penthouse comedies, comic fantasies; but there is no writer about whom one can say with confidence: 'Here is Broadway's sal-vation.' The hit-or-miss game goes on. The 'American' drama, though recognizable when met, is not easy to pin down. Neither Williams, with his long look at Southern decadence, nor Miller, with his reforming zeal, nor the dramatists who discuss mother-fixations and who tie themselves in psychiatric knots, can be held as fully repre-sentative of their theatre. Arthur Miller's preface to his *Collected Plays* is not a very bright torch in the mist:

My concept of the audience is of a public each member of which is carry-ing about with him what he thinks is an anxiety, or a hope, or a preoccu-pation which is his alone and isolates him from mankind; and in this respect at least the function of a play is to reveal him to himself so that he may touch others by virtue of the revelation of his mutuality with them.

Broadway has had very little place for the explicitly poetic drama by native authors; thus there is no successor at present to Maxwell Ander-son. Archibald MacLeish has written a strange work, *J.B.*, which Brooks Atkinson described as one of the memorable achievements of the century 'as verse, as drama, and as spiritual inquiry. In every respect *J.B.* is theatre at its highest level'. It is the story of Job related in modern terms, and in the setting of a circus tent: a morality that does not always gleam from the page, but that has won the strongest ap-plause for its effect in the theatre which, after all, should be its first quality. Rosamond Gilder has said of it that 'Mr. MacLeish has dared to weave the thundering voice of the King James version of the Bible into the warp and woof of its own poetry without injuring the fabric'.

J.B. is certainly not typical of Broadway, though—returning to

Benét—we can say to the American theatre, of most of the plays mentioned in this article,

> All these you are, and each is partly you,
> And none is false, and none is wholly true.

There remains, of course, the 'Broadway musical', which is presumed to be the world's desire, the most technically expert, and elaborate, of all light musical plays anywhere, and which is the subject of a separate article. Taking it as a whole one is forced to conclude that at the last, any attempt to pigeon-hole Broadway must fail. One cannot pack in the 'musicals' with the psychological documents, the studies of a 'beat' generation, the brash little comedies, the fantasias, the 'jet-driven roar' of plays that feel they should be important, and listen to themselves roaring. Broadway, as of old, has any amount of talent, but this has not yet fused into an 'American' theatre:

> For, as we hunt you down, you must escape
> And we pursue a shadow of our own
> That can be caught in a magician's cape
> But has the flatness of a painted stone.
> Never the running stag, the gull at wing,
> The pure elixir, the American thing.

There, with Benét, we are back where we started. But Broadway is always changing, and at any moment the drums may beat. Williams, Miller (and O'Neill) will not always be alone.

The Re-birth of the Musical

At unpredictable intervals, and sometimes simultaneously, the theatres of London, Paris and New York take to what the anxious doctors in attendance fear may be their death-beds. Hope is usually at the lowest when one of the perpetual invalids makes an astonishing rally. The other two capitals then become the dumping ground for its plays. As soon as this happens there is a bleat of concern from the scene of the dumping. How can the native patient possibly survive the shock of the keen alien air? We are all likely to find ourselves at one time or another among the bleaters. Experience may tell us that this is the see-saw way the interchange of plays between the three great play-producing countries has always worked. It is hard, all the same, as we contemplate the sadly ailing native drama to believe that, so far from dying of shock, it is more likely in due course to be stung by the rival invalid's remarkable activity into some competitive activity of its own. The see-saw way is, after all, the natural way. The smooth-running mechanism for the swapping of successes has long ago converted the three theatres into one theatre. Each section has, of course, its now racially characteristic colour and manner, but a burst of genuine dramatic energy anywhere is good for the whole organism. Patriotic Englishmen stand at present much in need of any consolation this generalization may afford. They like to think that they invented musical comedy. Its development into the American musical is something they still do not understand. Apparently the only practical way open to them of assisting in the development is to supply the audiences. This they do with a will; but there is a touch of impotent jealousy in their appreciation.

'London produces expansive musical shows,' wrote Mr. Brooks Atkinson, reviewing *Annie Get Your Gun* in the *New York Times*, though, if one may be permitted to be smugly isolationist, the London carousels have less animal gusto than ours. Before the war Paris used to produce luxuriously bedizened girl shows for the tourists and footloose males, but there was little fun in them. No country except America seems to have the tradition, the organization and the equipment for these knockabout capers that blow you out of your seat with explosions of brassy music and whack the funnybone with the slapstick.

This modest survey of how things were a decade ago is roughly true of how things are to-day. We are bound to add, however, that the 'knockabout capers' have since grown to a scarcely believable extent in artistic purposefulness. What disturbs competitors now is less the animal gusto of the American musical, which is perhaps a racial and inimitable gift, than its enormous confidence, its air of going somewhere, of adventurously pioneering with happy valiancy into new dimensions of entertainment where mayhap discoveries of some importance to dramatic art are to be made. We are ruefully aware that our own once impressive status in the musical comedy world has dwindled to that of imitators. No sooner do we fall painfully into step than the stride we are trying to match lengthens, changes direction unexpectedly, and we are left once more in the dusty rear.

Many years ago it was the fate of Americans to labour under the same sense of hopeless inferiority. *The Belle of New York* in 1898 was their attempt to muscle in on English musical comedy. George Edwardes certainly learnt from the challenge to handle his Gaiety girls with greater liveliness, and *The Belle* undoubtedly put new pep into the spirit of the genre, but it had no notable successors and the English musical comedy went on its triumphant Edwardian way to reach its apogee in *The Merry Widow*. A flourishing tradition seemingly takes on a bias persistently in favour of those who have created it. That, anyway, is how outsiders have come to feel about the American musical.

This defeatism was comparatively slow to take root in London. *Show Boat* in the last twenties was a spectacle much enjoyed by fanciers of the stupendous, but as a piece of story-telling it was obviously inept. We assumed it would be remembered by a song, 'Old Man River', as the earlier *Rose Marie* was remembered by a dance, the Totem Pole. All through the thirties we grew familiar with fast-moving, lavishly mounted American shows and distinguished between them chiefly by the attractiveness of the music, which might be Jerome Kern's or

Sigmund Romberg's or, if we were lucky, George Gershwin's or Cole Porter's. And since these composers often wrote for pieces that were not specifically American the Broadway importations had, on the whole, rather less to say to us than the indigenous musical romance exemplified by such successes as *Cavalcade, Bitter Sweet, Glamorous Nights* and *The Dancing Years*. We got into the habit of telling one another that musical comedy, Daly's and the Gaiety and George Edwardes and all that, was an exhausted form and had better be allowed to fade quietly away. It was *Oklahoma!* that broke it to us that musical comedy had been reborn in a shape that was basically American and, while impossible to resist, seemed to be constructed on principles we had never considered feasible.

All the features of this epoch-opening show conspired to take us slightly aback. Unlike all the musical comedies we had ever ourselves hatched, it told a story of reasonably adult interest and did not suffer the story to be intensified by irrelevant songs, dances, ballets and bursts of comic patter. On the contrary. The authors had aimed at making every song, dance, ballet and joke a means of advancing the story and of holding the mood which they had evoked in the very first words of the opening song—'O, what a beautiful morning . . . everything's going my way'. They achieved their aim with a degree of completeness never before attained in musical comedy and not in fact to be attained again in *Carousel, Guys and Dolls, South Pacific* or any other of its illustrious successors until *West Side Story* came along to refresh a tradition that was beginning after some seventeen years of intense activity to show signs of wear and tear.

Perhaps if you have written a musical as revolutionary in technique as *Oklahoma!* you feel when you come to write another that no sort of technical handicap will prove too onerous. That, at any rate, is how Rouben Mamoulia, Oscar Hammerstein II and Richard Rodgers seem to have approached *Carousel*. They found the new self-imposed difficulty in Molnar's *Liliom*, the fantasy of a disembodied spirit given by a celestial police court a day on earth to undo the harm he has done in his previous existence.

The action of *Carousel* 'shamelessly, consciously and even proudly' followed the rather tortuous symbolical action of *Liliom*. In spite of this staggering handicap the show went home to the publics on both sides of the Atlantic. One half of it was good fresh-air stuff, all nostalgia and period charm yet lively, audacious, taking; the other half rose or declined, according to individual taste, into an exceedingly well managed tear-jerker, with a rather fearsome brand of American sentimentality, as it seemed to some English critics, substituted for Hungarian naïvety. None of the Rodgers songs achieved quite the rushing exhilaration of 'O, what a beautiful morning,' but in 'June is busting out all over' he was as near to it as any composer can hope to get when he tries to say the same thing twice. The importance of the piece seems in retrospect to be that it bodly established the spirit of adventure and of fearlessness in experimentation that has always been the mark of the American musical.

Broadway has asked all sorts of difficult questions about the potentialities of the medium and some of the answers hammered out have been illuminating. Can a musical get by without a hero? Is a song and dance show conceivable without a gay, lovable rascal as its central figure? Rodgers and Lorenz wrote *Pal Joey* about an out-and-out heel. Joey is a terrible fellow with no brains, no morals and no manners. His only human quality is a ferocious ambition to see his name in lights as the kingpin of a night club. Something in him appeals for a short while to the simple heart of the heroine and piques the jaded taste of an adventurous middle-aged lady with a rich husband. The story shows the gigolo exhausting the patience of his protectress ('I have known a dance-band leader with a better mind,' she remarks savagely) and the heel grinding into dust the illusions of the heroine. Yet the show did get by, both in New York and in London, not simply on the strength of the faintly improper 'Bewitched, Bothered and Bewildered' but mainly through the vigour and expressiveness of the dancing.

The expensiveness of the Broadway musical makes it highly desirable that it should keep one alert eye on the London market. *Damn Yankees* asked itself the dangerous question whether it could punch home the excitement and glamour of baseball on audiences with a lifetime's loyalty to cricket. In the event, it turned out that much the most popular scenes in the piece were those dealing directly with the alien game. The team in all the glory of their strange clobber had been provided with some crashing good songs, and that celebrating the importance to players deficient in technical skill of the mysterious quality called 'heart' must be the loudest ever heard in the Coliseum and also one of the most exciting.

But if the musical during its brief career has ever been in danger of taking a wrong turning it is not in the English view through its rash

willingness to ask itself daring technical questions at the risk of not finding satisfactory answers. Rather it is the tendency which it shares with
the legitimate drama on Broadway to become journalistic. The American playgoer of the last quarter of a century is probably better informed than any other playgoer. His dramatists are inveterate realists
and they spend a great deal of themselves in reporting and investigating
along the whole range of what may be called newspaper topics. It is
possible that, though adding in play after play to his intellectual stock,
he remains rather short of the emotional experience that can come only
from feeling the stresses of elemental problems treated on the great
scale. However this may be, the journalistic style certainly sits somewhat oddly on an entertainment which cannot in the nature of things
cope effectively with controversial matter demanding close and patient
analysis. This style was most elaborately exercised in *The Pajama Game*
where the Grievance Committee of the factory had the heroine at its
head, her opposite number was the zealous Works Superintendent,
and what interrupted the course of true love between them was a dis-
puted wage increase of $7\frac{1}{2}$ cents.

We might be forgiven for feeling that not only did the dungarees
do little to propitiate the light playgoer's pleasure-loving eye, but that
we were told at once too much and too little of the rights and wrongs of
the dispute and that if this realistic tendency went much farther the
musical would soon have bartered its lyrical heritage for a mess of drab
and unsatisfying realistic pottage. But to generalize about the American musical is still to tread on an upturned rake which flies in your face
with a cruel smack. No sooner had we decided that the form was likely
to die of an excess of niggling realism than we were faced with *My Fair
Lady*, a musical comedy of the first water which we might have made
ourselves if we had come by the idea and had had the single-minded
organizing power to put the idea into effect.

The only serious word of complaint that can be made against this
extraordinarily happy adaptation of *Pygmalion* is that it does not con-
spicuously lead anywhere. It could be called old-fashioned English
musical comedy done in the slap-up modern American way. But to
suppose, therefore, that the American musical is losing its pioneering
sense is to be at once contradicted by the recent appearance of *West Side
Story*. This is adventurous enough to satisfy anybody, for it is the first
attempt that the musical has made on Shakespearian tragedy. Two
things are obviously crucial in the experiment. Every note of music

must say something germane to the action, and this responsibility Leonard Bernstein discharges with a cleverness which makes a distinct advance on the notable music that George Gershwin wrote for *Porgy and Bess*. His success in providing an aria for Juliet and a love duet for the lovers may not quite meet the needs of the whistling errand boy, but his efforts to enforce a unity of sound on the action and to merge the preparation for the high dramatic moments with the high moments themselves are a sinuous succession of small triumphs.

The other vital necessity for the transference of *Romeo and Juliet* to the musical stage is poetry. This could be found in words, in melody or in motion. It is natural that Jerome Robbins, the director, himself trained in the rigour of classical ballet and in the freedom of American dance styles, should opt for movement. Besides, the choice merely continues a tendency which has been growing in the American musical for nearly a generation, for the dancer to take over and run the show. It comes from the instinctive wish that everything should become more fluid, more mobile, faster. Nobody will deny that, in this instance anyway, the choice was the right one. How else could the young street thugs of the rival teen-age gangs of Puerto Ricans and home-bred Americans have been made plausibly to produce even a measure of tragic poetry? Clearly the only way to touch these morons with poetry was by group treatment; and it is remarkable how effectively the transmuting art of the dance draws out the tragic pathos of their social condition and brings them within reach of our sympathy. All the dancing has vibrancy and emotive power, and the total effect of the piece is strongly to confirm our faith in the Broadway musical as an art form in process of evolution. One feels it will never for long be parted from its great maternal images, especially while Miss Ethel Merman, the greatest of them all, who has recently triumphed again as Mama in *Gypsy*, a fine musical made out of the memoirs of Miss Gipsy Rose Lee, has such abundant life and strength. *Candide* was no less ambitious, but less carefully planned.

The American musical is obviously determined to eat up one by one all the world's literary classics. It will some day probably try desperately to resolve into snappy lyrics the highly Latinized, rhythmically complex periods of Sir Thomas Browne's *Urn Burial* and itself perish of a catastrophic indigestion. It would be a noble death. There is no sign meanwhile that its enviable confidence in itself is misplaced.

The Off-Broadway Mixture

The Off-Broadway theatre is probably the only point on our globe from which you ascend to hell. Patrons of the Rooftop Theatre, Greenwich Village, made the ascent in the fall of last year to see Burgess Meredith's conception of Joyce's Nighttown which reached London this summer. 'Fantasy in a firetrap,' a wag murmured as we got out of the elevator; it is, though, a roomy little auditorium when finally you reach it, and in case you are worried about how to get out in a hurry, it says on the programme that 'the exit indicated by red light' (not of course in this instance to be confused with the décor) 'and sign nearest to the seat you occupy is the shortest route to the street. In the event of a fire please do not run—WALK TO THAT EXIT'. Some Off-Broadway theatres like this one have picture-frame stages, others are designed in a shape which might very loosely be described as the round. There was the case of the lady who rang up and asked if they had a seat left for to-night's performance. They had one left at $3.75. (Prices Off-Broadway are not, by London standards, at all cheap.) What row was it in, she wanted to know. 'Oh,' came the answer, 'I'm afraid we don't have rows.' There are times when these physical limitations may help the director. The Theatre East, which is a basement on East 60th Street, for example, beautifully caught the atmosphere of M. Genet's short work, *Deathwatch*, when it was played there toward the end of last year: the whole of the action takes place in a prison cell in which three men are incarcerated, one of whom is a murderer. Incidentally, this absorbing drama of the fantasies that run riot in the minds of the imprisoned (not all Off-Broadway productions are about this, one had better add, though a great many are) tersely confirms much that is said in that infinitely looser piece, *The*

Quare Fellow, which was performed with wider ripples of interest off Broadway somewhat later in the season.

But, before proceeding any further with these comparative issues, there insist the inevitable questions, where exactly and what exactly is Off-Broadway? Alas, we are now in a realm where exactness is about the last criterion that may be satisfactorily applied. Equity has ruled that, 'Use of the Off-Broadway contract will not be permitted in any theatre located in the area bounded by Fifth and Ninth Avenue, 56th and 34th Streets, in the City of New York.' But that only tells us where Off-Broadway, for purposes of salaries, is not; the question is, can one find the Off-Broadway spirit as far west of Times Square as Dallas, or in some of the smaller groups that perform around Los Angeles? What about the admirable theatre in the round in Washington, D.C.? What about the Actors' Workshop in San Francisco? The editors of a volume of seven Off-Broadway plays that has just been published (*The Off-Broadway Theatre*. Edited by Richard Cordell and Lowell Matson, Random House) are, in their interesting and scholarly introduction, quite firm in putting out of court anything that happens away from New York.

The term 'Off-Broadway' in any really definitive sense applies only to those New York *professional* groups actively engaged in theatrical production in places exclusive of theatres in the Times Square area. At the height of the theatre season, in the winter, these groups, thus defined, number anywhere from thirty to fifty. It is partly the success of their predecessors of thirty to forty years ago which sparks the creative drive of workers in the current Off-Broadway theatre, partly the discovery by the commercial theatre of such recent Off-Broadway talents as Ben Gazarra, Geraldine Page, José Quintero, Carmen Capalbo, Albert Salmi, William and Jean Eckert, and Jason Robards Jr.; and it is partly an irresistible urge to work in and contribute to the dramatic art which causes Off-Broadway to burgeon and produce so prolifically.

The Off-Broadway movement began just before America's entry into the First World War, it really began to flourish in the 1920s and, so far, its finest hour was probably in the 1930s. These writers give 1915 as the year dot. It was then that there came into existence the Washington Square Players, later the Theatre Guild, who included Kathleen Cornell and Lee Simonson; the Provincetown Playhouse, which moved in 1918 to New York and gave the first ever performance of a

play by Eugene O'Neill, *Bound East for Cardiff*, and the Neighbour-
hood Playhouse, run by Alice and Irene Lewisohn, which had a far-
ranging international attitude to the drama, and in 1923 started a
hare that is still running when it invited Richard Boleslavsky to train
its actors in the Stanislavski Method.

These now venerable pioneers of the Off-Broadway movement are
seen by Mr. Cordell and Mr. Matson as the spiritual heirs and heiresses
of the Little Theatre movement in Europe in the 1890s. In a sense they
undoubtedly were, but to create something out of nothing it not quite
the same as becoming the leader of a revolution in taste. Antoine
changed the style of the French theatre, Grein brought Ibsen to England and hence gave Victorian morality the knockout punch that
Gissing and Moore had failed to administer; Lady Gregory's anti-
Ibsenism, on the other hand, provided a theatrical focus for Irish nation-
alism at a crucial time. Has Off-Broadway wrought a comparable
change in American life? Or if these comparisons seem a trifle remote,
let us ask if there is a little theatre Off-Broadway, however widely one
may conceive the term, that has had an impact on American life comparable to that of the Royal Court Theatre on the life of London at two
different periods of the theatre's history? Ironically, the most important and influential 'Off-Broadway' theatre, the Group Theatre, with
which such names are associated as are to-day very much part of the
significant history of the American theatre—those of Mr. Clurman,
Mr. Strasberg, Mr. Odets—was not geographically off Broadway at
all, but on it—though at the time of the Depression, the Group
Theatre's heyday, the distinction was perhaps academic.

But then the whole theatrical situation in America was, and still is,
utterly different from the one in Europe. When Off-Broadway began,
a serious indigenous tradition of playwriting was hard to seek, the
repertory movement had not taken hold and there was no universal
style in the theatre. In the past Off-Broadway has done much toward
the creation of the American drama—which is still itself in the melting-
pot—and at present much toward the exposure of the American
theatre-goer to the great playwrights of modern Europe. The 1958–9
season for instance was distinguished by a successful production
Off-Broadway of *Ivanov* and by an even better one in the round of
A Month in the Country in Washington, D.C. Yet the sad and surprising fact remains that if one glances down the list of Off-Broadway
shows listed in the 'Goings on about Town' section of the *New Yorker*

they rarely include a single play by a young contemporary American playwright. New musicals are easier to find; at present there is an engagingly youthful one by Mary Rodgers, Richard Rodgers's daughter, called *Once Upon a Mattress*, a modern version of the fairy-tale about the princess who can feel a pea through twenty soft mattresses 'garnished to modern taste with hints of incest and premarital pregnancy'.

If the Off-Broadway theatre were functioning properly it would be showing plays by writers like Mr. James Baldwin and Mr. John Updike, or their theatrical equivalents if any such exist, rather than, or as well as, reviving such period pieces as *The Boy Friend* and *Leave it to Jane* by Jerome Kern, P. G. Wodehouse, and Guy Bolton, fun though these are. It is in fact difficult to think of one new play of any quality by a young American writer that has had its première Off-Broadway since the beginning of the new season in the fall of 1958. Mr. Cordell and Mr. Matson candidly admit this paucity of the native product and at least four out of their seven representative Off-Broadway playwrights are among the best-established names in modern literature, to wit: Sean O'Casey, Jean Anouilh, Jacquetta Hawkes with J. B. Priestley and James Joyce; of the other three it is gratifying for the British reader to discover Mr. James Forsyth finding honour outside his own country: his *Héloise* was the first success of the past season; the remaining two plays consist of *The Girl on the Via Flaminia*, a skilful dramatization of his own novel by Mr. Alfred Hayes (even he was born in London) about a wartime love-affair in Rome, and *Career* by Mr. James Lee, a piece about the suicidal cost of success in the theatre.

It would be untruthful to paint too gloomy a picture. Where are the young? is a hard question which it is always easy to ask, and, as Mr. Cordell and Mr. Matson explain, in New York the Off-Broadway theatre has several functions other than the promotion of the work of the young playwright. One of these is the conversion of the Broadway failure into a success, another is the revival of plays of some importance that came to the end of a run on Broadway a few years back but which large numbers of people still want to see. In this Off-Broadway emulates one of the best characteristics of the theatre in Paris. Thus, although Mr. Miller has not come forward with a new play since his *A View from the Bridge*, *The Crucible* has been running in an admirable production at the Martinique Theatre all through the season, giving the lie to those critics who said the play would not outlast the McCarthyism for which it presented an analogue: and at the same time another work by Mr. Miller, his adaptation of *An Enemy of the People* (a play that has had such great consequences for American drama), has been revived. Nor is Mr. Miller the only writer of successful Broadway plays to permit his plays to be performed off Broadway. One of the most valuable ventures during the past season has been the re-creation in the round at the Sheridan Square Playhouse of two plays by Mr. Arthur Laurents—author of the 'book' for *West Side Story* and *Gypsy*—specially rewritten for the occasion. *The Time of the Cuckoo* was a hit in the Broadway picture-frame; yet with a moving performance by Miss Kathleen Maguire as the heroine, this contemporary version of 'the international situation' in which an American spinster is forced to come to terms with Latin morals during a summer vacation in Venice (the temperature in New York was down to zero when the present writer saw the piece) came across superbly in the round, where the presence of the lagoon at the back of the audience, the players going through them to reach it, worked very well.

Mr. Laurent's second play to be done in this fashion (a series of four is planned), *A Clearing in the Woods*, a most ambitious piece of work, is a natural choice for a performance in the round in a small theatre. It is based on the notion that all time is eternally present; in it the American woman on the threshold of middle age (much the same character as the heroine of the earlier play) goes back to the point of origin, a space in the woods, by her childhood home, to try to find out why her life went wrong, and thus to be confronted by her former selves. The most remarkable feature of this production was the extraordinary physical resemblance between the different actresses playing the composite role of the heroine; it did much to support Mr. Laurents's often tottery illusion. Mr. Jack Ragotzy was the director of both plays, and his scheme of giving a retrospective one-man show to a playwright is surely a bright one and only possible in Off-Broaway conditions.

What else does one remember particularly? Dr. William Carlos Williams gave us in *Many Loves* some quick, disconnected insights into the private lives of New Yorkers, the whole smothered in a Pirandello dressing, but most intelligently performed by the Living Theatre Company in their pleasant new home of 14th Street, *The Threepenny Opera* continued to run, there was a fine production of *Our Town*, there were revivals of *'Tis Pity She's a Whore* and *The Beaux Stratagem*, Sean O'Casey's *Cock-A-Doodle-Dandy* was performed in a stridently insensitive production at Carnegie Hall Playhouse, there was a wonderfully crazy evening when Miss Leueen MacGrath pulled out all the stops in *Maidens and Mistresses at Home at the Zoo*, a one-act fantasy about a Southern Californian Lady Chatterley who hires out her Arab slave to her friends in order to pay the rent. But here one returns to the night- and day-mares of the imprisoned, and undoubtedly in this stock line the great things were the comic genius of Mr. Zero 'Bloom' Mostel, and the vigour with which Mr. Vic Morrow, Mr. George Maharis and Mr. Harold Scott brought to life the love-hatred subsisting among Jean Genet's strange cell-fellows.

The Nature of American Ballet

B allet in the United States survives without state subsidy. The two chief companies are the San Francisco and the New York City; they have a working association, sharing repertory, dancers and policy. Both enjoy token municipal sponsorship, and, after years of tottering, both begin to look like permanent institutions. They depend on loyal local audiences rather than individual patronage. Both have made extensive foreign tours, aided by the State Department. The San Francisco Ballet, a model of a well-run, neatly trained small-scale company recently flew back from Greece, the Near East and North Africa; in Addis Ababa the Lion of Judah gave the young dancers gold medals. Previously they had toured Latin America and South-East Asia. The New York City Ballet has made six trips to the European continent since 1950; in 1958 it performed in Tokyo, Osaka, Manila, and for sixteen weeks between Melbourne and Sydney. Next it will go to South America. With rehearsal periods, three annual New York seasons averaging twenty weeks of performances, tours and television, this company now affords continuous employment. The New York City Ballet withdrew from the State Department programme. Making friends and influencing people is the Department's justification before the Congress, but there are never sufficient funds to guarantee the response desired, particularly in countries which have to pay for their tickets. In Japan, for example, miscellaneous dancers from the Bolshoi, performing brief excerpts, had packed houses. Tickets were well distributed in advance through the Soviet Embassy to trade union groups. The Americans, being either above this sort of thing or poorer, had a large theatre one-third empty, except for 'student' performances when a massive public waited all night for

97

nominally priced seats and the hall could have been filled ten times.

Two other American companies, historically familiar, Ballet Theater and Ballet Russe de Monte Carlo, are in reduced circumstances. The former is inoperative; no coherent policy and the evaporation of persistent but unresourceful patronage paid off in collapse. The latter survives like a bad joke. It has not risked New York in many years. Even the State Department, notoriously generous toward any exportable attraction, boggles at the Russian Ballet of Monte Carlo, although it has less contact with Russia than with Monaco and none with good theatrical dancing.

The greatest financial success in the history of ballet in America has been the cross-country smash of the Bolshoi. Its enormous apparatus of deep conviction and absolute efficiency satisfied sold-out houses at advanced tariff. Aside from *The Stone Flower*, the repertory had been seen previously on the films; there were few surprises. The performances of this great company gave hope to Americans that one day support might even be extended to their dancers in the all-out race against the Soviet Union. Three-quarters of the audiences in big towns had never seen ballet before—many might never again. They came, hoping such husky boys and lovely girls would be too artistic to guide missiles at the American people. There was some carping, to be sure, at the taste of the Russians, which meant music, costumes and scenery. On any absolute basis, Soviet visual preference, while ignoring Bakst, Benois and Bérard, is no more rigidly codified or predictable than the run of Broadway good taste; Soviet scenery had the scale and solidity of the Moscow subway. No flats wavered; stairs, platforms, set pieces and drapes had a monumental solidity. The Bolshoi flattened America, not by choreography, which was elementary, nor music, which was unprogressive, but by the explosion of joy in their work: stupendous display without narcissism, coquetry, apology or refinement. Living under so famous a tyranny, how could they seem so *happy*? There were no new Nijinskys, but merely extreme capacity prodded by the State to a desired supremacy, not luxurious but necessary to its foreign affairs. The Bolshoi attended a rehearsal, arranged by Balanchine, of *Agon* and other works. The Russians said of the Americans just what the Americans said of the Russians: their dancing was interesting, their choreography was not. Ulanova, who had been two years later than Balanchine at the Marie Theater from 1914 on, inquired if this was by that same Stravinsky who had written *Petrouchka*. No one asked her when she last enjoyed that score.

It is hard for Americans to support local ballet with any generosity reflecting a basic need. Dancing is all right on television, in musicals or by foreigners. Balanchine's New York City Ballet, described by John Martin, the doyen of American dance critics, as a 'puny company', is a troupe of less than seventy dancers including apprentices and guests, with an orchestra of under sixty. It has its troubles. Dancers well trained by Balanchine's own teachers at the Imperial School over the last quarter of a century are not the problem; musical curiosity, an arrogant assertion of visual poverty, a contempt for expressive pantomime and incessant novelties of a cerebral nature do not leave much fat for the box-office. The company has always been run like a gentleman's folly and it is surprising that it has survived at all. America is currently attracted by Art, as long as it is speculative or negotiable (like highbrow musicals and French painting), but given a performing art which has no financial return—well, what's the use of it if you can't use it?

It is hard to imagine anything more useless, in terms of exchange, than Balanchine's last season (his twenty-third since 1947). In late May, hard on the draining of Broadway by the Bolshoi, he produced a single novelty, the hour-long association between himself and the eminent free-form concert-dancer, Martha Graham. It was not, as advertised, a collaboration. *Episodes* was based on the complete orchestral works of Anton Webern, starting with Graham's Passacaglia (Opus 1) and Six Pieces, ending after numerous episodes with Balanchine's Bach-Webern Ricercata from the Musical Offering. Miss Graham played it safe, timing the last moments of Mary, Queen of Scots. For the first time in her honourable career she enjoyed a large orchestra, magnificently prepared by Robert Irving, formerly of the Royal Ballet, Covent Garden. Bothwell was briefly seen, tiger-hunting for the Crown. The four Murrys as a mourning chorus; Darnley, Rizzio, Chastelard, named in the programme, were the only male figures in an efficient pantomime employing Graham mannerism. A delicately measured game of battledore and shuttlecock between Mary and Elizabeth proved the peak of this historical analysis. Balanchine's contributions were in the mood reaching from his Schönberg *Opus 34, Ivesiana* and *Agon*. It was visitors' day at his reasearch laboratory, where sonorities, intervals and texture were visually calibrated, clocked by free fantasia

H   99

in rearrangements of spare parts of the biped mechanism. Critics were quick to report how Balanchine 'hates the human body'. He hates it as a doctor hates it; it has become so familiar and fascinating that he is far beyond any superficial manipulation. He plays with its reversibility, dislocation and unhabitual extension, just as a virtuoso surgeon, released from benevolence, loves to cut. His *Episodes* had the residual atmosphere of reports from the Soviet Union detailing dogs that bark with two heads, ferocious, logical, unfunny, but not exactly grotesque. Webern was probably shot by a trigger-happy G.I. at the end of the war, when he came out in the dusk to light a cigarette. Balanchine's distressing and often beautiful ballet was a wry *amende honorable*; Webern's scores were heard oftener, more accurately than ever before in the United States or probably anywhere else. John Martin, who told Balanchine twenty-five years ago to go back to Europe where he belonged and who has been suspicious of him ever since, characterized the mood, with exceptional clarity as 'ultimate electronic pulp'— people dissociated from ordinary motor mechanism, galvanized impersonally with force but no pathos, in an absolute subordination to dictated energy. It was also a popular success with added performances and much stimulating discussion.

In the same season appeared Gagaku, musicians and dancers of the Japanese Imperial Household. The oldest constituted dance-company in the world, dating from A.D. 703, in Nara, they have performed at Court and shrine continuously since they followed the Emperors to Kyoto, and finally, under Meiji, to their Music Pavilion in Tokyo Palace. They danced on an exact replica of their cinnabar lacquer and green brocade platform, studded with gilt-bronze, hung with purple peonies. Would that Mr. Arthur Waley could have seen and heard these imperturbable men and boys, cut in jade, accoutred as Prince Genji's guard, as Korean bargemen, as T'ang polo-players. At the ballet's final production of the season Asiatic music and dance of the tenth century were performed next to Webern's serial fragments: a dainty feast. *Variety*, the trade-paper of the American amusement industry, considered that Gagaku was 'no go for B.O.,' but box-offices in Washington, Boston, Seattle, San Francisco and Los Angeles spelled sell-outs to fascinated audiences, astonishing the Japanese consular service, few of whose members had ever been privileged to see them at Court. Balanchine was so impressed by their immaculate presentation, the grave simplicity of their determined movement, that he began to eliminate a superfluity of over-interesting steps from one of his works. Mr. Dag Hammerskjöld, again waving his magic wand (he had previously arranged for Madame Birgit Culberg's *Medea* to be performed by this company), had offered the General Assembly Hall of the United Nations for the American *début* of Gagaku, thereby breaching the wall of a strictly isolated Imperial Household. But, after Prince Akahito's marriage to a commoner, which preoccupied local royalists almost as much as the visit of Queen Elizabeth II to Chicago, the Japanese wisely licensed this unprecedented tour, which in the future may be repeated in London and Paris.

The first figure in ballet here has long been George Balanchine; the school he founded in 1933 with his own teachers from the Marinsky turns out highly trained apprentices for his brand of developed classic dancing. It has often produced good girls; now boys of brilliance are appearing. Jerome Robbins, the best native-born choreographer, has had a long leave-of-absence supplying profitable and tasteful musicals for the world market. His recent serious work in jazz has had astonishing moments, but the focus is unresolved between popular hit and a repertory piece. Dancers are attracted to Balanchine and Robbins like moths to a candle. The fascination of authority does not mitigate the wariness of heartless manipulation. Balanchine forbids the prime American theatrical commodity, typecasting for personality. Balanchine, and Robbins too, transform chosen candidates into the athletic and asexual. Smartly groomed acrobats with long legs, long musical memories and little self-expression, perform as in a lay retreat, waiting for what Mr. B. or Jerry has decided is good for them. An almost cloistered anonymity is required to stand the gaff, but there are not many other places where it is possible to perform in an atmosphere of such iridescent possibility.

It is often held against Balanchine that he acts alone, without seeking those fabulous collaborations which enriched Diaghilev fifty years ago. Diaghilev has been dead thirty years, Balanchine has lived here twenty-five; the School of Paris, or its local imitators, would only have confused Balanchine's determined split with western Europe. He has had neither Cocteau nor Kochno; this has rendered his company inexportable to those centres which most appreciate these men of genius, but he has always hewn close to the greatest of Diaghilev's discoveries: Stravinsky. The composer is a constant companion and corroborator; he has written three new ballets and provided scores for a dozen more;

he is paternal patron and dynastic guardian. Close to Stravinsky is Robert Craft, his amanuensis and musical administrator, from whom Balanchine received the complete Webern and who makes constant hints from specific pieces of *musique concrète* to jazz combos. W. H. Auden and his partner, Chester Kallman, are long-standing friends; Balanchine directed the American *première* of *The Rake's Progress*; Mr. Auden introduced his new version of *The Nutcracker*. Auden and Kallman made the translation of Brecht's and Weill's *The Seven Deadly Sins* which has brought all Broadway to the ballet during the past year to watch the spectacular performance of Lotte Lenja, Weill's widow. The poets Marianne Moore and Edwin Denby, the director of the American Shakespeare Festival, John Houseman; Philip Johnson, the architect, and a fringe of young art-historians, painters and journalists provide a shifting background of appraisal which has no formal entity, but which provides a continuous warmth once exercised by Misia Sert and Madame Chanel.

Lincoln Kirstein, Balanchine's lieutenant, is ubiquitous, but so unreliable—as anyone having read Richard Buckle's charming memoirs can guess—that an exact estimation of his position is difficult. Well off, erratic, with a public manner so prickly that his chief talent seems to be for making enemies and alienating people, it might seem that, after so long a time, he could afford to relax. At the outset he was aided by the late Otto Kahn and Mrs. William K. Vanderbilt, whom he met while ghost-writing the Nijinsky biography by his widow. He was supported by the son of Kahn's partner, Edward Warburg. Governor Nelson A. Rockefeller sent his company to South America in 1941, and has often helped since; he sent a special train to transport the whole company and orchestra to Albany to appear at his recent inauguration. In recent years the principal patron was Alice Astor (Mrs. David Pleydell-Bouverie); her loss was keenly felt; it was she who enabled Frederick Ashton to produce two brilliant works for New York. Kirstein's latest caprice was his resignation in ill-concealed rage from the vast Lincoln Square project for all the performing arts, where, ostensibly, he should one day have received a permanent home.

Instruction in ballet in the American provinces is on a fairly high level, not only from the wave of Russian-trained teachers that have settled here in the past forty years, but from the first generation of their pupils who, having retired as dancers, are now teaching. Notable is the San Francisco Ballet School, which is much more than a 'studio' or a loose aggregation of differently trained teachers. This large and strong institution is captained by the brothers Lewelyn, Harold and William Christensen, Mormons of Danish stock, whose masters were the famous Luigi Albertieri, best of the Italian teachers in America, as well as Fokine, Pierre Vladimiroff and Anatol Oboukhoff. Lew Christensen's wife is Gisella Caccialanza, Maestro Cecchetti's god-child. William has for many years directed an excellent extension programme at the University of Utah, in which academic credits are granted for ballet instruction. This is a precedent that will be of significance when a national academy of the dance is established, which cannot be very far away. Harold Christensen is a West Pointer, and brings to the organization a military precision unusual in dance training here. It is known that Balanchine recommended Lew, a fine classic dancer of the thirties, to effect the reformation of the Metropolitan Opera Ballet School and Company which is quite disorganized. The Met, in a fit of compulsive competition with one and all, attempted to create four large-scale new works in one evening. This disaster seems to have summoned aid from the West Coast in the person of Christensen, but it is doubtful if he can succeed where so able a professional as Anthony Tudor has failed.

What became of Tudor? Even before his self-exile as director of the Metropolitan Ballet School he had done little work for a decade. His latest piece, for the Met evening, was set to disjunct pieces of Richard Strauss (his *Dim Lustre* is no longer danced but should certainly be revived). Miss Eleanor Steber sang the Last Four Songs very well, but there was almost no dancing. Return to the soil that nurtured *Lilac Garden* might help Tudor's great gifts.

The Abstract Image

During the past decade the European art world has grown increasingly conscious of the status of modern American painting, especially of that group of artists generally known as the New York school (though its affiliations stretch as far as San Francisco), who have emerged as the protagonists of a new non-figurative movement. Strongly favoured by the Museum of Modern Art, which has sponsored several impressive exhibitions of their work, championed by such robust critics as Clement Greenberg, Thomas Hess and Harold Rosenberg, and supported by European as well as local dealers, the school has made a startling and swift impact on many European artists, provoking enthusiasm or dislike, according to the degree of pro- or anti-Americanism prevalent among the interested parties. A Jackson Pollock, a Rothko, or a de Kooning, rightly or wrongly, are felt to express a new vision, one symbolical of a particular form of transatlantic experience.

The international status of this younger generation is undeniable, as is made clear, for instance, in the large-scale exhibition devoted to art since 1945, on view at Kassel. There American painting is not only well represented but shown to be quite capable of giving a good account of itself. It is, of course, not the first time that American art and artists have achieved a notable situation on this side of the Atlantic; Benjamin West's importance as an historical painter or Whistler's influence upon the course of late nineteenth-century English painting hardly requires emphasis. Yet it is perhaps only now that American artists in general have shown themselves capable of repaying with interest their debt to Europe. That they have been able to intervene so effectively is partly due to the present situation in Europe itself; in spite of the significant achievements of a Staël or a Bazaine, or the emergence of such brilliant younger men as Sergio de Castro, a certain weariness, a certain lack of grasp even, is discernible among European painters. The war years have taken their toll. As a consequence, a vacuum is apparent and while it would be absurd to pretend that the contemporary American school has filled it, its energy, its boldness and its determination have provided a welcome fillip.

The prowess and reputation of the new men comes over all the more strikingly because at first sight their work is by no means clearly American, and one of their number, Mr. Sam Francis, has largely made his reputation in Europe. Unlike the members of the Ash Can school, for example, who went in for the local scene and who were intimately concerned with political and social struggles, their preoccupation with local questions would seem scant, or, at best, oblique. Moreover, broadly speaking, they must be classified as abstract painters, although Kooning is vitally concerned with an ostensible subject-matter. However, their contribution to an international style is all the same endowed with certain national characteristics. They could hardly be anything other than American.

Naturally it would be wrong to assume that non-figurative painting or a concern with *avant garde* trends is a quite recent phenomenon in America. It is not. The genesis of the movement may be traced back to those stimulating years just before the First World War when a revolutionary spirit was in the air. Men like Weber, Maurice Prendergast, Feininger, and Marsden Hartley—to name only a handful—were receptive to these fresh currents, and a general knowledge of the radical movement was spread through the Armory show of 1913 or by the activities of Alfred Stieglitz. Indeed, two painters in particular, whose relevance for the abstract trend has only recently been seized, Morgan Russell and Stanton Macdonald-Wright, evolved a style, Synchronism, which was all their own, however close it might seem to be to Delaunay's Orphism.

The First World War only served to release a fresh spurt of experimental energy. In the ebullient jazz era, American painters, like their colleagues in Paris and Berlin, were agog to paint in a novel manner, and they succeeded. Experiment, in any case, was only to be expected in a country that prided itself upon its awareness of new techniques and where progress was an established article of faith. Some artists, like Sheeler, were practitioners of a style, verging on the abstract, that de-

rived its sustenance from observation of machines and factories; others
—like Joseph Stella in his *Brooklyn Bridge* of 1917–18, went in for
Futurism. All the same, this style, which might well seem to have
accorded with the period, yielded sparse results and

> perhaps Leo Stein was right when he argued in 1925 that it was rooted in
> an essential fallacy, that this was a machine age which should be reflected in
> a machine art—whereas, said Stein, it is the least machine-like of all ages, in
> which the perfection of our modern inventions is as nothing compared
> with the imperfections of all our social machinery.

However, experimentalism was no longer felt to answer when the
crash came; the trend toward realism, toward a closer examination of
the American way of life in so far as it was reflected in men and manners, was dictated by the stern conditions of the era. Painters were
lucky enough to earn some sort of a living; and Thomas Benton,
Grant Wood and John Steuart Curry became the exponents of the new
'American' style. Not that their work ever attained the direct force-
fulness of an Eakins or a Winslow Homer; their range was too narrow
for that.

All the same, too much can be made of the realistic triumph at this
date. An undercurrent of abstract painting, and of experimental art in
general persisted. In 1935, for instance, a survey of abstract painting
was held at the Whitney Museum, while in 1937 a group of artists
founded the Abstract Artists' Society; indeed, as Mr. Thomas Hess,
one of the earliest historians of the New York school, has pointed out,
'abstract art became as American as baseball or Archibald MacLeish'.
It was a trend, moreover, that was assisted by the influx of refugees
occasioned by the advent of the Nazis and the outbreak of war; men
like Hans Hoffman, Joseph Albers, and Fernand Léger, and Miro,
came to America and contributed to the enlargement of artistic
sensibility.

Foreign art, in fact, and in Pollock's case that of the American
Indians, has greatly influenced the painting of the New York school. Its
members have looked far and wide, as is in keeping with the eclectic
traditions of the country. For such painters, surrealism and an examination of the subconscious have meant much, as is also to be expected
in a land where psychiatry is so widely practised—and required. Instinctive painters, romantic painters even, like the Fauves before them,

they have gone all out for sensibility. As Grace Hartigan, one of their number, well says:

> I have found my 'subject', it concerns that which is vulgar and vital in American modern life, and the possibilities of its transcendence into the beautiful. I do not wish to *describe* my subject matter, or to reflect upon it—I want to distill it until I have its essence.

The essence, in short, is what the New York school seeks; the kernel of life, a variant perhaps on the theme of the Golden Bowl.

Like all such movements, whose theories tend toward the esoteric and the elliptical, their aims are apt to be misunderstood. Almost to a man they deny that they are abstract. In 1943, for example, Gottlieb and Rothko in a letter to the *New York Times*, announced that: 'We assert that the subject is crucial and only that subject-matter is valid which is tragic and timeless. That is why we profess kinship with primitive and archaic art.' Then again, one must differentiate between the popular vision of the school as consisting of hit or miss men, sloshing on their paint without any concern for surface qualities or for design, and their actual achievement. Naturally, inevitably, the drip technique has come to be hailed as symbolical of their outlook; it has supplied too tempting a myth to be shelved. But one ought to remember that they are not linked by adherence to a common vocabulary as were the Fauves or Cubists. What, indeed, could be more different than the work of Rothko and de Kooning. The one is an exquisite, delving into gentle layers of paint, creating a world of pure aesthetic contemplation, in which the allure of the tones takes on the refulgence found in a piece of Sung porcelain. The other is dramatic, questing, a Northern expressionist, fastening on to *Das ewig Weibliche*—those tormented females that summarize the conflicts of his art, and as he declared: 'Art never seems to make me peaceful or pure. . . . I do not think . . . of art as a situation of comfort.'

They are related, however, by certain technical similarities. They have discarded the conventional easel picture; they have endorsed the large image, the striking note; and the grandiose, the gigantic are part of their pictorial baggage. The very size of their canvases would seem to suggest, moreover, that, although prepared to particularize one aspect of experience, they desire to make the fragment reveal the whole, as did Monet with his paintings of waterlilies, the influence of which on Philip Guston, for instance, is demonstrable. In their own way, which is determined by the conditions of our age, they are trying to paint on an epic scale—to create, in fact, an epic which has not a conventional subject for its theme, but which divulges the full range of an individual's sensibility.

That a desire to render the fullness of life should have arisen in America is understandable enough. The consolidation of America as a great world Power is evident for all to see. It might be argued, as well, that such a period of expansion must necessarily be vented in creative terms; that it will be matched by an explosive art, as was the case in Britain during the Industrial Revolution when Constable and Turner revealed in their painting the inner dynamic of their environment. America, whether she wants to or not, has assumed the leading role; that an art form should now emerge to correspond to her vitality is perhaps inevitable.

All the same, could it not be said that the old realist tradition provided, and still does, a better reflection of national aspirations? Certainly, one can hardly deny that one aspect of American society—the world of the underdog, for instance—has been effectively rendered by the realists, by a Dreiser or a Reginald Marsh; but what is so exciting about the American complex of cultures is that such views of life in the raw are complemented by more introspective analysis as revealed in the novels of Henry James or Scott Fitzgerald. Such manifestations have also to be taken into account. Nor ought one to overlook the debate, continuous and agonizing, concerning man's role in organized society: the desire, so often manifest in American life, to cut through to the heart of the matter, in spite of the complications of taking such a line.

In this connexion, the New York school of painters must be seen as explorers of personal reactions—as delvers. Thus, when Robert Motherwell writes that 'without ethical consciousness, a painter is only a decorator', he is speaking for a country which believes in moral dilemmas, which surrenders to analysis and which adheres, as Mr. Dulles adhered, to the concept of a foreign policy, rightly or wrongly, based on a moral standpoint. Their adoption of a non-figurative style, their belief that they can only vent their feelings in a free and untrammelled manner of painting, reflects, too, some of the special characteristics of the environment. In view of the diversity of national strains existing in the country—German, Japanese, British, Russian—a style had to be found capable of providing a language in which racial self-consciousness might be submerged or transmuted. Such a style, indeed, has provided a way out from the 'frontier fallacy', so well analysed by Mr. E. P. Richardson. This contention may be valid only at this particular stage; before long, the general move toward a more figurative approach may require some shift among the leaders of the American *avant garde*. The nature of the problem they feel called upon to tackle may alter of its own accord.

Since the early nineteenth century American painting has oscillated between two positions: absorption in the native soil and expatriation. The latter course, it would seem, is no longer necessary—or rather, the metamorphosis of reality, of the actual, into another plane has proved possible owing to the liberation provided by abstraction itself. In this respect New York has offered a convenient setting: in spite of its sweat and rush, in spite of its compelling personality, it somehow lies outside the boundaries of reality, and, like Venice, it can take on an air of hallucination. The painter resident there, once he has abandoned the overt realism implicit in the daily round, once he has said farewell to his grass roots, can ride on air; he can and does mount into his own private realm.

Fundamentally, such painting is opposed to rationalism. It could well be, as Jean Cassou has suggested, that it expresses the elemental forces, the Whitmanesque sides of American life; some of the school's reckless, pulsating canvases—those of Pollock, for example—can give off the rhythm of the anonymous crowds that move to rock and roll. Is such painting the equivalent of this almost frenzied paganism? Up to a point, one may agree, and yet . . . the fineness of the perception, so apparent once the language has been mastered, is a sign rather of a sort of aristocratic devil-may-care, a dandyish disregard for convention.

Perhaps Mr. Greenberg put his finger on the distinctive quality of so much modern painting—and not only American—by stating that

> uniformity, this dissolution of the picture into sheer texture . . . seems to answer to something deep-seated in contemporary sensibility. It corresponds perhaps to the feeling that all hierarchical distinctions have been exhausted, that no area or order of experience is either intrinsically or relatively superior to any other.

The refusal to accept such distinctions in life is characteristic of contemporary American society. Yet American democracy, while very real, is also very superficial; it does not go more than skin deep. Away from an agreed heritage, or rather the victim of a multiplicity of heritages, the American is ever in search of some niche; he can turn against life and beat it or, like so many painters, he can seek to find his place by endeavouring to render the essence of his sensations in terms of private symbols. Hence also the connexion with Oriental art and thought, which is more apparent with an older painter like Morris Graves than with the younger set; Nirvana, abstraction, can become a reality owing to their absolute quality. Such artists, after all, can call cousin to the Last Puritan.

Within its limitations, the New York school has made a real contribution to American culture, even if the praise sometimes lavished on it may sound excessive. To some of its critics, it has seemed to represent the brashest sides of national life; nevertheless, a determination to be oneself, to venture far, to go all out for an experience, come what may, without counting the cost, can yield results. Even if such painting, as André Chastel has observed, may find the greatest difficulty in growing old, it has surprising relevance; as much as anything else, it incorporates a belief in the individual. 'Paint quality is meaningless if it does not express quality of meaning,' wrote Gottlieb. In an age that has tended to think only of American materialism, the action painter, the abstract expressionist, call him what you will, must be saluted. He has kept alive a faith in the perennial qualities of disinterested values; he stands out as an upholder in his own setting and in his own fashion, of *l'art pour l'art*. For that, if for nothing else, his contemporaries and posterity have every reason to be grateful to him.

The Music Man

To the time-weary European, American music has a strange
fascination: for we can hear in it a civilization coming to birth.
We are enriched by centuries of tradition; yet there are times—
since we live in a world conscious of violent change—when our traditions seem to shackle rather than to satisfy us. The American composer
is neither enriched nor shackled. He had nothing to start from but old
rags and bones of European culture that, imported to a new environment, soon lost their savour. Then gradually, in the pulping machine
of a polyglot society, the rags and bones began to acquire a taste of
their own. The process, however, took time; and perhaps for this
reason the earliest American compositions to manifest a creative
spark tended to be technically inexpert. William Billings, in the late
eighteenth century, had little ambition except to produce devotional
music in the tradition of the Puritan hymn. His mistakes in text-book
harmony have, however, a whiff of creative genuis: so that he is an
original who can still move us, while the professional competence of his
European-trained contemporaries and successors can move us no longer.

The first authentic American composer is undoubtedly Charles Ives
(1874–1954), who knew that if the loss of tradition means the loss of the
wisdom that tradition brings, it also offers a supreme opportunity. He
could not be content, like Macdowell, to write second-hand academic
music in the German tradition, with 'American' titles appended. If he
was to be an honest creator, he had to take his material from the world
around him. Since he was born at Danbury, Connecticut, this meant
the town band, ragtime, the corny theatre tune, the chapel hymn. The
remoteness of this music from academic convention stimulated the
aural imagination. The music was not what it would seem to be,

rudimentarily notated on paper. It was unpredictable sound-stuff which was also human experience: the vast body of camp-singers yelling slightly different versions of the same hymn; the horn player who gets left behind his fellows in the town band; the four bands that, at celebration time, play different music simultaneously in the four corners of the town square; the chapel singing heard over water, mixed with the sound of wind and rustling leaves.

Ives's empirical approach to technique relates him to Whitman; he shares the poet's all-inclusiveness, his ubiquitous love of humanity, of every facet of the visible, audible and tactile world. His gargantuan appetite 'absorbs and translates' experience as the original Leather-stocking pioneer attempted to subjugate the physical world. Yet the obverse side of the American myth is present in Ives, too: for the Ego that would swallow all experience becomes progressively more aware of its loneliness. Beneath the gregarious bustle of life is the isolated consciousness that, in communion with Nature, seeks not aggressive domination but sublimation. For Ives, as for his heroes Emerson and Thoreau—and for Emily Dickinson too—artistic creation was funda-mentally a mystical act, an attempt to apprehend Reality beneath the flux of appearances. In a New World—both physically and spiritually speaking—the Transcendentalist must first put his own house in order.

One might almost say that America compressed its musical past, present and potential future into the personality of Ives. The strife in his music is a still more violent development from the European sonata principle (he admired Beethoven above all composers); and its very violence leads him to a new, in part serial, search for order. His ex-perimental techniques are not always adequately realized, for he suffered, as any artist must, from working without a public. Yet his polyphony of independent ensembles, explored more than forty years ago, may have more to suggest to the future of music than any of the European composers who are, in intrinsic achievement, greater. Nor is his significance limited to his experimentalism. In spite of its 'newness', his finest music, such as the marvellous *Hausatonic at Stock-bridge*, sounds now as ripely and inescapably a part of the past as the Mahler and Berg whom it fortuitously resembles; and when one has allowed for the Whitmanesque diffuseness in the two piano sonatas there remains an authentic note of grandeur. It is a note that is becom-ing rarer; we should be grateful for it.

Carl Ruggles, born in 1876, is a man of the same generation as Ives:

but whereas Ives is both gregarious democrat and solitary visionary, Ruggles is unequivocally the isolated spirit. (He is almost literally a hermit; and the walls of his study, in his house at Vermont, are symbolically papered with the exquisite calligraphy of his own manuscripts.) Thus the texture of Ruggles's music has nothing like the multifarious complexity of Ives, the ragbag into which all experience is poured helter-skelter, to be re-created. Yet although Ruggles's music contains no direct reflection of the chaos of the American scene, he is still concerned with the New: for he is a solitary in New England, where so much that went to make America is rooted.

Though Ruggles has written only a handful of works his music is singularly consistent. His is a dedicated art, affirming the freedom of the human spirit; and his affirmation runs parallel to Schoenberg's 'free' atonal period, in the Europe of the second decade of the century. As an American, indeed, with no past, Ruggles sought freedom—from tonal bondage, from the harmonic strait-jacket—even more remorselessly than Schoenberg. The harmonic sound of his music, with its preponderance of minor seconds, major sevenths, and minor ninths, is similar to Schoenberg's; but in place of Schoenberg's tense Germanic opacity, Ruggles cultivates a clear, 'open' resonance in his singing, winging polyphony. This spacious texture and resilient rhythm are perhaps Ruggles's representatively American qualities, which have their counterparts in the polyphonic textures of Ives in, for instance, the Emerson movement of the *Concord Sonata*. But Ruggles differs from Ives in his desire to clarify, to refine and to concentrate. Ives 'accepts the Universe'—the trivial and tawdry along with the sublime. Ruggles is concerned with his own soul—with the 'great things' that are done when 'Men and Mountains meet'. It is revealing to compare Ruggles's *Men and Mountains* with Delius's *A Song of the High Hills*. Delius starts from the burden of his own passionate heart—the appoggiatura-laden harmony that tries to drag down the singing lines. Ruggles's chromaticism is not, historically speaking, so far from Delius's. But for him singing polyphony overrides harmonic tension, seeking the One in the Many. Delius is a (belated and weary) humanist; Ruggles is a mystic in a non-religious society. Paradoxically, his mysticism is part of his Americanism: for it is also his 'newness', his search for personal integrity.

A more radical 'newness' is, of course, possible. Ruggles starts from the twelve equal semi-tones of European tradition; Ives, in exploiting noise and non-European elements, hinted at their abandonment. Edgar Varèse (born 1885) from his earliest days discarded the conventional materials of diatonic melody and of harmony, as well as rhythmic patterns related to harmonic tension. For him the post-Beethoven approach to music as psychological drama, rooted in the self, was irrelevant. He rather sought a musical complement to Action painting; music should be created, like the dance, as an act of the body itself, manipulating tangible and audible material 'concretely'. So he starts from the sound-characteristics of each instrument—what he calls its 'density', its timbre and quality independent of pitch-relationships, let alone harmony. The instrument is a sound like any other, relatively accidental, noise; and Varèse's music is a polyphony of timbres, each instrument having its own typical melodic figure and rhythmic pattern (both of which never develop). Construction, for Varèse, is an achievement of the sense of space. Harmonically constructed music achieves this through the development of themes, the movement to and away from a central key. Varèse achieves his 'opening of space' through the addition and contrast of rhythms and timbres.

Clearly such a conception of music is more ritualistic and magical than 'expressive': and has much in common with Oriental music and with the music of primitive cultures. Varèse believed that this was necessary because the hyper-self-consciousness of modern man was one of the reasons for twentieth-century chaos; art's duty was to encourage forgetfulness of self, if not in mysticism (which is accessible only to dedicated spirits) then in magic. But he has always insisted that his ritualistic approach is twentieth century as well as primitive, being related to a machine-dominated civilization. The percussive noises and rhythmic patterns in his music have affinities with the sounds of modern city life that have become part of our everyday consciousness. The artist's task is to |help us perceive the patterns of order and beauty that lie beneath mechanistic chaos, if we have eyes to see and ears to hear.

Ives, Ruggles, and Varèse are the three grand old men of American music: from whom the multifarious evolution of composition in the (culturally not very United) States can be traced. Of the composers born around the turn of the century Roy Harris has something of the rugged, Whitmanesque quality of Ives in his regional, folk-hymnodic vein; and the essence of his music, as of Ruggles's, is in the sustained flow of his melodies. The enormous opening theme of the Third Symphony (his best-known and perhaps best work) is vocal and modal in character, half-way between folk-song and plainchant. Its primitive religious feeling, its pioneering aspiration, relate it to Puritan tradition; and the unbroken 'sections' of the symphony are a germination from this single seed: an empirical process rather than a matter of conscious integration.

The American flavour of Harris's language centres in its 'vernacular' line and rhythm. If the opening theme suggests plainchant that is not only because it is religious in feeling but also because plainsong is close to speech. The racy vigour which the movement gradually acquires and the open texture—with a prevalence of rising fourths, minor sevenths. and major ninths—rejuvenate the continuous Wagnerian flow of the enharmony and the shimmer of the Sibelian *moto perpetuo*. So, imperceptibly, the *moto perpetuo* is transformed into the brusquely American fugued dance with which the work concludes. This exciting if curious mating of the jaunty middle-west dance-hall with the medieval hoquet is the most obviously 'contemporary' section of the score; and the closest in spirit and technique to the music of Harris's contemporary, Aaron Copland.

The pioneering, quasi-religious vein of Harris is remote from Copland's early music. In an arid machine civilization he, like Varèse, seems to have felt that he had to sacrifice the natural technique of lyrical growth. In the *Piano Variations* of 1930 he starts from skeletonic fragments: from declamatory 'blue' notes and percussive rhythms, By disintegration and reintegration, by investigating all possible serial permutations of a tiny five-note figure, he extracts what human nourishment he can, creating music of stark power, yet also of unexpected tenderness. If Copland came to feel a need to humanize his music it was not because his early works were not created out of the fullness of his being; it was simply because an artist—as Ives found— cannot long subsist without an audience.

The more direct style of Copland's ballets and film music does not deny the technique of his earlier works: though the music's deliberate lack of progression is less disturbing when allied to immediately recognizable, folk-like tunes, and to physical action or visual drama. Certainly the folky vein of Copland's ballets, especially *Appalachian Spring*, is not an evasion of the steel girders—within which Copland so miraculously discovers a human warmth—of the *Piano Variations*; for he sees the prairie as a symbol of the irremediable loneliness of big cities, the hymn as a symbol of the religious and domestic security that urban man has lost. The uncompromising austerity of Copland's earlier work and the more popular mode of his ballets meet in the mature music he has created since about 1940. It is not fortuitous that these works should include a fine song-cycle to poems of Emily Dickinson: nor that in the last movement of the *Piano Sonata* percussive machine-noises should be transmuted into the eternal solitude of the prairie. The 'open' fourths, fifths, sevenths, and ninths, the immensely slow rhythmic organization, carry us outside time and still the heart's agitation. The serenity Copland attains here is the more impressive and (to most of us) moving because Copland is not a religious mystic in the sense that Ruggles and (sometimes) Ives are.

The regional, Robert Frost-like aspects of Harris and Copland have had many imitators; yet most that is vital in American music seems to derive from the tradition of solitariness, if the paradoxical phrase is valid. Elliott Carter's music, for instance, though more sophisticated than either, has hints of both Ruggles and Ives in its sturdily independent polyphony of line and rhythm; and he like the later Beethoven in his attempt to create order from chaos, through a conscious exercise of the Will. Like Ives, Carter uses both 'dualistic' tonal techniques and 'monistic' serial methods in seeking order. Other composers, notably Roger Sessions, have gravitated from traditional tonality to a complete acceptance of the serial principle. The Puritan austerity common to the composers we have mentioned thus far (except possibly Ives) is alien to Sessions; his music is richly sensuous, with a quality of Jewish rhetoric that suggests Mahler and the earlier Schoenberg, though his rhythms are much more kinetically extrovert than those of the Viennese school. There is nothing obviously American about Sessions's music. His Reality, like that of Wallace Stevens, is the truth of the imagination; and the external world obtrudes into his music scarcely at all. Yet it is significant that he and Carter have had far more influence upon the younger generation of American composers than the regionalists or those that have followed the more consciously European stylizations of Stravinsky. Perhaps this amounts to an admission that a socially acceptable idiom is, for a 'serious' American composer, no longer a practical possibility.

Some 'advanced' composers have, indeed, relinquished the notion of an audience altogether. The music of John Cage, for instance, starts from Varèse's radical preoccupation with sound as such, in time; but whereas Varèse remains always conscious of the physical world, Cage attempts, through his music, to obliterate the physical and temporal. Music becomes therapeutic, an agent of Zen Buddhism: hardly discussable in the same terms as traditional Western music. It is perhaps interesting that his work appeals strongly to those concerned with the visual arts.

Though superficially surprising, it is not really odd that so obsessive a concern with the integrity of the human spirit should exist in a world dominated by mass-produced entertainment. Perhaps, moreover, the case of George Gershwin suggests that we should beware of glib distinctions between art and commerce. An instinctive musician, nurtured on the restricted diet of Tin Pan Alley, Gershwin used as his basic material the 32-bar tune, with a no less machine-made harmonic idiom dating from fifty years back. Yet the songs Gershwin wrote within this convention revivify cliché, perhaps because—like the hero of his urban folk-opera, Porgy—they preserve a radical innocence. Both their lilting ecstasy and their nostalgia speak to us with the voice of genius, however modestly; for we are all, like Gershwin himself, in some sense dispossessed, spiritually isolated, living in the moment, poor boys who hope to make good. The Jewish and Negroid elements in Gershwin (as in Copland) are not merely racial. The authentic essence of jazz came from a dispossessed and oppressed people. Its techniques, being incantatory and hypnotic, tend to negate the 'Western' concept of progression in time. So it is, after all, understandable that there should be affinities between jazz—whether in a state of nature or in a sophisticated, even commercialized form as used by Gershwin or by Blitzstein and Bernstein—and some of the most apparently esoteric music of our time.

Certainly to an outsider, viewing the American musical scene, it would seem that what matters most is the extremes. On the one hand stand the grand old 'progressives'—Ives, Ruggles, in smaller way Varèse—with the more experimental Copland, Carter, to a lesser degree, Harris, Sessions, and some of the more recent experimentalists. On the other hand is the authentic element in jazz, as urban folk art; Gershwin when he is not writing symphonic works; Blitzstein and the Bernstein of *West Side Story*. Comparatively, the middle-of-the-path men, even such an excellent musician as Samuel Barber or such a clever theatre-man as Menotti, have little vitality and not much social or artistic justification. Perhaps there is a moral in this, for a new if not for our old community. Certainly it suggests that the split between the 'esoteric' and the 'popular' is not necessarily to be deplored. In the long run the real split may prove to be between the creatively vigorous on the one hand, the emotionally and academically safe on the other. And that split has been with us since civilization began.

Red and Black

Two causes of guilt lie heavily on American history. One concerns the Indian, the other the Negro. Neither has, as yet, been fully redeemed.

To-day we are most likely to think of the Indian in terms of Western films, of cowboys and gunmen and wide open spaces, but the first Indians met by the settlers at Jamestown were not hostile. They believed in hospitality, and the English, though ready to suspect treachery at every turn and mindful no doubt of the fate of Raleigh's colony at Cape Henry, were impressed by their friendliness. The Indians taught them new methods of agriculture and showed them new crops of corn, sweet potatoes and maize. It was the massacre of 1622 which was seized on to justify war:

> Our hands which before were tied with gentlenesse and faire usage [wrote Edward Waterhouse in his *Relation of the Barbarous Massacre*] are now set at liberty by the treacherous violence of the Sausages [Savages]. . . . So that we, who hitherto have had possession of no more ground than their waste, and our purchase at a valuable consideration to their owne contentment, gained; may now by right of Warre, and law of Nations, invade the Country, and destroy them who sought to destroy us. . . . Now their cleared ground in all their villages (which are situate in the fruitfullest places of the land) shall be inhabited by us, whereas heretofore the grubbing of woods was the greatest labour.

From that moment the Indians were attacked and massacred, and as the white man explored farther and farther into the new continent the Indian was pushed farther and farther to the west. But what was the legal justification for European settlement in territory occupied by another race? If the English had refused to accept the unqualified sovereignty of the Indians, were not the Indians right to attack? These questions troubled Thomas Jefferson and they are still troubling many to-day; only five years ago the Supreme Court, in the case of the *Tee-Hit-Ton Indians versus the United States*, adjudged that these Alaskan Indians were not entitled to compensation for the seizing by the United States of lands in their possession prior to the purchase of Alaska by the United States in 1867. Justice Reed delivered the opinion: 'Every American schoolboy knows that the savage tribes of this continent were deprived of their ancestral ranges by force and that, even when the Indian ceded millions of acres by treaty in return for blankets, food and trinkets, it was not a sale but the conquerors' will that deprived them of their land.'

The modern white American, then, lives among the remnants of a race whom he has dispossessed by force, and among the more numerous members of another race who were dispossessed of their homeland to be transported forcibly to North America. It is impossible to compute accurately the number of Negroes taken from Africa over several centuries; estimates run as high as twenty million. Certainly nowhere near half that number ever reached American ports. For after the warlike raids on the villages, the march to the coast, the branding and the chains, came the Middle Passage. A slave ship could be smelt for miles down wind. Sickness raged. Manacled bodies were chained side by side, with sometimes as little as eighteen inches between floor and ceiling.

> I saw pregnant women [reports one slaver, Alexander Falconbridge] give birth to babies while chained to corpses which our drunken overseers had not removed. . . . The younger women fared best at first as they were allowed to come on deck as companions for our crew. . . . Toward the end of the run, which lasted nearly six weeks, the mortality thinned out the main hold, and some scores of women were driven below as company for the males.

The ships were unloaded in the West Indies; the diseased were weeded out and the fraction that remained fit for sale were taught to wear clothes, speak English, do plantation work and worship the Christian God. There were two million slaves by 1830, almost four million by the outbreak of the Civil War.

Nothing distinguishes the modern American, for all his optimism and material success, more from the European than that he lives in a land with this double image of guilt upon it. Vast recompense has already been made. There are Indian tribes to-day richer than whole counties of England. Negroes in the United States have a greater chance of raising their standard of living and achieving a higher education than anywhere else in the world. But below the surface the old sores still run to erupt, spilling violence and confusion. The present school trouble in the Southern states is one of them.

Of the two races it is the Negro who has made a longer impact on white consciousness and white imagination. The Indians withdrew leaving the land almost empty behind them, except for the names, the melodious and tongue-twisting names of the rivers and mountains, plants and animals—Shenandoah, Allegheny, persimmon, succotash, chipmunk. Though Pocahontas became a legend, based largely on a chapter of John Smith's *General Historie* of 1624, and Longfellow published his 'Indian Edda' *Hiawatha* in 1855, James Logan, chief of the Mingo Indians, Chief Joseph of the Nez Percé tribe or Captain Jack of the Modoc Indians have not become national figures. The frail and energetic Francis Parkman lived for some weeks in 1846 with Sioux Indians near Fort Laramie in Wyoming, taking part in their buffalo hunts and their ceremonials, and later dictating his prose epic, *The Oregon Trail*, to his cousin and companion, Quincy A. Shaw, but it was James Fenimore Cooper, a generation earlier, importing the manner of Sir Walter Scott to the land of the Mohicans, who has made the life of the frontier, the Woodsman Natty Bumppo and the Indians, romantically familiar to generations of schoolboys.

Cooper's Indian, like Uncas, was still the idealized noble savage, close relation to Chateaubriand's Natchez Indian Chactas (of *Atala*), or the very incarnation of villainy and treachery like Magua. Cooper's wilderness is without the terrific storms characteristic of North America, without mud, sleet, snow, without squalor, human depravity or obscenity. The only cruelty is the cruelty of Indian warfare which Leatherstocking continually explains away as the product of the savage's peculiar 'gifts'. Cooper's frontier is a kind of paradise that is forever passing before the advance of civilization, just as the frontier is passing in the classic cowboy story, *The Virginian*, by Owen Wister. In fact, between them, it might be said, Cooper and Wister have supplied the framework of that whole epic romance of cowboys and Indians which, as the saga of Greek heroes once filled Western imagination, now fills the West's cinemas and television screens. The black and white of the morality, the good Indian and bad Indian, the Christian and pagan, the whole idealization of the primitive life, which is part of its enormous appeal, derives ultimately from Cooper.

The white Americans have seldom lived side by side with the Indians. To-day Indians are gathered mostly in reservations impinging little on public life. Yet whether he has been cast in an heroic role, as in J. G. Neihardt's *Song of the Indian Wars* or in the savage role of the Apache making their last stand against the gunmen of the West, the Indian has really always been seen as a figure in a romance. Perhaps it was because he never threatened sufficient danger, because he was an easy enemy and easily conquered, that the Indian has so quickly entered the world of legend; or rather, that he has never left the world of legend. To-day, when not shown as the warriors of the Westerns, they are the ancient people of New Mexico and Arizona, in contact with the time-lessness of rock and sand, uncluttered by mechanical occupations and mass-produced possessions, to whom writers like Willa Cather, as well as D. H. Lawrence from the other side of the Atlantic, have escaped from the modern city and the modern world.

If the Indian became quickly legendary, the Negro was actual enough. Working under the overseer on the plantations, or as a house servant, or on the fields of a smaller farm with the master himself, white man and black man have lived side by side for three centuries. At first the Negro was almost entirely a financial property. Advertisements such as this would appear:

> Negroes for sale: A girl about twenty years of age (raised in Virginia) and her two female children, one four and the other two years old—remarkably strong and healthy—never having had a day's sickness with the exception of smallpox, in her life. The children are fine and healthy. She is very prolific in her generating qualities and affords a rare opportunity to any person who wishes to raise a family of strong and healthy servants for their own use.

We may recall the conversation Miss Watson's Jim overheard one evening at the door between his 'missus' and the Widow Douglas:

> 'I hear old missus tell de widder she gwyne to sell me down to Orleans, but she didn't want to, but she could git eight hund'd dollars for me, en it 'uz sich a big stack o' money she couldn' resis.'

And Jim, remember, like Uncle Tom, was a family man with a wife and two children.

The whole history of the Negro in America is that of his emancipation from the status of financial property, with no rights even within his own family, to the slow and often grudging recognition of his full human stature and dignity. For the earliest picture of the Negro, still segregated in his shanties far from the white folk, playing his drums and conducting his voodoo ceremonies, we must go to the Negro songs and folk-legends, especially the spirituals which tell of the year to year hopes of Negroes in slavery, longing for escape either north to the free states, or to Liberia, the promised land of the American Colonization Society. Though written in the language of spiritual aspiration, their hopes ('Go down Moses, way down in Egypt Land, tell ole Pharaoh, Let my people go') are more often for this world. The hero of one of William Faulkner's first wholly successful stories, *Sunset*, published in 1925, is a poor backwoods Negro, who has run away from his plantation and knocks about the port of New Orleans asking: 'Cap'n, suh, is dis Af'ica? . . . Ah'm tryin' to get to Af'ica, please suh, is dis de right way? . . . Ah wants to go back home, whar de preacher say us come fum.'

In 1774 a British traveller, Nicholas Cresswell, gives us a glimpse in his diary of some slaves he saw in Maryland: 'In their songs they generally relate the usage they have received from their Masters or Mistresses in a very satirical manner. Their Poetry is like the Music—rude and uncultivated. Their Dancing is most violent exercise, but so irregular and grotesque I am not able to describe it.' But to get at the character and mind of the plantation Negro, we must read Joel Chandler Harris's Uncle Remus stories.

Harris's own parentage was a cross between Georgia and Ireland but his tales of Brer Rabbit, Brer Fox, Brer Possum and all the other animals have achieved the status of folk-legend. He himself wrote: 'It is a fable thoroughly characteristic of the Negro; and it needs no scientific investigation to show why he selects as his hero the weakest and most harmless of all animals. . . . It is not virtue that triumphs but helplessness; not malice, but mischievousness.' Mischievous Brer Rabbit may be, and nothing is more typical of him than bursting out 'in er laff', or rolling on the ground 'laffing fit ter kill'. Yet this world of brothers is no children's world of stuffed toys. Brer Possum is killed in a bonfire, Brer Wolf is scalded to death in a chest, Brer Fox murders

Brer Tukkey Buzzard. This is nature red in tooth and claw. Harris's Negro is never sentimental about animals in the Enid Blyton manner; nor are these tales allegories in Æsop's manner; there is ultimately only one moral, as Uncle Remus explains to the little boy after the treacherous death of stupid lumbering old Brer Possom: 'Folks is folks en creeturs is creeturs, en you can't make um needer mo' ner less. Creeturs is natally got ha'sh idees, en you may take notice: wharsomever you see ha'r en bristles, right dar youer mo' dan ap'ter fine claws en tushes.'

Some have said that Harris patronized the Negro; that he was fascinated with the Negro as he wanted him to be—part devoted child, part dangerous animal—rather than as he really was. Yet his world is still the closest thing to Negro folk-tale that exists and was based on close and exact knowledge of the real Negro story-teller and the real Negro folk-tale.

The ballads (or work songs) tell of other folk-heroes, such as John Henry, sometimes the steel-driver in the building of the 'Yaller Dog' or 'Yaller Ball' railway line for 'Mister Billie Bob Russel', sometimes a roustabout on river boats; Winslow Homer painted the Negro on shore and at sea; Booker T. Washington, son of a slave, wrote his own autobiography; yet in white men's eyes the slave or emancipated slave of the later nineteenth century had developed into a series of stereotyped portraits. One type, created by Mrs. Stowe, was Uncle Tom, the noble, high-minded, devoutly Christian slave who is finally flogged to death by Simon Legree, the drunken, degenerate planter. Uncle Tom bred a progeny of like menservants, such as Mingo, in Joel Chandler Harris's novel. Another stereotype was (and remains) the Negro seen as a barely suppressed primitive savage who under duress will run berserk, true to his inner jungle self. Eugene O'Neill gave dramatic expression to this theme in *The Emperor Jones*. All who have seen or read the play will remember the giant Negro, Brutus Jones, former Pullman porter and ex-convict, breaking down amid the incessant beating of tom-tom, retracing his own steps and those of his race to the chain-gang, the auction-block, the slave ship and the crocodile god in the Congo. This, too, is the theme of the first part of Vachel Lindsay's *The Congo*:

> Then I heard the boom of the blood-lust song
> And thigh-bone beating on a tin-pan gong.
> And 'BLOOD' screamed the whistles and the fifes of the warriors. . .

Some such clichés are still with us. The savage has become the Negro in the Harlem razor-fight: the servant, the family mama whom in actuality or fiction we all recognize, whether from the film of *Gone with the Wind*, or the infinitely true and warm Berenice of Carson McCullers's *The Member of the Wedding*.

There is no need to list here the anti-slavery novels, such as J. T. Trowbridge's *Cudjo's Cave* and *Neighbor Jackwood*, or *Marie* written by Alexis de Tocqueville's companion on his American tour, Gustave de Beaumont. These books were mainly propaganda. Some authors, however, pondered deeply the relation of white man and coloured man. In 1851 Melville published his *Moby Dick or the Whale* and one of the first of many astounding incidents is Ishmael's night at the Spouter Inn, sharing his bed with Queequeg, the pagan South Sea island harpooner:

> Upon waking next morning about daylight, I found Queequeg's arm thrown over me in the most loving and affectionate manner. You had almost thought I had been his wife. . . . I tried to move his arm—unlock his bridegroom clasp—yet, sleeping as he was, he still hugged me tightly, as though naught but death should part us twain.

And again, echoing this passage toward the end of the book when Ishmael and Queequeg are both fastened to a 'monkey-rope': 'For better or worse, we two, for the time, were wedded; . . . an elongated Siamese ligature united us. Queequeg was my own inseparable twin brother.' Queequeg, it is true, was not a Negro. It is Flask's harpooner, Daggoo, who is the Negro; but Queequeg, the heathen, is the only friend the solitary Ishmael finds in the strange world of middle-class Christian New Bedford. Together they attend Father Mapple's sermon on Jonah in the Sailors' Bethel, together they worship Queequeg's idol Yojo, and together they sleep 'a cosy, loving pair'. Thanks to Queequeg, wrote Ishmael, 'no longer my splintered heart and maddened hand were turned against the wolfish world. This soothing savage had redeemed it.'

The deep truth this symbol expressed for Melville, Mark Twain explored in *The Adventures of Huckleberry Finn*, published after the Civil War, over thirty years later. We all remember the incident when Jim and Huck are separated by fog and how Huck (in a somewhat Tom Sawyerish prank) pretends there had been no fog and no chase and that Jim had dreamed the whole thing. Jim believes Huck's story until in the light of dawn Huck points at the leaves on the raft and the smashed oar. Jim is silent for a while and then, from out his hurt pride, comes a withering speech, ending:

'En all you wuz thinkin' 'bout wuz how you could make a fool uv ole Jim wid a lie. Dat truck dah is *trash*; en trash is what people is dat puts dirt on de head er dey fren's en makes 'em ashamed.' Then he got up slow and walked to the wigwam, and went in there without saying anything but that.

At this, the last shreds of Huck's white pride finally disappear:

It made me feel so mean I could almost kissed *his* foot to get him to take it back. It was fifteen minutes before I could work myself up to go and humble myself to a nigger; but I done it, and I warn't ever sorry for it afterward neither. I didn't do him no more mean tricks, and I wouldn't done that one if I'd 'a' knowed it would make him feel that way.

In fact, Huckleberry Finn nowhere condemns the institution of slavery and in the very next chapter has a crisis of conscience about the right and wrong of helping Jim to escape. But Huck had recognized Jim as a brother and this recognition is the central event of Mark Twain's story.

Jim is the conscience of the book, Jim who burst out crying to think how he had struck his little daughter for not obeying a command only to find an attack of scarlet fever had left her deaf and dumb, Jim who becomes Huck's foster-father, treating him as gently and warmly as Huck's real 'pap' had treated him roughly. Together black man and white boy form an ideal society of freedom and brotherhood on their raft as it floats irrevocably south, farther and farther into slave territory. Together their life is an unspoken criticism of all the surrounding society on the banks of the Mississippi, with its greed and feuds, deceptions and violence, including the 'morality' of Aunt Polly, the Widow Douglas and Miss Watson who had considered selling her Negro to a slaver for eight hundred dollars.

In the end the novel returns, on the Phelps' farm, to the world of Tom Sawyer's relations and the hardbitten puritan ethos of frontier St. Petersburg. This, as many readers have remarked, is a flaw. For there Tom's imagination, which romanticizes experience, and no longer Huck's, gains control and the quest for freedom degenerates into farce. Though Jim is freed in the end, neither his freedom nor Huck's (in spite of his famous last words) is quite what the glorious chapters on the river had promised. Was it a failure of nerve on Mark Twain's part, or a failure of the imagination? Who knows? Such a brotherhood as existed on that Mississippi raft was perhaps only possible through a boy's vision. It needed a civil war and several generations since, and it will need several generations more before the mutual easy respect between black and white, as Mark Twain envisaged it, can be achieved, or, in Huck's words, before everybody is 'satisfied, and feels right and kind toward others'.

If not from Jim, it is clear from his portrait of Roxy in *Pudd'nhead Wilson*, that Mark Twain could draw a warm full-blooded Negro. Not, in fact, until William Faulkner's novels were there again such Negroes—Dilsey, the old Negro woman of *The Sound and the Fury*; Sam Fathers, 'son of a Negro slave and an Indian king'; the nameless, lonely Joe Christmas walking the city pavements in *Light in August*; or Lucas Beauchamp, the dignified old Negro of *Intruder in the Dust*, who is accused of having shot a white man in the back and is held in Jefferson gaol with a threat of lynching. Faulkner's society, far from fulfilling the promised 'marriage' or brotherhood held out by Melville or Mark Twain, is a society tortured by the triple doom of slavery and civil war in the past and the mechanized industrial revolution of the present. Faulkner is a moral author groping for the human truth which is neither that of the decayed and decaying old order nor of the spreading poison of the new order. But the Negro's role throughout is one of heroism—'a people who had learned humility through suffering and learned pride through the endurance which survived the suffering'.

Most Negroes, the descendants of those that came in the slave ships, endured; only a tiny fraction were returned to Liberia. Gradually, and increasingly, the Negro became part of the texture of American life, until to-day he feels himself to be fully an American; when, like Richard Wright, he returns to Africa he knows that only the colour of his skin is still the same: his whole way of life has become utterly different.

Since his arrival in the New World the Negro has passed through many roles: he has been slave and cotton-picker, house servant, funnyman minstrel (Mr. Tambo and Mr. Bones), city slicker in Harlem, student, writer, glamorous jazzman, and a dozen more.

To-day the dominant image of the Negro is two-faced: he is the pea-
sant, in a land without peasants, but he is also the city rebel, living a
life of the emotions in a complex, puritan civilization. It is a dual
image of a race which is gay, uninhibited, natural, easy, lazy, passionate, feeling life straight from the heart, whose songs (though often
written by white men like Stephen Collins Foster) are folk-songs,
whose music is jazz, whose world is the world of folk-opera, of *Porgy
and Bess* (book and music by white men)—a race which is, in some
indefinable way, free.

Such is the final irony that the white man's idea of a Negro, often
operating below the level of consciousness, stands for freedom. This
is what drew the flappers of the 1920s to the world of Harlem, Negroes
and jazz. This is what draws the Beats to-day. This is what draws the
young, and not so young, all over the industrialized world not only to
the excitement of Negro music but to the rebellious jargon of city
streets that goes with it, to be 'hip' and not 'square', to be 'cool' or
'gone' or 'way out', or whatever the cult word of the moment is.
This image is not very different from that drawn by Aimé Césaire:

> Hélas pour ceux qui n'ont jamais rien inventé
> pour ceux qui n'ont jamais rien exploré
> pour ceux qui n'ont jamais rien dompté
> mais ils s'abandonnent saisis à l'essence de toute chose
> ignorants des surfaces, mais saisis par le mouvement de toute chose
> insoucieux de dompter, mais jouant le jeu du monde.

'Not intent on conquest, but playing the play of the world'—so speaks
a sophisticated Negro poet from Martinique. But the new bohemians
are as vehement in rejecting Ford and Edison, the inventors, the explorers, Teddy Roosevelt and his Rough Riders, all those Americans
who by aggressive self-reliance and guts made modern America what
it is. To take the side of the Negro is, for them, to take the role of
protest and freedom.

But is this final image very different from that with which we began,
that of the happy, noble savage, except that now he is seen from within
Western society and no longer from without? The legend of the
Indian, which dominates the past, and the myth of the Negro, which in
large sections of the United States dominates the present, are still, as
they have always been in one form or another, images of escape from
our modern, newly mechanized and complex society. The Negro

novelists of the 1920s (Jean Toomer, Countée Cullen, Claude McKay and others) a James Baldwin or Richard Wright can tell us what it feels like to be an American Negro to-day, but what the Indian and Negro will think when the majority of his race attains full stature and full equality, and how he will then transform his heritage, still remains for the future.

The Realist's Predicament

Advance guard Americans are convinced, not without reason, that the current style of painting known as Abstract Expressionism radiates the world over from Manhattan Island, more specifically from West Fifty-third Street, where the Museum of Modern Art stands as the Parthenon on this particular acropolis. Indeed, Alfred H. Barr, Jnr., has issued from that supreme court the *mot d'ordre*—'Since resemblance to nature is at best superfluous and at worst distracting it might as well be eliminated.'

Given this fact, and given the high international rate of conversion to the new aesthetic order, it may surprise Europeans to learn that non-abstract painting, although under the weather of fashion, is still widely practised in the United States. Lack of familiarity abroad with twentieth-century American realism, be it straightforward, poetic, symbolic, magic or expressionist, exists for a number of reasons. Foremost among these is the fact that, with the exception of a few cosmopolitan stars of the past like Whistler and Sargent who actually imposed their vision on European art, American painters have, on the whole, been derivative from European traditions. Their work is naturally often marked by a strong Yankee flavour, but it hardly travels. Nor could a European have been expected to enthuse, say, over the singularly delicate impressionism of Theodore Robinson, Monet's pupil, when the Master of Giverny was close at hand. Thus, inevitably, it has required something new from the New World to upset the balance of the Old.

To-day's American realists trace their earliest descent to one or the other of two main pictorial traditions, the outspoken realism of Copley, Eakins and Homer, and the romanticism of the Hudson River

School, of followers like George Inness who poured deep draughts of mysticism into landscape and of the ultra-poetic Albert Pinkham Ryder. But since 1900 many powerful and turbulent tributaries have joined the majestic main stream, mixing social comment with realism, fantasy with romanticism, and expressionism—personal feeling at its most intense and engaged—with both. As the twentieth-century picture broadens and loses its sharp outlines, isolated figures such as Arthur B. Davies, a transatlantic Redon; Charles Demuth, poker-faced at one moment and Firbankian the next, and the rhapsodic John Marin have staked substantial claims on interpreting the visual world. And last but not least Grandma Moses, now in her ninety-ninth year, a favourite at the White House and the ultimate triumphant exemplar of 'Do it Yourself' art.

So much for the complicated inheritance come down to contemporary realists. No one persuasion predominates among them. Unlike the abstractionists, closely and often jealously banded together, forming and dissolving one unpopular front after another, non-abstractionists heed no single guiding tradition and show little concern with one another's work. This state of their individual isolation provides a further reason for the faint impression they make abroad. There may not always be strength in union but, grouped together in no matter how struggling a fashion, a school of artists has the means of imposing an aesthetic point of view denied the solitary performer.

Any review of American realism to-day must begin with—and then swiftly pass by—the National Academy, whose unsullied conservatism continues to exist like the dead calm in the centre of a hurricane. Pursuing a shelved and ineffectual way, it maintains an art school, distributes awards, and provides a refuge for the 'official' art of other years, for the New England seascapes where sunset-coloured waves dash on mossy rocks, and for conversation pieces and portraits whose specific respectability would baffle even the cultural seismograph of Osbert Lancaster. The absence of a strong academic background, either as a help or hindrance, contributes largely to the instability of American art as a tradition.

This instability, the fact that new movements have a way of lasting for a few years only before being quietly deposed, means that the number of artists who once enjoyed a brief moment of fame is legion. Some few have stuck to their guns, but most have spiked them. Among the former still active the most important are Edward Hopper and Charles Sheeler, both of them in their different ways exponents of the tradition of the American Scene. Hopper paints landscape and figures with a sort of stoical sentimentality which excludes any personal involvement. He sees the pathos of city streets at dusk and the loneliness that afflicts urban and suburban life. This quality of quiet desperation has been the theme of many American writers, but no one has distilled it in paint with Hopper's poignancy. As a member of the older generation of realists he derives from an exclusive focusing on visual facts and degrees of emotion that younger artists prefer to convey symbolically.

The literary values that Hopper makes so much of in his work are kept sternly at bay by Sheeler, whose fastidious precision of style leads to utter emotional detachment. He is the artist as scientist, exactly delineating a scene with an eye to its formal complexities, in which his subtle and ruthless observation delights. For his intensity of vision he may well be considered a forerunner of the Magic Realists.

Charles Burchfield is another member of the older generation of realists for whom landscape has not withered as an inspiration. He deals with it nostalgically and with no small degree of fantasy, vividly animating trees, flowers and ramshackle buildings, giving each a 'personality', sometimes in the manner of Walt Disney and again in that of Graham Sutherland. On the whole, realists of all generations concentrate on rural scenes. For some reason the painter's eye appears to be surfeited by the big city, which no longer excites him as it excited John Sloan, doyen of the New York school of 'incorrigible window-watchers' that reached its zenith just before 1914, and of which Louis Bouché is the last follower of any consequence.

Having never deviated from a style that suited them, and still being popular enough to command high prices, these men occupy a sufficiently secure position to ignore the sensational success of abstract expressionism. Their point of view is well summed up in some recent observations by Burchfield:

> I would just as soon not comment on the arts of to-day other than to say that I think any comment is futile. When a decadence sets in, and really gets rolling, there is nothing that can stop it. It must run its course before a renaissance can begin. I cannot possibly see what a course in design would do for an artist if he did not also have *academic* training in life drawing, still-life and composition—in fact the renaissance in the arts I mentioned will be impossible unless these subjects are restored to the artist's training.

Otherwise we will continue on the barren road of decoration most artists are now travelling. Thank God there are a few individualists who still refuse to conform.

Burchfield is speaking from a position of strength. He and a few others, notably Andrew Wyeth, can outride the abstract storm. But for one Burchfield there are ten conservative realists whose market has largely vanished. Not surprisingly, their feelings toward the fauves of 1959, toward the fickleness of public taste, the Museum of Modern Art and even the Whitney Museum, are exceedingly bitter. They may paint, in President Eisenhower's recent phrase, 'what America likes', but they win small support for their efforts.

Actually, realism unaffected by overtones of one sort or another rarely appears in American painting. In art at least America is not the land of fact. Romantic, psychological or social values keep breaking in, translating visual phenomena into the language of a 'message'. Surrealism's more extravagant flights found barren ground here, but the school of Magic or Symbolic Realism, carrying as it does observation to a point of extreme intensity, invades the territory of surrealism. This sect, in the hands of Paul Cadmus, Peter Blume, Jared French, George Tooker, Andrew Wyeth, Bernard Perlin and, more recently, John Wilde, Elwyn Chamberlain and Robert Vickrey, has lost strength in the past few years but still appeals to those who admire technical finesse and are roused by 'problem' pictures. As a style, with its minutely realized fantastic subjects, it stands in absolute opposition to abstract expressionism, a position of some strength. For those who thoroughly dislike the latter are also impatient of the kinds of realism that smuggle in abstract mannerisms. So Symbolic Realism holds its own to-day, attracts gifted newcomers, but is a little short on pictorial themes of serious relevance. Too often its most accomplished productions are devoted to trivial and far-fetched ideas that fail to live up to the wealth of technical eleboration that brings them to being. But, as a school, Symbolic Realism is a going concern and will receive fresh impetus when abstraction becomes less fashionable. And, in a negative sense, it is at least keeping standards of technique high until the moment when they will be widely demanded.

The collapse of social realism from its heyday during the 1930s is directly attributable to the general decline of interest in politics, to to-day's prosperity, which affects many artists themselves, and to the fright given to intellectuals by McCarthyism, a spectre that has by no means entirely vanished from the scene. This collapse represents a real impoverishment. For a great strength of American art in the past lay in its ability to reflect, no matter how crudely, the outside world. Generally to-day, and this is true of realists as well as of abstractionists, American art is aloof and bent on wrestling with private problems. Even Ben Shahn, the outstanding social realist of twenty years ago, has come to prefer the expression of emotion through symbolism of his own devising from which political satire is absent.

Nor can portraiture, although thriving in a commercial sense, be considered to be in a healthy state. Ironically enough the camera, which once threatened the very existence of portraitists, has now gone abstract itself and again leaves the field open to painters. This could promise well but we have at the moment the simultaneous absences of a John Singer Sargent and a Julia Margaret Cameron. The majority of to-day's portraits, painted for banks, clubs and an occasional private person, are timid, begging-to-please affairs and emphasize status and conventionality rather than individual character.

These categories do not exhaust the whole range of non-abstract activities to-day which are admittedly being given a bad time by the international vogue for abstraction. Whatever the historical and cultural justifications of this vogue, it is taken tremendous advantage of in America by dealers, publicists and high-pressure salesmen who have no difficulties with collectors who want at all costs, and at great costs, to be in the swim. Nor do modern architects, not at all the most generous of patrons, care to commission works of art which are not essentially decorative. The goose is still golden but its keepers are taking risks.

The realists' predicament finds its counterpart abroad, although probably not to such a drastic extent. However, the fact remains that things change very rapidly in America and there is every possibility, as well as certain definite indications, that the high tide of unmitigated abstraction is ebbing. The Museum of Modern Art will shortly present an exhibition devoted to the figure in modern art, and visual impressions lead a secret existence in many a picture that seems but faintly inspired by them. The late Turner may well succeed the late Monet as a 'discovery'.

No one can claim that non-abstract painting is passing through a particularly brilliant or creative period. Like a political party defeated in a landslide it is disorganized, bewildered, decidedly out of power and temporarily short of leaders. But it holds on to hopes, not simply that the party in power will run out of ideas, but that its own principal idea, which is an affirmation of what lies beyond the mind's eye, will come again to a significant agreement with contemporary thought.

The New Grand Tour

'With the architect and with no one else rests the praise or blame for that architecture which has no accepted name, but which is now the accepted architecture of the twentieth century: the great nineteenth century engineers and theorists prophesied it and made it possible, but the architects have made it currency.' Thus writes Ian McCallum in his remarkable book, *Architecture U.S.A.** In his context that 'accepted architecture' is American architecture—we here have not accepted it, not as currency and not with comprehension. Yet those prophets, those 'engineers and theorists' were both American and European, some of them were even English. There is to-day no 'international style', no world-wide uniformity as is so often assumed. True, there is no vernacular either. 'We are not living in a time when the artisan-workman can make a contribution to architectural style' and an industrialized building industry—based more on metallurgy than on geology—precludes any regional vernacular. For all that, the skyscrapers of, say, Milan or Caracas are as 'Latin' as those of New York or Roehampton are 'Nordic'. The regions are merely bigger than they used to be. The most vital of them is the United States of America. There are (as has been noted elsewhere) three conditions for great architecture—'a prosperous and lively building industry, creative freedom and conspicuous expenditure', and to-day all three exist in the United States and nowhere else. For the young European architect an American Grand Tour is becoming as important as the Italian was to the eighteenth-century English gentleman.

It has not always been so, not until quite recently. Mr. McCallum,

* Architectural Press.

136

writing just before the death of Lloyd Wright, says: 'Four pioneers are still living and practising, Walter Gropius, Mies van der Rohe, Frank Lloyd Wright and Le Corbusier, all but the last resident in the United States of America.' It might have been more to the point to say that only one is American. America may be 'The New World' in more senses than one, but in the event the story is its architecture was so chequered as to make the actual parturition of the new architecture from the old a mainly European event. Even a new architecture may need a tradition—whether to build on or to revolt against —and in the nineteenth century the American tradition was only that of Europe—second-hand and mainly second-hand *via* the École des Beaux Arts. Two of Mr. McCallum's living 'pioneers' are products of the Bauhaus; a third, le Corbusier, is the world's symbol of anti-Beaux Arts; while the fourth, Lloyd Wright, has been as much concerned with giving America the tradition it lacked as with modernism for its own sake.

It is the complexity as well as the brashness of American architecture that has prevented it until now from being the objective of a Grand Tour. The Chicago pioneers were the greatest of all, either side of the Atlantic, but a hundred years ago in the Middle West they were also necessarily archaic, primeval. Then, again, a new American architecture, it would seem, might have flowered in the 1930s; nipped by the frosts of the depression, it came to little. That twenty-five-year delay was heaven-sent, for now—as would have been impossible then—the brashness is passing, the complexity resolving itself, in face of a more unified technology, into a more unified total picture.

To understand that picture, however, one must also understand those complexities whence it is derived. There are, first of all, the two genuine but purely domestic traditions—European in origin but American in fact—the English colonialism of the Atlantic seaboard, and the Spanish genre of California. The domestic simplicities, the white-painted windows of colonialism are still there, in the newest Massachusetts homes, interwoven with the Germanic sophistications of the Gropius-Bauhaus group. The patios, pools and sun-grilles of that other tradition are there too, but reinterpreted, almost beyond recognition, in the Californian houses of men like Eames and Neutra. But that is all, that is the whole of America's debt to the past, perhaps because it is the only bit of the past that is her own. Of the classicism that came from the men trained in Paris, of the classicism that made the

Federal Bank or The Capitol, the mansions of McKim, Mead and White, or the Neo-Georgian campuses, not a trace remains. The origins of America's new architecture, urban and public, must be sought elsewhere—in her own pioneers.

It was in the days of saloon-pistols, buggies and covered wagons, before even Lloyd Wright was born, that America herself laid the foundations of her own, her very own, modern architecture. If the Lever Building is now the Parthenon, then a hundred years ago in Chicago they were building Paestum and Girgenti. Mid-century had seen the end of the master-builder and amateur architect; the civil engineers formed a society in 1852; the American Institute of Architects was founded in 1857; the first school, Massachusetts Institute of Technology, was started in 1866, fifty years before either Reilly in Liverpool or the A.A. day school. The era of the shack was over. The great argument concerning historical precedent versus a 'modern style' had begun. It had begun, moreover, in America, at a time when we were still drowned in the Gothic Revival and when France was building only the Opera House and the Grand Boulevards.

It must have been in the early 1850s that Horatio Greenhough stated the basis of functionalism. 'God's world has a distinct formula for every function and we shall seek in vain to borrow shapes; we must make the shapes by mastering the principles.' He then told his fellow-architects to 'study the functional beauty of ships'. It was not until 1927 that Le Corbusier, in *Vers Une Architecture,* said the same thing as if it were a discovery. It was not until 1908 that Adolf Loos made his famous remark: 'the engineers are our Hellenes', but it was Greenhough, in 1852, who said that 'the men who have reduced locomotion to its simplest elements, in the trotting wagon and the yacht *America,* are nearer to Athens at this moment than they who would bend the Greek temple to every use'. Eighteen fifty-two—the year that Ruskin wrote *The Stones of Venice!*

Greenhough can hardly have thought it possible that his theories would be realized. He forgot the American tempo. 'The system of building we have hinted at cannot be formed in a day. . . . Whether we are destined soon to see so noble a fruit may be doubtful; but we can at least break the ground and throw the seed.' The fruit, when it came, was H. H. Richardson (1838-86). Beaux Arts trained, Richardson could hardly escape historicism of some kind; the style he chose was not classic but, oddly enough, Romanesque. He used it in an utterly new way. He had to, since it was for an utterly new purpose. The Ames-Pray Building in Boston, 1886, and the Marshall Field Building in Chicago, 1887, have round arches—the former even has machicolations—but the plain surfaces, the organic plan and the plate glass are all new, and all essential to the architecture. Richardson's technique was necessarily that of solid masonry—eight storeys was his limit—but his office, operating in two cities, was a twentieth-century organization. The 'Chicago School' had been founded.

So far as Europe was concerned, Chicago in the 1880s was only a great roaring Yankee city, famous for pork and railroads but not much else. The English, beginning to buy Morris papers, were not interested in urbanism and can hardly have envisaged Chicago as the birthplace of a new architecture. After all, the period of gestation was to be nearly a century. And yet, if the United States to-day really is, as one suspects, destined to be a new Grand Tour, how much more significant were those first crude towers by Lake Michigan than were, say, that score of country houses by Philip Webb, Cowles Voysey or Norman Shaw —those 'pioneers of the Modern Movement' who were, one sees now, no more than a mere eclectic rearguard of the Gothic Revival. True, they played their arty-crafty variations upon the theme of gable and mullion to such effect that a few Shavian shingle-clad mansions were actually built in New England. But it was historically small stuff. In Chicago, meanwhile, they were inventing the 'city block'—the city block of the twentieth and the twenty-first centuries—big, light and high.

'Louis Henri Sullivan,' writes Mr. McCallum,

[forms a bridge between the ground-clearing pioneers . . . like H. H. Richardson, and those who, like Frank Lloyd Wright, began to build on that new ground an architecture not merely bold and fresh in its externals, but renewed to the marrow of its bones by the fusion of a down-to-earth approach to design with revolutionary materials and techniques.

Like Lloyd Wright after him, Sullivan was born on a farm and loved nature; some of the most astonishing ornament in history is found in the cast-iron sheathing of his buildings. With Adler—'the engineer-constructor'—as his partner, the basic principles of all our steel-framed buildings were now thrashed out as an utterly new architecture. In the 1880s the population of Chicago had doubled itself to more than a million, and something speedier, larger, more flexible was needed for its monuments. The old masonry technique was inadequate. The sixteen-storey Monadnock Building had walls at ground level twelve feet thick . . . so the steel-frame simply had to come into history. In Sullivan's words, 'the trick was turned and there swiftly came into being something new under the sun'. Immediately moreover this genius realized that a new technique implied a new architecture. Fifty years later London architects were still casing their steel frame in grotesque imitation of solid masonry, as if they wished the steel were not there. The Wainwright Building, Buffalo (1891), the Bayard Building, New York (1898) *look* like steel-frame buildings—vertical stanchions clearly emphasized, metal panels between the windows. And the Carson, Pirie, Scott Store, Chicago (1899), is, perhaps, *the* landmark of the Modern Movement. It is fresh, modern, clean-cut, remarkable in its own right—not merely as a forerunner—still, after sixty years.

After 1900 it is Frank Lloyd Wright who emerges as the giant. He dominated American and, indeed, the world's architecture until his death this year. He is the link between the hustling, self-assured men of the Chicago boom, and the whole romantic culture of Western man. His work was to be haunted by a curiously uncertain taste—curious touches of Aztec or Jazz ornament—but that is a small thing compared with his main achievement. Most things in the new American architecture can be traced back to this or that building by Wright, but when a future generation has assessed them all his main achievement, though expressed through architecture, may prove to have been something more imponderable. His writings, not least this final *Testament*,* are scrappy, contradictory, angry, irrational, sentimental, messianic—not quite without parallel in *Praeterita*—but out of them, somehow or other, as out of *Praeterita*, the bigness of the man does emerge.

At the heart of a very complex achievement there was a marvellous reconciliation of opposites, of the technical and the romantic. In his earlier years, in his Chicago days, he had partnered Sullivan, and was therefore nothing if not a modern architect. 'I invented the plate-glass door,' he was wont to remark. His Unity Temple, Oak Park (1906), was the first building to be conceived as a reinforced concrete mono-lith, with 'services'—lighting, heating, etcetera—an integral part of the architecture. His Larkin Building in Buffalo (1904) had been the first conception of an 'environment'—light, clean, warm, comely—for a

* Architectural Press

large clerical staff, the first building with metal furniture and 'designed' sanitary fittings. The Imperial Hotel, Tokyo, in its ornament shows him at his worst, but was far and away his most popular success because, thanks to concrete raft foundations, it had dramatically withstood the great earthquake. Even the ornamental pools had served their purpose in fire prevention—as he had foreseen. In 1924 he designed, but never built, a skyscraper for Water Tower Square, Chicago—a double-cantilevered structure sheathed in copper, it would have been an 'advanced' building in 1950. The Johnson Wax Factory, Racine (1936), was, like the Larkin Building, an 'environment' for office workers; with remarkably graceful 'mushroom' columns— more like water-lilies than mushrooms—and curved tubular-glass walls; it reminds one that Wright coined the phrase 'stream-line'. Its later laboratory tower (1949) rests its full weight of 7,000 tons on a single central point, thus leaving the floors and windows free from all structural walls and columns. In 1936 he had also built the famous Kaufmann House, 'Falling Water', at Bear Run. It is a design based on a series of big concrete platforms cantilevered out over waterfalls, and set among birch trees.

Thus does Bear Run illustrate that reconciliation of opposites. Wright, as spiritual heir to Sullivan, could indulge in unlimited structural adventures. Setting this structural *tour de force* among cascades and tree trunks he emerges also as the poet, the eternal romantic. He would often quote Victor Hugo, that the Renaissance was hailed as a great dawn whereas it was in truth a great sunset. He realized fifty years ago that there was no place in Chicago or the Middle West for William Morris's medieval dreams, but he worshipped Morris all the same, Ruskin only a little less. At Taliesin West, out in the Painted Desert of Arizona, he set his bed beneath warmed southern stars—the eternal pantheist. As a romantic, however, he missed the force and value of a vernacular tradition; at eighty he was bowled over by the English Cotswolds. In his 'organic' architecture he arrived at the long, low house of broad eaves and wide terraces hugging the earth. If America had no vernacular of her own, she at least had the great Walt Whitman myth—redwood, elm, granite and the open hearth. In his own homes—with their studios for the apprentices—both at Taliesin in Wisconsin and in the winter home in Arizona—Wright managed to give a very full expression to this pantheistic romanticism. He did so in innumerable houses over a period of more than half a century. He had tried to do what is for one man, almost by definition, an impossibility. He had almost given a tradition to a nation.

But if Lloyd Wright had provided the main inspiration, other things were happening too. In the Lovell House, California, Richard Neutra, a Viennese, had emerged in 1927 as something more 'Latin', superficially more glamorous than Wright. His contribution has been to modernize the Spanish genre, to build low, spreading, lavish, richly planted houses, with their swimming pools, terraces, patios and flowing 'open' plans. He calls it 'constructed human environment'; that, however, might apply to any architecture; but for all that he does it superbly well.

If the Chicago pioneers had spotted the potentialities of steel and glass, then it was Mies van der Rohe—last head of the Bauhaus, 'poet, prophet and pace-setter'—who turned the steel frame itself, with its opaque and transparent infilling panels, into an art form as cold, as subtle and as 'classic' as anything the Greeks or Chinese had ever done. In the Farnsworth House (1950) he resolved a dwelling into a 'glass box'—refined and polished to the nth degree—not, like all other houses that ever were, a conglomeration of forms (roofs, windows, walls) but in itself a single object, as it might be a Ming pot. Mr. McCallum makes the contrast with Lloyd Wright:

The Seagram Building by van der Rohe is sheathed in autumnal bronze; crisp and rectilinear, it soars to the sky without emphatic termination. Wright's Guggenheim Museum is curvaceously moulded, ground-hugging, even ground-penetrating with a spiral terminated by a glass dome, reading as much downward as upward. The two buildings represent the polarities of modern architecture: metallurgy and the machine serving the purpose of the multi-cellular building on the one hand; and the structural versatility of reinforced concrete . . . on the other. Both are as valid as they are necessary.

Buckminster Fuller is a key-figure but scarcely an architect. He works beyond the boundaries of architecture. With his geodetic domes and his synergetic geometry—discovered in 1917—he is designing not buildings but, rather, methods of enclosing space that others may one day make into an architecture. A 375-foot dome, with hundreds of hexagonal facets, is his limit so far. If Mies van der Rohe has made rectangularity into an art form, Buckminster Fuller's work hints that the days of the rectangular are numbered. More than one young architect is making that break; the hyperbolic paraboloid dome, the geodetic dome, sprayed concrete on curved armatures, and so on, are appearing. Such domes already span the concourse of more than one airport building, more than one assembly hall or university auditorium.

American architecture to-day is poetic, structural, febrile, self-confident, lavish. Saarinen's buildings, for instance, are exalted. Industrialists are patrons in the old sense. For the first time in 200 years there is an accepted Western architectural style—as opposed to fashions, revivals and movements. Like the very different architecture of Ancient Rome or of the eighteenth century, it is an architecture of materialism . . . that does not make it any less an art, but it does leave Greece and the Middle Ages still supreme.

The Small Screen

Observing his countrymen glued, as he put it, to their television sets, Mr. Adlai Stevenson thought that they were ill-prepared to cope, in war or in peace, with more austerely nurtured peoples behind the Iron Curtain, and then added, 'They aren't even having a good time.'

The addition may be taken as a prime instance of the egg-head fallacy which invalidates so much of the bill of complaint against our mass media entertainments. Generously endowing the entire public with his own cultivated perceptions and his own range of interests, Mr. Stevenson has yet been arrogant, he has said, in effect, that no one can really be having a good time with such tawdry stuff as television programmes seem to him and the implication is clear that if we do, we should not. The same overtone can be apprehended when professional critics (or those who 'wouldn't have a TV set in the house') assert that television has not educated, not informed, and certainly not stirred the imagination of, the American people. It can be held that television has not done any of these things as well as it should have done, and it is quite possible that certain forms of television blunt the mind and dilute the sensibilities so that it seems at times that the creation of apathy is the manager's definition of operating 'in the public interest'. But this does not mean that the general public has had nothing of value from television and it emphatically does not mean that the general public has not enjoyed it.

The effect of television on the higher faculties has not been deeply studied, but we have a clue in the nature of the response to the radio daytime serial. A recurrent phrase, when women spoke or wrote of this type of programme, was 'visited with', a mid-western expression

144

for chatting with one's neighbour. The listeners visited with Aunt Jenny or Big Sister and not only had a sense of participating in the troubles of John's Other Wife; they received from these people guidance, help in solving their own problems, to which they gratefully testified. The lives of the heroines were as turbulent and spectacular as the lives of the listeners were harassed and obscure, but the dailyness of radio cancelled out the difference. The dramatic programme was flanked on one side by the immediate news of the day, on the other by the soap and the soup to be bought to-morrow at the market. Whatever came out of the little box standing on the shelf over the kitchen sink had the reality of the morning paper or the wrapped package and when it said that men from Mars had landed near a village in New Jersey citizens of Kansas and Oregon took to the roads in panic.

There runs with this sense of the daily and the ordinary another attitude toward broadcasting which significantly affects the nature of the programmes it offers and, consequently, the nature of the response from the audience. With such minor exceptions as the magic lantern and the phonograph, all professional entertainment from the Comédie Française to the country-fair tent-show had to be gone to and paid for. The motion picture effected a partial revolution: it brought (a year late, perhaps) metropolitan quality to the village. But going to the movies still entailed leaving home and paying money, so that, like the theatre or a football game, the movies were a 'sometime thing' and a reward, identified as such for good behaviour in children, psychologically a reward to adults for having the time and the money and, perhaps, the congeniality within the family, to go. The box in the home knows none of this. It is, in America, assumed to be free. It is, of course, nothing of the sort—but it is *there*. Since it is always available, the enjoyment of it has become virtually a right and the exercise of that right is so prevalent that 'life, liberty, and the pursuit of *Maverick*' may now be taken as the declaration of a sizeable number of Americans.

Since the American thinks of his broadcast programme as a part of his daily life, as something that occurs whether he has earned it or not, his demands upon it are inevitably less insistent than his demands on the entertainment for which he plans and spends. And in spite of Mr. Stevenson's metaphor the attention he gives to it is not as close and single-minded as his absorption in the play he goes out to see. The chair he sits in is the one from which he rose to get a can of beer and the smell of cooking comes from the next room. The events on the 21-in. screen take place in the atmosphere of total familiarity. If Blake's apocalyptic vision rose before the viewer, it would still be somewhat diminished to the proportions of everyday.

It seems, then, that, quite apart from the economics of commercial sponsorship, the nature of the television apparatus and the conditions of reception in the home are not favourable to works of the imagination grandly conceived. The occasional production of Shakespeare can be noted and the prevalence of Westerns, the great manufactured myth of America, but these are not the inventions of television, they are transferences and are as irrelevant to the medium as its capacity to transmit twenty-year-old movies. The tone of television in its most effective phases is domestic: the comedian is the cut-up in the parlour, and the life of the party, interrupting or taking part in guessing games, playing charades. In the grandiose style, we have the Master of Ceremonies but he (or she) is known as 'your host' and so concentrated is the emphasis on this function that dramatic series bearing the name of the sponsor have given up this priceless identification because an actor or actress, with or without talent, appearing in perhaps half a dozen out of thirty-nine plays, but introducing them all, became the true attraction and the series gained a higher rating when known as 'John (or Jessie) Starr's Theatre'.

Clearly these are not the conditions in which the imagination flourishes. Yet we know that the apparent reality of domestic drama is deceptive. It is not intended to provide the 'shock of recognition' which is in itself a powerful spur to the imagination. Domestic comedy and its semi-serious counterpart in hour-long drama both start with a familiar situation in a faithfully rendered setting; a boisterous exaggeration promptly intervenes in comedy, as in the 'I Love Lucy' series, and in the longer plays a peculiar 'fudging' or compromising with the ideas or the central motives of the chief characters leads to an acceptable ending. In neither case do we get 'the contemplation of things as they are' which Bacon said was worth more than a host of inventions. But Bacon's maxim is for philosophers and aesthetes to whom television is not primarily addressed. Television programmes stick to inventiveness—a sort of psychological gadgetry.

The history of some other American entertainments indicates that the course taken by television is not entirely dictated by its situation within the home which has been emphasized. The rude and joyful Keystone comedies gave way to feeble polite comedy in the movies and the exquisite imagination of Krazy Kat and the violence, cheerful because it had no ulterior motive, of other comic strips were gradually edged aside by the 'realistic' comic strip of daily life which originated in Chicago. (So did the daytime serial which was, at the start, an account of what had actually happened day by day to the husband and wife bringing the report.) In the movies a return to insanity occurred with the coming of sound and of the Marx Brothers. In the comic strip L'il Abner and Pogo have successfully escaped the realistic method. But in both movies and comic strip the most common escape is by way of horror or a low grade of science fiction or a combination of both.

It is generally taken that in television the mode of escape from the prosaic is by violence. A vast amount does exist and it differs from the violence of the Keystones and the comic strip because it is not formal, traditional and comic: it is to a great extent cruel and central to plot—it is motivated and explicit. It is, in fact, another, concealed, version of the prose which seems to be television's natural mode of expression. The deceptively 'real', artificially laconic speech of Dragnet, a resounding success for several years, was itself a mask for hardness of heart (a debasement of the style which Dashiell Hammett had invented in his detective stories). The old, 'pure' Western, repeating the movies formula, was the only instance of patterned violence, and the case of the critics who tried to protect children from the exhibition of hundreds of killings a week was always weakened when they lumped the almost symbolic shootings of the Westerns with the stranglings and pistol-whippings of the straight big-city crime programmes.

In the past two years or so a variation has appeared: the adult Western. Even if one did not find them engrossing, they had a refreshing air: the hero was basically a coward or seemed to be, or, like the hero of Have Gun, Will Travel, was a restorer of justice and rescuer of damsels in distress who quoted Plato or Meredith or Kafka at least once in each episode. Neither irony nor wit precluded a deal of gun-play and the basic type, by way of repeats of television series or the transmission of old movies, to this day holds a firm place in the schedule.

In one significant area television has activated the American imagination—in its direct report on events and their significance. Before coming to it one more thing should be said about the trifling and often tedious fictions we have been discussing. Distressed the philosopher and the statesman may be by them, but they do make a start in engaging the mind and the emotions. When we say that the spectator is 'taken out of himself' we are also saying that for a few moments he is participating in a life other than his own. It is an exercise leading to no noble end—but it is at least an activity. And it may be a necessary beginning, the small shake by which one begins to awaken the sleeper. Along with these contrived fictions we do have in television an impressive number of plays, mostly derived from novels or the theatre, which bring at least a portion of *The Wings of the Dove* or *For Whom the Bell Tolls* to a significant part of the audience nurtured on crime and Westerns and domestic serials. We have, less frequently now than five years ago, a kind of elevated domestic drama itself, as in *Marty,* which was the story of an inexpressive butcher and a gawky girl, set in low circumstances; an honest story. We have a wholly unrealistic style of presentation in the non-commercial Camera Three—part reading, part acting, with a fold of cloth for backdrop and a few chairs for props, producing both modern and ancient classics—and the method as well as the principles of selection have their effect. Borrowing from the older arts, producing fragments in its own experiments, television touches the poetic level in which we, the inheritors of a culture based on the printed word, are accustomed to recognize the imagination of the artist and by which our own imaginations are stirred.

But, as has been said, prose is the natural medium here, and it is by a variety of reports on the actual world that television has chiefly redeemed itself from the charge of stupefying the imagination of its audience. Some of these reports are close to travelogues, but no one travels to-day without awareness of stresses and dangers and discontents. Some are reports 'in depth', carefully investigated cases, appraisals of the significance of events and of the individuals involved in them. Some are the confrontation of several interesting people and others give total freedom to a single philosopher or artist or scientist to present himself. The jeopardy and the excitement of our time are in these ways conveyed to us.

It would be idle to say that these things do not affect the imagination because they rise out of and are concerned with the actual. We who were brought up in the world of Keats and Leonardo, or in the world of T. S. Eliot and Picasso, want to feel sure that only the greatly conceived and the enduring can affect us deeply. We are, with some justification, afraid that the constant substitution of small things will end with the disappearance of the great. But we must keep in mind that millions of people are aware of and concerned with ideas and emotions, brought to them through avenues of information, and that this is a spur to the imagination, even if untouched by anything divine.

The situation is not helpful to the individual creator. Long ago, in contracts with movie studios, the writer acknowledged that 'the studio is the author' of his script—a legalism which conveyed a hard truth: by the time a script was ready for shooting so many individuals and teams had worked on it that it represented not what one writer, but what the whole studio, required. The writer for television is cribbed and confined by the requirements of the sponsor and in many ways the producer of the programme is far more free and more creative than the originator. For the moment the creator tends to escape by retreat, he goes first to Hollywood and, finding himself still unhappy, into the theatre or the novel.

It is hard to predict what will happen. A year ago one network, envious of the critical acclaim of its chief rival, is said to have circulated a memorandum the burden of which was 'from now on we are creative'. When one reads the annual reports of broadcasting executives, one has a sense that they take pride only in the exceptional production, not the daily 'bread-and-butter' programmes by which the exceptions are supported. And this points to a central issue: how to bring more and more members of the permanent audience into the audience for the special event. Many proposals have been made, and among them one of the most ingenious is that of John Fischer, the editor of *Harpers,* who asks for an autonomous authority empowered to produce programmes of exceptional merit, financed by a levy on the income of the broadcasters, who will also be under an obligation to transmit these programmes in the cherished prime-viewing hours. This would relieve the broadcasters themselves of the obligation to create superior programmes—a dubious consequence.

The feeling persists that something must be done. It rises from an apprehension about the nature of the core-audience, the millions who uncritically accept whatever is offered, moving from one station to another to receive variations of the same thing. In the recent debate on television in the House of Lords it was said that desires are created and then satisfied, and this process is spoken of as if it actually gave the viewer a choice. This has long been recognized in America, and it has also been recognized that the producers must create those desires only which they can satisfy. The consequence is not only that broadcasters serve the interests of a large majority, which is inevitable, but that they serve this majority only in small part. The average man has more curiosities, latent if not active, than any of the mass media are concerned with. The few that are satisfied are so abundantly satisfied that no urgent want is felt. And the proof of it is that while almost everyone who is asked says he would like more of this or of that in television, no one feels empowered to demand of television anything which it does not give.

One reason has been here suggested: that what it gives is of relative goodness and of vast copiousness; it is better entertainment than most people could get elsewhere. But it tends to create an apathetic mass, poor in spirit and without strong wants. It is here that television, along with other entertainments and other institutions (such as advertising and parts of the educational system), deaden the imagination, and it is quite probable that the critical question for the statesmen of broadcasting is to find a way for the public to express its inward wants, to share with the broadcasters the right of defining 'the public interest'.

Publish or Perish

Whatever else may be said about American scholarship, one must grant it the quality of copiousness. Dozens of university presses, scores of private institutes and foundations, hundreds of journals and newsletters, thousands of surveys and reports exhibit the results of an unceasing, nationwide, solemn-eyed activity which every American citizen has learnt to regard as sacred and indispensable: Research.

From one point of view, this extraordinary output is easy to explain. The principle of systematic scholarship is a reflection of the nineteenth century's love of science, which the United States imported in the 1880s and 1890s when it established its graduate schools. From these schools 'researching' has spread throughout the literate world and has been reinforced by all the requirements of a complex technology. Trade, industry, and government have multiplied the demand for fact-finding and the educational system has responded by making the instruments and techniques of research accessible and commonplace.

But how much of this ferreting and publishing can be called scholarship in the honorific sense? It depends on how honorific one wants to be. America has a way of turning out from time to time a piece of definitive research which is also a literary achievement and a contribution to thought and feeling—in short, a book. One thinks of Samuel Eliot Morison's *Columbus* or Lionel Trilling's *Matthew Arnold* or Henry Nash Smith's *Virgin Land: the American West as Symbol and Myth*. Yet the conventions by which scholarship is encouraged in American academic life, though they do not precisely prohibit the emulating of such triumphs, do not favour it either. The conventions have not been consciously designed; rather, they have grown out of the programmes for the higher degrees, which were established seventy years ago in hybrid imitation of Germany and France. The central idea of these programmes is that a scholar is made by taking the courses and writing the dissertation which will earn him the Ph. D. degree. Since this preparation is to launch him into the profession of research, the young scholar's promotion in the academic hierarchy depends on his continuing to 'contribute' to the literature of his field. No Ph.D., no scholar; no production of articles, no promotion.

At the present time one can see in the United States a violent exaggeration—indeed, a caricature—of these commandments, and hence of their results. One can therefore understand why American scholarship is what it is only after looking a little further into the conditions that produce it. Two considerations out-top all others: the young scholar wants to move rapidly to a tenure position; the college or university wants scholarly prestige. The young scholar, if he is wise, will neglect the teaching duties for which he is paid and will devote his time to research in a field which his superiors deem important at the time. These superiors meanwhile are looking for older scholars to invite to their university so as to 'strengthen the department'. The 'strength' comes from a reputation acquired by scholarly publication. This prestige is at all times accurately gauged as by a sort of intimate Lombard Street of ten or twelve specialists in each field.

Their judgment is not false, but it may be faddish—as it is in the branches of physical science. In fact, the impetus behind modern scholarship is the desire to imitate as closely as possible the conditions that obtain in scientific research. The latest symptom of this is characteristic. The institution of higher learning that wants to demonstrate how high its learning is tries to lure a scholar of high reputation by promising him unlimited opportunities for research—no teaching, frequent leave of absence, and money for books, microfilm, travel and research assistants. The scholar is set up like a *grande cocotte* to shed radiance exclusively on the lavish protector. It is but fair to add that the purchaser of these favours sincerely believes that the scholar's presence will bring the institution not only prestige but also some mysterious quality inherent in research. The students will benefit even though kept at arm's length; colleagues will be inspired, even though the scholar is on his travels; the whole tone of academic life will be raised by this tribute to scholarship, even though the purport of the work in progress is unknown.

In a recent book which is itself a notable piece of research and which is called *The Academic Marketplace,* Professors Theodore Caplow and Reece McGee, of Minnesota, describe the ordinary procedures by which scholars are chosen when they are not the 'great names' in the profession. What a man has written plays a major role in these decisions, too, for no department wants to take to its bosom someone who is not 'a productive scholar'; even if they did, his chances of being appointed by the central authority would be slight. Yet in more than 200 interviews with those responsible for such choices and appointments Professors Caplow and McGee did not find one man who confessed to having read the scholarly productions of the prospective appointee. The books and articles were submitted, glanced at, leafed through, weighed in the hand, but not read. It would be wrong to infer from this fact that American university professors do not really care for scholarship. They are passionate about it, obsessed with it; few instances are known of a true scholar's being left to languish in an inferior post. A young unknown who 'brings out a good book' will be dragged from his hinterland college and given a position in one closer to the limelight. But in spite of this theoretical and practical devotion, the arrangements in force to foster scholarship in America foster at the same time faddishness, lip-service, make-believe and a great deal of unnecessary publication.

What we are witnessing in the United States is not due to a purely American error. It is part of the universal error of believing that all good things can be deliberately procured. The modern world wants art and scholarship, and it sets about *providing* for them. If the world usually comes back from its labours with empty hands, it may be because in its comings and goings it has passed by what it was busily trying to make out of whole cloth.

For the facts about the scholar's work teach a simple lesson. In the preface to her latest book, *Mountain Glory and Mountain Gloom,* Professor Marjorie Nicolson tells us that its preparation took twenty years. She explains in detail how the idea of the work arose in the course of her teaching, and she relates the vicissitudes of its execution. If this is the way of achievement, as the history of thought confirms, then the academic imperative of 'Produce' is plainly ridiculous. And by the same token, so is the requirement that the doctoral dissertation shall be a piece of scholarship. Professor Trilling's *Matthew Arnold,* already mentioned, was indeed a dissertation, but it took him twelve years to write it. Professor Abrams, of Cornell University, whose study entitled *The Mirror and the Lamp* added so much to our understanding of Romantic criticism, has been for more than a decade at work on his next work. Clearly, if the scholar's worldly prospects are made to depend exclusively on getting frequently into print, what follows is what one finds—an abundance of trivialities designed chiefly for committees on promotion.

An American classicist has estimated that in his field scholars wrote four times as much as they could read. He based this estimate on the fact that all the scholarly journals he knew had enough articles for four years ahead. And his was a relatively unpopulous branch of learning. Psychologists, one hears, are so short of printing space that the practice of paying the journal for the additional pages which, if accepted, one will occupy has become a respectable custom.

This apparent surfeit of knowledge points to another characteristic of modern scholarship—its indifference to form. A scholar takes thought about everything except his prose and the length of his chapters. He is suspect if he writes well; he is mistrusted if he does not overwhelm the reader with details, quotations, and indiscriminate bibliographies. The American scholar no longer heeds Emerson's advice, 'Tell us what you know'; he tells us what he has found, which is a longer and drearier story.

In an excellent and laudably brief survey of scholarly publishing, prepared for the American Council of Learned Societies, Dr. Rush E. Welter, of Bennington College, reports that it is the monographs of medium length—too long for an article, too short for a book—that are being denied publication. To a university press, publishing 200 pages is a nuisance: the price must be low and the trouble will be as great as for 600. It is also significant that Dr. Welter found much resistance among scholars to the suggestion that they write better and more briefly.

Now the question of size is not purely material in its effects. From the moment, nearly a century ago, when history, philosophy, philology, literary criticism, political economy, and the rest of the humanities repudiated the literary art in an effort to resemble the objectivity of natural science, the contempt for The Word has increasingly bred an unawareness of The Idea. Frederic Harrison was already pointing this out in 1893 in his delightful dialogue, 'The History Schools'. The false analogy with science which suggests to the scholar that any fact will ultimately be valuable now makes him willing to spend his time on inquiries of which he himself is unable to state the point. In literary studies, particularly, the modern mode is to count images or themes, detect far-fetched parallels and generally worry a poem or a novel until Raggedy Ann is nothing more than a heap of sawdust. And each grain, though without value in the market-place for ideas, is scholar's gold.

This resignation to pointlessness is especially conspicuous in the scholarship of art and literature, these subjects being the very antithesis of futility and incoherence. But the willingness to ignore intellectual import also governs much of the work done in American history, economics and sociology. Here again, of course, the exceptions are notable: Professor Arthur Schlesinger, Jr., Professor Henry Steele Commager, Professor C. Vann Woodward and a dozen others who could be named are men to whom ideas matter, being native growths. But the bulk of the scholarship done upon American historical sources lacks both ideas and scale. Obscure state politicians of eighty years ago are treated to painstaking biographies. The history of banks and timber merchants is retold with a minute fidelity worthy of the greatest revolutions of States. In economics, as everyone knows, description and synthesis are in disfavour, having given place to the construction of mathematical 'models' which are supposed to symbolize the exact relations of certain elements abstracted from our bread-and-butter life. Similarly in sociology, the study of types and professions yields a tonnage of books and graphs unencumbered by philosophic thought and comprehensive views.

Is all this the democratization of learning, the new mass scholarship, in which persons of average intelligence but uncommon energy are half-lured, half-driven to collect, compile, and report, without the benefit of reflection, without the incentives of a generalizing purpose, and often without the critical implement of literacy? If, indeed, the routine products of American scholarship answer to this description, the phenomenon is not, or will not long remain, American alone. What we commonly attribute to the fact that America is not lucky enough to be England or France is but the necessary consequence of tendencies and purposes that Europe is becoming proud to share—democratic education, the division of intellectual labour, professionalism in life and letters, regard for technique as a good in itself—in a word, the standardization of talent.

What should give hope and encouragement to the societies undergoing this change is that America, in spite of the tremendous forces that grind its intelligence into these common shapes, continues to produce scholars of the first rank, original minds in the fullest sense of the term, as well as perfectionists in technique. From the late Bartlet Brebner, whose premature death left unfinished his ripest work—a re-examination of the Industrial Revolution—to Professor Bertrand Bronson, of Berkeley, who has just brought out the first volume of his annotated collection of the music of the Child Ballads, America can be proud of her scholars. But just as England did well a generation ago to cast a critical eye on her own tradition of amateurism, so the United States might with profit reassess her present cult of research *à outrance* and scholarship unlimited.

Religious Enthusiasm

'The religious instinct had vanished, and could not be revived. . . . That the most powerful emotion of man, next to the sexual, should disappear might be a personal defect of his own, but that the most intelligent society, led by the most intelligent clergy in the most moral condition he ever knew, should so thoroughly have solved all the problems of the universe seemed to him the most curious social phenomenon he had to account for in a long life.' So Henry Adams wrote, at the beginning of this century, about the conditions of his youth in the 1850s. It must be conceded that this essentially secular quality, both of American life and of American literature, has been commented on by other writers in plenty. Indeed, with the colossal exception of Melville and the minor note of Hawthorne's *The Marble Faun*, 'the most powerful emotion of man next to the sexual' seems to have been by-passed almost entirely in classical American literature.

George Santayana, discussing the comparable absence of religious emotion in Shakespeare, finds it present only in one sonnet, in a few lines in *Henry IV*, and in one in *Hamlet*. He suggests various reasons: the traumatic effect of the Reformation, which drove the playwright to a 'pest on both your houses' attitude; the neo-Paganism of the Renaissance. The Founding Fathers followed close in time on Shakespeare's heels, but it is not easy to find reasons for the absence of *eidos* in American literature, nor to attribute it to some one historical break such as the Revolution, which cut the umbilical cord. Certainly politics played their part: for example, John Wesley's open approval of George III did his followers great disservice; all eight of his original preachers returned home. And in the fall of 1958 a Catholic priest apologized to his flock for the Feast of Christ the King: Jesus, he assured them, was not the old-type wicked monarch, like George III or the Roman emperors!

In America, whatever the historical reasons, the order of the two great commandments is certainly reversed. The most important thing in life is to love one's neighbour, or, at least, to get along with him: the most important relationship is that of neighbour. For Americans, at all times in history, at all times in their lives, are forever on the move. So it was in the days of the Pilgrims; of the Indian wars; of the treks west; of the gold rushes to the Klondike and the Yukon; of the opening up of Alaska; so it was on Iwo Jima and Guadalcanal; at Monte Cassino and in Korea; so it is among the millions of unionized labourers; among the millions who move their dwelling annually, for many good reasons or for none; so it is for the enormous groups working for Government or industry in satellite cities; for the thousands of slum-dwellers re-located annually by federal, state or urban housing projects; so it is for the thousands of 'senior citizens' retiring in trailers to Florida. For each one the most basic and vital confrontation, historically and actually, is with the neighbour. A mother, as an already classic American children's book has it, is to cook, as a hole is to dig; parents, once one is through college, are for Christmas; in-laws are for jokes; siblings and cousins count only in Social Register circles or among the still foreign-tongued immigrants.

And for Americans generally the paramount importance, the predominance, of the moral has filled the lacuna occupied by religion elsewhere. The twin worship of the Golden Rule and the Golden Calf has usurped the veneration for the altar, and the practice of the Presence. And as that of neighbour is the key relation, so social action, unpreceded by thought and uncomplicated by retrospection, has for touchstone neighbourly approval or disapproval. To be a good buddy, a regular fellow, is the ethical, as well as the social, imperative. 'The children', wrote Henry Adams, 'reached manhood without knowing religion, and with the certainty that dogma, metaphysics and abstract philosophy were not worth knowing.' To-day's student asks, 'What can I—or anyone else—get out of it?' when offered Plato or Aquinas, and on learning how little training in the humanities can produce in cold cash, scornfully rejects them in favour of science or business administration. The garbage collector honestly pities the professor or the minister his much lower salary, and would not recommend either profession to his son. Recently the president of Brandeis College publicly admitted that he could get all the millions he needed, and more, from the Government and from industry for chemistry, biology, medicine, or, indeed, any scientific project or research. But to raise a paltry few hundred dollars to reward the most promising young novelist, musician, painter, poet or dramatist each year was, he said, a matter of months of hard begging. So, too, in religion. Albert Schweitzer or Cardinal Spellman attract big money for their hospitals; but a single small community of contemplative Benedictine nuns has a hard time existing in a country of more than forty million practising Catholics. Yet, as a visiting British novelist wryly remarked, contemplation must be America's destiny, since it needs it so much! Certainly since the Second World War the amazing rush to the cloister has not been to the active orders but to the contemplatives, to the Trappists, the Carmelites and the Carthusians, the latter only now for the first time established on this side of the Atlantic.

The history of American faiths has been, at least in part, a matter of individuals surviving sectarian differences around them; of individual intermarriage and group interpenetration leading to one nationally and passionately, held conviction: that religion, one of the four essential freedoms, is definitely an individual affair. Not at all a private one: in no country is religion so advertised, so publicized, so worn on the sleeve. No other country has such a flurry of Catholic and Protestant publishing houses all pouring out denominational 'literature' and spending vast sums barking their wares; in no other country do the big networks allocate so much radio and television time to the different religious denominations (never 'prime time', however, be it noted). In no other country would one atheist mother's protest at the social discomfort suffered by her child while his companions went for their 'released time' (religious training on church or synagogue premises during school hours) have reached the front page of leading newspapers all over the country, as did that of Mrs. Vashti McCollum, of Illinois. Whether or not parochial school children may ride on the buses provided for public school children is a burning question that has split the Supreme Court, and has been the subject of several angry books; whether a verse from the Bible may, or may not, be read in state schools is a perennial subject of furious debate. Indeed, newspaper editors to-day regard religion as among the main 'beats'—as significant as business, crime, education, or science: all the big weeklies carry a 'Religion' page.

Americans are tremendous joiners, and their religious expression almost always included *belonging*: to the 'Y' if Protestants, to the Knights of Columbus if Catholics; to B'nai B'nith if Jews. There are religious sub-groups in many of the big organizations: in Shell Oil, or the Telephone Company; in the big unions or Johnson and Johnson, for example. The Roman Catholic employees will have their annual Communion Breakfast and Day of Recollection; the Protestants their get-togethers, the Jews their special *tomarshas,* all addressed by television stars or big politicos or best-selling authors, as the case may be. Quite a few recent novels have dealt with this side of the 'religious life': the very popular Taylor Caldwell's story of a young minister, *Tender Victory*; *Marjorie Morningstar,* Herman Wouk's epic of one Jewish girl's seven-mile Odyssey from the Bronx to Central Park South; and Joe Dever's *Three Priests.*

Although American religion is individual, it is also racial. Thus most Negroes still to-day are either Baptists or Methodists, having received, when slaves, from their masters the inestimable gift of their own faith. The second, third and sometimes fourth generation of Irish, Italians, Hungarians and Poles generally remain Roman Catholic. Discrimination to-day is subtler than it was: the old sign—still often seen in the 1920s on job-notices—'No Jews or Catholics need apply' has completely vanished.

A 'restricted' community is still, however, one that is free from Jews, and in the 'better' suburbs, though many mothers will allow their children to play with Jewish children on the street or in school, many still do not ask them to their homes. The social gulf between public, private and parochial schools is narrowing, and Dr. John C. Bennet, co-editor of the Protestant *Christianity and Crisis* wrote recently: 'That Catholics have "arrived" is a matter of fact, and we believe that Protestants are coming to accept this and to recognize that this is a religiously pluralistic society and not a Protestant one.'

One symbol of the social and political arrival of American Catholics is Senator Kennedy. For, while religion is individual, it is also political: the much-discussed availability of Senator Kennedy for the Presidency turns, as did that of A. L. Smith, on his religion, which is his biggest handicap, greater even than his eggheadedness, though he has written (not had ghosted) a book, and an excellent (and best-selling) one at that. However, in a nation-wide poll as to whether his religious affiliation would deter voters from him, although nearly a third said it would, 12 per cent. said they did not realize he was a Catholic. General Eisenhower's 'religious affiliation' was widely commented on before his election; he was 'raised' a Mennonite, but shortly after his election was received into the Presbyterian Church to which his wife already belonged. In his currently best-selling *The Status Seekers* Vance Packard has one chapter entitled 'the long road from Pentecostal to Episcopal' and an oft-quoted jingle summarizes this journey: 'A Methodist is a Baptist who has been to High School; a Presbyterian is a Methodist who has been through college; an Episcopalian is a Presbyterian who has gotten into Society, and a Catholic is an Episcopalian who has gotten religion.' Vance Packard notes that Roman Catholics are outside any of his status-seeking categories or groups— probably because they belong in the first instance to groups too far down the social ladder to emerge individually, they generally remain Catholic, except for individual seepage.

Religion in the United States is still very geographical: Methodism is to the Middle West what Puritanism was to New England; California is the spawning-ground for cults unlimited; the biggest Catholic concentrations are urban: Chicago, Boston, Brooklyn and Detroit are four of the largest Catholic archdioceses in the world. When a Negro wished to write a realistic novel about the Chicago slums, he chose a Roman Catholic family for his protagonists: *Knock on any Door,* by Willard Motley, is a sensitive study of two brothers suffering identical social pressure and reacting in opposite ways.

The political pressure of religion is felt differently in different areas. There were 873,071 Presbyterians who registered disapproval when the National Council of Churches urged the recognition of China, and 1,200 Alabamans met in Birmingham to launch a Methodist layman's union whose object was to abolish the separate Negro jurisdiction in the Methodist Church. The tremendous power of the Catholic Legion of Decency to 'censor' films has aroused nationwide protests; at the same time the fact that a book is 'banned in Boston' (by Catholic pressure) ensures it magnificent sales elsewhere. Most of the big movie companies submit their scripts to Legion of Decency officials before they start shooting (even if they do not always act on Legion advice) and during the filming of a Roman Catholic novel such as *The Nun's Story* ecclesiastical assistance is sought—and found—continuously.

The fact that Boris Pasternak's *Dr. Zhivago* beat Vladimir Nobokov's *Lolita* to first place on the best-seller lists for something like twenty straight weeks was no doubt partly because most Americans are much more anti-Communist than they are naturally sensual men, and no doubt partly because some preferred U.S.S.R. citizens to White *émigrés*. But also it was, at least in part, because of *Dr. Zhivago's* deeply religious undertow.

For very few contemporary Americans is religion 'fear of power invisible'. Where it exists as alive and important, religion is generally a dialogue, continued in other terms: with a Person, instead of between persons. So, too, in twentieth-century literature, religion first appears as a concern, rather than as an emotion or a *mystique*. In Henry James, as in hell, God is present by His absence: the moral imperative is all. In J. P. Marquand—one of the most perfect portraitists the white Protestant upper middle-class has ever had, the peer of John Galsworthy—ethics are entirely dependent on class. Certain income-brackets refrain from certain types of conduct as surely as they choose other types; their motives are as instinctively snobbish as are those of the people who change each evening for dinner or who use the parlour on Sundays. In such authors as Marquand and James Gould Cozzens the Puritan conscience seems to have evaporated—in literature at least—into a miasma of good breeding. Cozzens adopts a rather dated attitude to Roman Catholics and Jews as being 'lesser breeds without the law'—the law being what is done on the right side of the railroad tracks.

At the other end of the religious scale writers such as Eugene O'Neill (in his last personal cycle of plays) and John O'Hara flail the Catholic piety they have cast off, and the Protestant *mores* to which they aspire, with equal venom: *Long Day's Journey into Night,* O'Neill's posthumous, highly successful play, is like an over-long visit with a social worker. Where the Puritan conscience rears anew an unexpected head is in the novels of the Beat Generation. Writing of the Beat novelists in *New World Writing,* Kenneth Rexroth (himself a Roman Catholic) describes them as 'debauched Puritans' and, for all his much-vaunted self-identification with Zen techniques and discipline, Kerouac certainly seems to be reacting rather to Puritan than to Buddhist antibodies.

It was between the wars that the American novel got religion. Paradoxically, it was the total destruction of the American dream—of the continually improving, everlastingly expanding and ever-happier, better and richer world, that brought about a revulsion among writers against the moral, the normal, and the optimistic.

William Faulkner, Ernest Hemingway and F. Scott Fitzgerald were the first three American writers of this century whose novels evidenced awareness of a quite other, religious dimension. With Faulkner, for the first time since Melville, the moral became religious by becoming myth. With his overwhelming Protestant certainty that 'there must have been some initial evil', with his sense of men as 'pawns of God' haunted by sin behind them and harried by fate around and before, Faulkner is the Protestant Dostoevsky, and the only American novelist with a comparable religious and literary rating. Sean O'Faolain has called attention to Faulkner's 'boss words' *doom, doomed immortality, destiny, fate, fatality*, and *immortal doom*. Faulkner has exteriorized, almost in parable form, the permanent struggle between moral liberty and the servitude of the flesh, in the struggle between the Sartorises and the Snopes. And in his later novels—from *Light in August* on—the references to the Saving Victim increase in every book. At first only casual and alliterative—Joe Christmas's name, his feet-washing by Mrs. McEachern, the Holy Week dates in *The Sound and the Fury*, the sacrificial undertones of *Soldier's Pay*—they increase in blatancy and number, until, in *A Fable*, Jesus Christ surfaces like a submarine. In *Requiem for a Nun* (especially in the play adapted from the novel by Faulkner himself and produced on Broadway in the fall of 1958) he is openly thundering from a magnolia pulpit, and what he is preaching is, as he puts it, 'more than the divinity of individual man (which we in America have debased into a national religion) but the divinity of his continuity as Man'. Man made God by the free choice of God made man.

It had to be in the South, where the ghastly dichotomy between the great American Declarations and the 'peculiar institution' and its contemporary consequences creates a schizophrenia in all thinking persons, that the always latent conflict between religion and morality found fictional expression. It has done so in every line of the great Yoknapatawpha Saga.

Faulkner is, perhaps, the watershed writer in the history of the religious imagination in America. In the stories of Flannery O'Connor, born in Georgia in 1925, the whole world of the South—the horrid children, the healing preachers, the godless spectators, the veterans of three wars, the displaced persons, the new industrial rich settlers from the North—is described with brutal irony and merciless humour. She can show a convent bred child entertaining two prurient-minded cousins for the weekend, or the murder in cold blood of a whole family by a misfit, or a Pole run over deliberately by poor white trash in a tractor, with extraordinary composure and a compassion so universal that it raises all her local characters to a universal scale. And her stories are not merely religious, but theological. Another remarkable young Catholic Southern writer is the Texan, John Howard Griffin. Griffin gradually lost his sight as the result of wounds suffered in the Second World War. His first novel, *The Devil Rides Outside,* tells of a young American who goes to study plain-chant at Solesmes. Gradually he comes to understand the life of the monks, but, as he does so, the flesh begins to bother him. The first part of the novel ends when the young hero leaves the cloister precincts to board in the contiguous village: and would the story had ended then. The second part, where the devil, who 'rides outside' every monastery, overcomes the hero, is bad Mauriac: a no doubt valiant, but foolhardy and almost completely unsuccessful attempt to understand what makes a French village tick. Griffin's less known second novel lacked the spiciness of the first but was actually much better: a contemporary *Erewhon* tragically true.

The hero, a happily married professor of sociology, is flying home after a conference, and when his aircraft crashes, is the sole survivor. He lands on a Pacific shore, where he is nursed back to health by the savage inhabitants. He finds no difficulty with their life or their language: only gradually does he come to realize that they are totally and absolutely without love. The mounting horror of what this means—sex without love, maternity without love, religion without love, death without love—is gradually and excellently developed.

Cornelia Jessey, a young Californian, in her first novel, *Treasure of Darkness,* handles the Faulknerian theme of total guilt: it is not what we do but what we are that is sinful. The heroine has murdered her mother; her father has taken the rap, and no one blames him for his supposed deed. During a long, wartime journey to the Pacific coast the heroine comes gradually to accept and to acknowledge her guilt. Truman Capote alone, of contemporary Southern writers, seems to escape this almost omnipresent sense of guilt: perhaps because he seeks his material below the surface of ordinary life, in persons not wholly rational.

Ralph Ellison, one of America's foremost Negro writers, has pointed out that the American novelist cannot live to-day without an 'awareness of chaos'. This is particularly true since the Second World War, when American readers generally, even when they do not know what ails them, have shown, like algae moving with the tide, how disturbed and unsatisfied they are. Such mammoth sellers as Joshua Liebman's *Peace of Mind* or Bishop Sheen's written and spoken words, such auto-biographies as *Seven Storey Mountain,* by Thomas Merton, or Lilian Roth's *I'll Cry Tomorrow* show that the feeling of a need for a salve is fairly general.

Perhaps the most deeply religious of the younger writers is J. D. Salinger, whose 'discipline' (to use a horrible jargon word in use at Columbia University) is Zen. Zen first appeared in the literary life of the United States about 1925, with the translation into English of D. T. Suzuki's books. Its influence ripened slowly, until the present craze for Zen of the 'hipsters', who all claim to 'dig' it. But Salinger is a serious writer. The hero of *The Catcher in the Rye,* disgusted with the falseness of adult values, finds his only possible communication with his ten-year-old sister. He wants only one thing of life—to be the one who catches those about to fall. In Salinger's *Nine Stories* (all first published in the *New Yorker*) religious love is even more surely, as light was to Cézanne, the 'hero of every picture'. The pregnant girl whose lover is trying to persuade her to have an abortion repeats the prayer of Jesus between her retches; the soldier, sickened by all he sees, is saved by Esmé's watch; and one story ends with the Tolstoyan discovery that Christ Jesus is the fat woman, the fat woman is always Jesus Christ. In everything he writes, Salinger calls in the spiritual world to redress the balance of the material.

Mary McCarthy, who, like her master, Ernest Hemingway, trails Catholic clouds, writes with more than a hint of *eidos*: sometimes with almost an embarrassed genuflexion. She writes too with brutal bravado: her accounts of a girl having her first abortion, of a middle-aged matron having an affair with her ex-husband on the present incumbent's sofa, leave nothing to the imagination. Yet her bitterly touching *Memories of a Catholic Girlhood* reveal her as a fundamentally religious writer: her description of her loss of faith at boarding school is tragically hilarious. J. F. Powers, too, in his two volumes of short stories, *The Presence of Grace* and *Power of Darkness,* owes something of his almost feline delicacy of spring to Hemingway—surely the most imitated of all writers. But where Hemingway sometimes misses his fish by overcasting, Powers works a small vein, the Irish-American clergy, their friends, foes and foibles, and produces gems 'of purest ray serene' in which the holy and the horrible both are windows for the reader.

No young writer of to-day can provide the meridional, garlic-Gallic *Romanitas* of the early Hemingway, and perhaps he is still the most hard-boiled eschatologist among American writers. William Gaddis, in his first novel of more than 950 pages, was a valiant ox-imitating frog, but, alas, he burst. W. Lederer's and Eugene Burdick's *The Ugly American* is a far cry from the expatriates of the 1920s, yet it could not have been written without many antecedents, of which Hemingway's *To Have And To Have Not* is one.

The popularity of Samuel Beckett's very religious plays, the huge success of Archibald Macleish's *JB*, and the recent revival of Arthur Miller's *The Crucible* (which can be seen now, removed from the McCarthy context in which it was written, for the very fine play it is) are all indications of the growth of a religious appetite in the American public. Such frankly religious foreign films as *He Who Must Die* and *Marcelino* also appeal to a large audience, as do Gian-Carlo Menotti's religious operas.

But it is perhaps the large body of young poets who distil most truly America's new literate concern with the Deity. The older men had begun: Wystan Auden in everything he writes, however humorously; Peter Viereck, Phyllis McGinley, John Ciardi (poetry editor of the *Saturday Review* and a great influence on the younger men) and Robert Lowell. But there is a whole crowd of young ones among them: Daniel Berrigan and Ned O'Gorman, the last two years' Lamont poetry prize winners; John Logan and J. F. Nims from the Mid-West; Isabelle Gardner from Boston. For all of these one of the greatest American poets has well spoken when he wrote:

> how should tasting touching hearing seeing
> breathing any—lifted from the no
> of all nothing—human merely being
> doubt unimaginable You?

Guys in Advertising

What most strikes native observers of American advertising is its apparent lack of imagination. The word itself is not highly prized by advertising men. It seems to carry a hint of 'imaginary', a risk of removal from that reality which contains the client's product, the consumer's dollar and the advertising agency's commission. Far preferable within the advertising community is the word 'creativity', with its interesting connotation of making something real which was not real before. One speaks of a 'creative department' or even a 'creative committee', as one could not (without contradicting all experience) speak of 'an imaginative committee'. The word 'creative', moreover, passes through most American conversation in a magnificent, luminous aura; all one can see usually is the aura, because the sun inside is so bright one dare not look right at it. Enshrined at the heart of an advertising agency, the word 'creative' casts its glow over the entire enterprise, and enables the agency to secure in the labour market, if not the best, at least a good selection of the second-best brains of a generation.

When people who know about advertising talk about its imaginative content they usually reserve their highest praise for work done in the graphic arts and in the construction of research projects. (More cynical commentators have been known to linger over the sometimes remarkable imagination displayed in relations between the advertising man and his corporate client; but the arts of the confidence man are not susceptible to accurate analysis.) It is no exaggeration to say that the best photography in the world appears in American advertising. Trading on the relative scarcity of their mysterious talent, and on the general view that they are all crazy anyway, photographers have established in advertising an independence and a scale of pay which make the work highly desirable.

Artists are somewhat less happily placed. While the photographers are independent contractors, the artists are salaried personnel of the agencies, subject to constant and often irritating supervision. A talent for the sort of design required by advertising is less hard to find than the genius for giving life to the dead chemicals of photographic film. Moreover, the imaginative possibilities of photography do not extend far beyond the limits of what can be done in an advertisement, while the realm of art is infinitely greater than the design which can be used for commercial purposes. Nevertheless, a printed advertisement must offer people something interesting to look at if it is to stand out from the boundless seas of its fellows, and the people who pay for advertising understand quite well that only an artist's imagination can supply the necessary distinction. Art is useful, too. Someone once observed that the notion that a picture is as good as 10,000 words could have arisen only in a culture which wrote its language in pictographs. But there are some arguments which *can* be made more concisely in an illustration—such as the advantage of travel by a fast aircraft, expressed through a photograph of the ocean, with the right-hand quarter of the picture torn away.

An astonishingly high quality of imagination has gone into the best advertising research—indeed, looking at some of the studies, it is sometimes difficult to see where intuition ends and research begins. All successful scientific investigations, of course, grow from the imaginative accuracy of the hypotheses to be explored, and much of the customary failure of the 'social scientist' rests on his self-denying belief that he must 'consider all the facts', his fear that he may be accused of bias if he approaches his work with a strong hypothesis. In the advertising field, many of the inhibitions that limit academic social psychology have been removed by the need to reach an immediate, usable answer—an answer that may be true or false on the most profound levels of thought, but can be successfully employed here and now on the surface levels of advertising. One could not ask women to describe the sort of housewife who puts instant coffee on her shopping list without perceiving that the use of powdered 'nowork' preparations is considered a mark of laziness. The man who assigned investigators to count the eye-blinks of shoppers in a supermarket had first experienced the imaginative notion that people buy packaged foods in a kind of trance. The one who turned machines to measuring the tension of automobile accelerator springs began with the hunch that people judged the power of their cars by how hard they had to stamp their foot to get the maximum result.

In such cases, of course, it is the researcher—the sociologist, psychologist or salesman-with-pretensions—who has come up with the essential advertising idea. Some of the complaints about research which are an audible mark of the American advertising copywriter doubtless grow from this usurpation of the writer's imaginative role by the supposedly soulless researcher. Often, however, the copywriter's anger has justifiable cause. Most advertising research, like most of the work in the social sciences generally, is mere plodding accumulation of inert material. Under the long tables of statistics, and the sheaves of paper reporting what some unperceptive graduate student thought a housewife at 110, Main Street meant when she said the words 'toilet paper', the copywriter struggles haplessly for *lebensraum*. His imagination suffocates, and inevitably he turns out a simulacrum of what someone else has done before. He then complains, not without reason, that research stifles imagination.

The copywriter is hedged around with too many restraints, too many bosses, too many collaborators. Though the imaginative accomplishments of the best researchers and artists may be more interesting than anything done by a copywriter, the entire structure does rest, finally, on a copywriter's ability to find, completely comprehend, and phrase an argument. One can reasonably doubt that the worst advertising would be any more appalling than it is without research to prove it and art to prettify it; and one can easily believe that the best advertising might be more effective if it were no more than one man's intuition of the consumer *vis-à-vis* the product to be sold. For that intuition—that imaginative perception of what can bind a product to its market—will always lie at the centre of successful advertising.

The copywriting intuition is not so stale or used up as might appear from an examination of an average hundred American advertisements (and a hundred can be found in most issues of most popular magazines, or in a day of watching television). The fact that certain assorted sets of ten advertisements look alike does not mean that imagination is absent: it means merely that *one* imaginative presentation has drawn imitators. Commercial pressure is always exerted toward the imitation of what has been successful. Both the original imagination and the imitation are most obvious when something entertaining has started the parade. One of the advantages of vodka is that the beverage has no odour: thus, 'It leaves you breathless.' Large automobiles are an obviously wasteful luxury, and the case is admirably stated as one of 'The dinosaur in the driveway'. Even the most sombre philosopher might yield a smile to the combination of spoof and sense in the recommendation of a concentrate, beginning, ' *Who* put eight great tomatoes in a itty bitty can?'

But it is not the clever advertisement which is, in advertising terms, the most imaginative. Art may or may not have a purpose, but the purpose of advertising is unavoidable. The greatest problem in advertising is to take a common, noisily advertised product and by imagination to impress a name deeply on the public consciousness. What is required is the kind of insight and ability that produces popular songs, crowning a cliché with precisely the correct bargain hat. The ultimate expression of imaginative advertising is not the man in the eye-patch who can sell moderate quantities of shirts to a luxury audience, but 'Winston tastes good like a cigarette should'.

One understands and sympathizes with the general reluctance to award the accolade of imagination to something so essentially offensive as this ungrammatical jingle. But the argument that 'it's all a formula' will not bear examination. There is formula advertising to be seen, but only in holes and corners:

> The three gentlemen pictured [runs the text of a recent mail-order book advertisement] are *Lionel Trilling*, literary critic and Professor of English, *Jacques Barzun*, Dean of the Faculties of Columbia University, and *W. H. Auden*, Professor of Poetry of Oxford University. They will screen, from the best books published each year, the ones they want on their own bookshelves. These will be offered for your selection through The Mid-Century Book Society.... Members will enjoy the following advantages. . . 3). The accounts of members will receive individual attention from the Society.

You could not sell soap with such stuff, but there is a naïve community to which it appeals. Its sole resemblance to the degraded genius of 'Winston tastes good like a cigarette should' is in provoking melancholy reflections about the things intelligent people will do for the sake of money.

We are here meeting a question to be met everywhere in these pages:

where is the line that separates the imaginative from the not-imaginative? Is imagination in itself a purposeful activity, or is it (as Beethoven once proposed) a by-product of the exercise of a craft? Need it be 'original', constructing a new world from the chaos of the senses, or may it be merely an improvement on what is found, incompletely structured? Must it be successful, in that others find themselves stimulated by it, or can it be completely private, a simple joy in the breast of its originator?

Des Esseintes went to great trouble to create a criminal; the best of advertising copywriters struggles with his higher instincts and lower passions to create a cliché. The quality of his imagination can be measured only pragmatically—by the extent to which his cliché becomes, in fact, part of the hideous, old-fashioned mental furniture in the heads of his readers and audience. Most advertising ideas and slogans pass so rapidly from one void to another that only the advertiser is even conscious of their transient presence. What distinguishes those few which achieve relative permanence ('Halitosis', 'BO', 'Cleans your breath while it cleans your teeth', '99-44/100ths per cent pure', 'There's a Ford in your future', 'I'd walk a mile for a Camel', 'Betty Crocker', 'Which twin has the Toni?', 'She's lovely, she's engaged, she uses Pond's') must in all logic and fairness be granted a quality of imagination.

To say that there is something peculiar about this sort of imagination is to discover salt in the sea. What poet could have conceived a bald Turkish eunuch, wearing a single ear-ring, as the proper symbol for a liquid cleanser? What novelist would have found in the wave of national enthusiasm for scientists and scholars an argument ('thinking man's filter, smoking man's taste') for a brand of cigarette?

But the conclusions which should be drawn from the fact are too often neglected. The imagination which designs the visible images of advertising and its fellow which designs the research projects are both comprehensible in terms of allied endeavours. The imagination which finds the right advertising slogan or idea, however, is *sui generis*. Its only close relation is the gift of writing successful popular songs. The recognition and reward of this sort of imagination, as something rare and commercially precious, is one of the lesser contributions of America to the twentieth century.

Like all talents, that of finding advertising ideas can be schooled but not acquired in school: thus the disappointment of the industry in those who have been graduated, often *cum laude,* with degrees in advertising (which the industry's leaders, however, continue to push on more or less reluctant universities). And, like most talents, the advertising imagination does not transfer easily into other areas. Every year writers regretfully decide to sell their souls and enter advertising—only to find that they lack the kind of imagination necessary to succeed in the trade they despise. Every year, high-paid, discontented advertising copywriters decide to chuck it and write that novel which teems within them, only to learn that their abilities when confronted with the expensive blank page of a magazine are useless before the challenge of the cheap folio. Intellectuals lament the loss of artistic talent in the Sodom and Gomorrah of the movies and advertising, but talent, in a society as free as that of mid-century America, usually finds its proper outlets. The imagination which has gone into the creation of advertising is well employed—though one could wish that those who have the necessary gift, and those to whom they give it, were just a little less unhappy about their situation.

A Vocal Group

Since the war Jewish assimilation in America has made its widest, deepest and easiest gains, and one result is that the Jew, for most practical purposes, is counted in to-day with the majority. With everyone's eye on the Negro problem and, in a number of cities, on the Puerto Rican, he moves more easily than he had expected into the older suburbs, into a position with a Gentile corporation, a Government agency, an English department, and in the liberal, eager-beaver ethos of American community life, business, or research, he is perfectly at home. He finds that his aggressiveness and shrewdness, his love of the politics of life—like most of his other tags—are transvalued now into assets that promote acceptance rather than merely tolerance. Also to have Jewish friends, to use a Jewish pediatrician, to read *Marjorie Morningstar* or *The Magic Barrel,* or *I and Thou,* are currently signs of urbanity at the different cultural levels rather than of oddity, much like having a Yiddish phrase or two to season one's speech.

The sense of Jewish difference remains, but it is a painless one— easily accommodated to the suburban point of view, easily overlooked, easily moralized, if one likes, into the special capabilities and vision of the talented outsider: what one remembers of Bloom or Swann without having to be reminded of what they suffered as Jews. But mostly the Jew is taken for granted in America. The real outsiders are the Negro and the Puerto Rican; the images they offer to the imagination are still too violent and bleak for most Americans to transvalue, moralize, or overlook.

Much of the same development has occurred in the different atmosphere of the literary scene. The emergence of first-rate Negro novelists such as Ralph Ellison and James Baldwin has been widely noticed.

173

The noisy disturbance produced by the literary juvenile delinquents—the Beat writers—has been taken as an important development in current letters—the latest rise of the Redskins against the Palefaces. There is the growing feeling that the formalism and decorum that have characterized serious fiction, poetry and criticism since the war, deriving mainly from the influence of the New Criticism, have had their say; and Kerouac, Ginsberg, and Mailer are being viewed, at least in part, as an over-reaction to an Alexandrian decline into rituals of recondite style and sensibility.

However, while attention in America has been directed to and distracted by the literary Outsiders, as well as by the English Angry Young Men, a more substantial and formidable development has been going on, as it were, from within—as indeed it has been going on under everyone's eyes since about 1950. This is the emergence of American-Jewish writing as a decisive force in American letters. Among leading critics to-day are Lionel Trilling, Alfred Kazin, Philip Rahv, Leslie Fiedler, Irving Howe; there are few younger fiction writers of unmistakable significance but among them are certainly Saul Bellow and Bernard Malamud; though inactive in recent years, Arthur Miller remains our most solid and serious playwright; in poetry there is Karl Shapiro (whose latest collection is titled *Poems of a Jew*), as well as Delmore Schwartz, Howard Nemerov and Stanley Kunitz, who is perhaps the most underrated poet to-day. Further, the unquestioned influence of *Partisan Review* has been largely the work of these and a host of lesser-known American-Jewish writers. The prowess and enterprise of this group also has helped to establish the rapid reputation and influence of *Commentary*—one of the first American-Jewish journals of any real literary distinction and impact. And even more indicative, perhaps, of this new literary energy is the growing group of younger poets, fiction writers, and critics who are just beginning to rise into prominence.

But first some necessary qualifications. The present writer is aware of the tendency—particularly marked among the more official Jewish literary historians—to name whatever prominent Jewish names there are and call it Jewish writing. He is also aware of their tendency to take whatever time they have happened to be writing at since about 1930 as the beginning of the Jewish millenium in American letters. The point is not that these writers are Jewish so much as that they are American ones. Some of them are actively affiliated with American-

Jewish letters, some are not: the range is from Irving Howe, who has been trying to make Yiddish literature accessible to American readers, through to Stanley Kunitz, who has written three volumes of poetry without any explicit signs of Jewish content. On the whole, most of them have tried to follow the same line as Louis Zukofsy:

> I'll read their Donne as mine,
> And leopard in their spots
> I'll do what says their Coleridge,
> Twist red hot pokers into knots.

Moreover, most of them are too dispersed by their individual interests to constitute anything like a movement or school. Though they give a distinct direction to American writing to-day, it is a very general one: we assemble them with the sense of the differences rather than the close similarities, of their positions in privately won outposts rather than as part of a phalanx. Still, they do represent a special energy in the literary scene and one of the things that does characterize them generally is that they play with 'red hot pokers'. And judging by the signs of activity and daring of the new generation of American-Jewish writers that appear in the writing they do for *Partisan* and *Commentary*, *Midstream* and *The New Leader*, we may still be only at the beginning.

A recent essay by Leslie Fiedler is entitled 'The American-Jewish Novel and the Breakthrough'. 'Breakthrough' is a good term: it suggests the initial location of an opening, and then the calculated aggression, followed by dramatic gains. Fiedler uses it mainly to describe the significance of Saul Bellow's *The Adventures of Augie March*. He believes it is the first American-Jewish novel that really enters, opens up, and takes possession of its true material—that which lies within the widening margin where the Jewish scene is simply the American scene with a certain difference. Further, Fiedler finds a clear advance in the characterization of the hero. Augie, he believes, is the classic *schlemiel* who comes fully developed out of Yiddish literature as one of its chief types and who previously found his way into the fiction of Daniel Fuchs and Nathanael West in the 1930s. Another obvious materialization is the hero of the Chaplin films; also Bellow's own free-swinging translation of 'Gimpel, the Fool'—probably the best *schlemiel* story in the literature—is relevant to Fiedler's point. At the same time he notes that Augie derives from an equally classic

American type—the uncommitted son of the open road whose most famous embodiment is Huck Finn. And in this sudden, resonant blend of the two literary traditions, Bellow is found to have made the same brilliant advance in method as he has in content.

Fiedler's notation of an inner breakthrough within the fiction is a telling one, and on the whole his survey of the American-Jewish novel is the first to open up *his* subject, the first breakthrough to be made against the ethnocentric pieties and apologies and spites, against the general provincialism that has characterized the more or less official account. At the same time, his penetration and energy of mind, the peculiar aggression he makes upon his subject, remind us how his essays have consistently been zealous assaults upon received ideas and settled points of view. His essays, for example, on the Hiss-Chambers affair, on the Rosenbergs, on life in Montana, on our contemporary liberalism and fiction generally, have had much the same shock-value as his more notorious study of the homosexual implications of American Innocence in general and of *Moby Dick* and *Huckleberry Finn* in particular.

The same willingness to revolt, to take chances, to trust one's own instincts and insights and standards, to risk a crushing failure and even ridicule, has marked the fiction of Saul Bellow. As he tells us on the first page of his first novel, *Dangling Man,* here was a revolt against the codes of hard-boiledness, impersonality, and suppression of the self which derived from Flaubert and Eliot notably, and which had produced in its American equivalent a novelist such as Hemingway, who, as Bellow later remarks, finally 'wants to be praised for the offences he does not commit'. In *Dangling Man,* he put it as follows:

> Do you have feelings? There are correct and incorrect ways of indicating them. Do you have an inner life? It is nobody's business but your own. Do you have emotions? Strangle them . . . on the truest candor it [the code] has an inhibiting effect. Most serious matters are closed to the hard-boiled.

In most of his best work, Bellow has continued to make fiction out of the direct expression of a leading character's mind and heart. At the same time, he has carried his attack to other sectors. *The Victim* broke through the conventions of the anti-Semitism fiction which was very popular shortly after the war. His hero, Asa Leventhal, is a homely, surly, at times distinctly unattractive Jew who is victimized by a clever Jew-baiter named Albee. However, years earlier in a fit of anger and frustration, Leventhal had caused Albee to lose his job and while he was later making his career in publishing, Albee was sinking into alcoholism and vagrancy. Working out the novel situation of the suffering Jew who has himself inflicted suffering on his persecutor and must recognize it, Bellow was able to complicate this short-lived genre and to open up its deeper implications. Similarly, his next book, *Augie March,* was an assault upon the contemporary social novel, upon its decorum and polish, its inability to handle the thickness and unruliness of social detail, upon its thinness of ideas. *Augie March* was as much a breakthrough in terms of social and intellectual coverage, in terms of its creative energy, intelligence and wackiness, as it was in the respects that Fielder notes. Bellow's next surprise was a story of the Depression, 'Looking for Mr. Green'. It can also be seen as a deliberate challenge to the well-mannered and pretentious tale of 'ideas'—specifically the ideas of the American illusion and reality to-day that has been much in vogue with the general attempt by our intellectuals to put themselves in touch again with America.

The two most recent works, 'Seize the Day' and *Henderson, the Rain King,* also dramatically exemplify Bellow's single-minded attack upon our major canons of literary technique and taste as well as his breaking open and revitalizing still two more of our fictional genres—the business man's story of failure and the story of the innocent and indomitable American abroad. In most of his fiction Bellow has tended to keep to a single underlying line of inquiry by which he has tested and extended the definition that appears in *Augie March*—'a man's character is his fate'. However, in his restless daring, his unwillingness to repeat his material, in his love of the sudden, one-man raid upon apparently played-out material, Bellow illustrates in his fiction, as Fiedler has done in his social and literary criticism, the energy of American-Jewish writers that has been flowing into contemporary letters.

For Bellow and Fiedler can be seen as only more extreme cases of the post-war venturesomeness of writers who finally have found the social and psychological conditions in which they can write boldly as Americans. Bellow and Fiedler are farther out in their assaults upon our current literary scene; they take longer chances and perhaps pay higher prices in terms of evenness of achievement, certainly in the critical response to their forays. However, in more restrained ways, many of the other writers previously mentioned have also developed their own brands of artistic or critical radicalism and opposition, have carried out their own quieter aggressions, and have found opportunities for their own breakthroughs. Take the, perhaps unlooked-for, example of Lionel Trilling, whose impeccable critical manners have masked the behaviour of possibly America's most brilliant and influential literary maverick. While the New York intellectuals—both Jews and Gentiles—were beating the drums of Left-Wing literature and thought in the 1930s, Trilling worked quietly away on what was to be the definitive study of Matthew Arnold.

In the 1940s, when the Liberal imagination arose again from the ashes of the Marxist one and prepared for what promised to be a spectacular flight, Trilling was already fingering its weaknesses and calling our attention to those that had already limited Parrington and Dreiser and Anderson and were soon to limit Liberalism itself. While the New Fiction was in vogue he was examining its essential narrative and intellectual deadness and was anticipating and calling for the novel of action and ideas and roughness of grain that has come back with such writers as Bellow and Ralph Ellison. He has championed the Romantic imagination through its lean years of disfavour and the historical approach to literature when close textual analysis to reveal the rhetorical strategies was the fashion. Critics of James were crowding and jostling about the poetic complexities of the later work; Trilling called our attention to the hard, clear, prose truths of *The Princess Cassimassima* and *The Bostonians*.

And so on. Most important, generally, has been Trilling's cool subversion of the Formalist position in the interest of a fundamental moral criticism of literature, one that can get at such things as the weight and permanence of the human content, the quality of a writer's values that may be detected in his literary voice, the opposition that the creative self puts up to the circumscriptions of a culture (his major theme recently, and one whose wide expression is near the centre of post-war American-Jewish writing). Steadily counter-acting the trend to make literature out as a kind of psycho-drama of rhetorical devices, Trilling has been instrumental in keeping up our awareness of the historical and biographical realities under which literature is written, and to the moral reference by which it still must finally make its appeal. And with the exception of such critics as Edmund Wilson and Morton D. Zabel, along with those earlier mentioned, he is one of the few leading critics who come to mind as having done this in recent years, and, for the most part, has done so a good quarter of a mile beyond anyone else. Trilling's two famous stories, 'Of this Time, of that Place' and 'The Other Margaret', and his novel, *The Middle of the Journey,* were also in their different ways advanced pieces of fiction, their daring again concealed by the smooth urbanity of his tone.

Thus Trilling's quiet attack upon the political and literary 'pieties' of his time (a favourite term of his and a revealing one) may well prove to have been the most successful intellectual aggression of all. In the criticism of such students of his as Richard Chase, Norman Podhoretz and Steven Marcus, one finds much of his moral orientation to literature, along with his vigour, independence and toughness of mind. Chase's recent book on the American novel is one of the real signs of life in our rather domesticated scholarly scene, and the present writer was elated for days by Podhoretz's courageous and incisive analysis of the nihilistic drift in Camus's latest collection of stories—at a time when the Nobel Prize award had persuaded one into seeing him as a positive moral force. Marcus's assaults upon the Wyndham-Lewis-Pound-Eliot-Hugh Kenner group have also been brave and intelligent, and needed. However, along with Trilling, the dominant American-Jewish critics are still Kazin, Rahv, Howe, and Fiedler; and their careers exhibit much of the same interest and virtues that we have been finding in his. At the age of twenty-seven Kazin had already produced the remarkably learned and independent *On Native Grounds,* in which he was already working out the moral-aesthetic position that since then has increasingly enlivened and pointed his practical criticism. Rahv's major aggression on American consciousness has continued to be his editing of *Partisan Review* (though *Partisan* is showing some signs finally of middle-age); however, Rahv's own essays have also had their own range and energy and willingness to take chances. For example, in his controversial 'Paleface and Redskin', collected in *Image and Idea,* he was willing to sort out the major American writers into these two classes and succeeded in establishing a distinction that has proved to be crucial in our present definitions of American literary traditions.

Like these other critics, Howe has been particularly attracted to the American imagination (a point we shall return to); and like theirs, his varied career has been marked by a similar preoccupation with content rather than with form and by a similar boldness in confronting literature as politics, psychology, morality. At the same time he has been the most committed and telling critic of the Jewish imagination; perhaps his best single essay is the long introduction that he wrote with Eliezer Greenberg on the Yiddish literary tradition for their recent *Treasury of Yiddish Stories*. This introduction is of first importance in opening the way to a remarkable and as yet little-read body of literature and also, at many points, illuminates the home base from which most of the contemporary American-Jewish writers still start out, and frequently these days return to—'a culture so thoroughly commited to the exploration of moral order'. In his double role, Howe is perhaps the pivotal figure on the American-Jewish scene, or, at least, stands most clearly for the divided energy that has explored Jewish consciousness as radically since the war as it has American.

The most dramatic expression of the former has been the recent work of Bernard Malamud. His novel *The Assistant* is a radiant fusion of its humane sentiment, comedy and ethical firmness: the story of an Italian drifter who slowly becomes a Jew through the suffering and aspiration that take possession of him during his relations with an impoverished Jewish grocer and his daughter. *The Magic Barrel,* for which Malamud won this year's National Book Award, is mainly a group of terse, tense fantasies upon the similar and central theme of the Yiddish literary tradition—the meaning of Jewishness. A young rabbi falls desperately into a marriage with a prostitute, while her father, the marriage broker, mumbles the prayer for the dead. In another story, a poor art scholar is unable to respond to an all-but impossible demand upon his generosity, and so has his precious manuscript on Giotto destroyed by the panhandling Jewish refugee from Israel: the scholar forgives him. Elsewhere in the collection a Job-like little tailor must make himself believe in a Negro angel named Levine.

Malamud's reverence for feeling, his preoccupations with the dispossessed and the weak (even most of his New York Jews live in timeless, spaceless realms of poverty and isolation), his essentially comic mode of moral analysis, his faith in the power of the human heart and will to discover and re-create the self—all of these place him in the mainstream of Jewish literature, and station him in his role as a translator of the eastern European morality into American terms. To be sure, Malamud is a sophisticated writer and, typically, is in possession of several literary traditions. However, a dominant one is the Hasidic tradition and it is not surprising that his emergence coincides with that of Martin Buber, its foremost student and philosopher, and with that of its foremost Yiddish fiction writer, Isaac Bashevis Singer. Hasidism can be described as the personal, the concrete, the intimate element that came into the religion in the eighteenth century; it has remained, at least theologically, the element that is on the side of self-awareness, personal moral aspiration, and a conscious joy in the world.

Finding a viable part of their religion still preserved intact in Buber's *Tales of the Hasidim* has been an exciting discovery for many American-Jewish intellectuals in the 1950s—a decade which has, in fact, been marked by a general rediscovery that they derive from Jewish culture as well as American and that these can be profitably connected in one's books as well as in one's life. Kazin's *A Walker in the City* is a notable example of the new effort to define a Jewish past in the light of the awareness and sympathy that has come with acculturation and accep-tance. S. N. Behrman's *The Worcester Account* is another such product of the 1950s, as is David Daiches's *Between Two Worlds*.

In the late 1940s, Isaac Rosenfeld (whose death at thirty-seven is the greatest single loss that contemporary American-Jewish writing has suffered) was already making the same attempt in fiction to explore what he calls in *Passage from Home* the 'minor world', to return to a Jewish past and to the boyhood strategics of revolt and return. Del-more Schwartz's *The World is a Wedding,* Paul Goodman's *The Break-up of the Camp*, Herbert Gold's 'The Heart of the Artichoke' also exemplify the first real attempt of sophisticated American writers to get in touch with their Jewish backgrounds and so get in touch again with themselves. Lionel Trilling's essay 'Wordsworth and the Rabbis' also strikes the note of personal rediscovery, of the effort to repossess an illumination that came in one's childhood as a professing Jew, how-ever reluctantly one did so. In a recent essay on the American Negro and the Jew, Leslie Fiedler also finds his way back to the Jewish roots of his racial attitudes.

Here and there in the work of the rising younger poets such as Chester Kallman, Donald Finkel, Jascha Kessler, Irving Feldman, and particularly in that of Harvey Shapiro, one finds the sudden, tense engagement of Jewish content and modern poetic technique that has given such resonance to many of the poems of Delmore Schwartz and Karl Shapiro. In fiction, James Yaffee and Sylvia Rothchild, and per-haps more notably Philip Roth and Wallace Markfield, like the young South African writer, Dan Jacobson, are handling Jewish life with a new colour and curiosity and candour. American-Jewish fiction has long been disabled—and some of it still is—by the writer's inability to stay away from the played-out veins of local colour and by his inability to write his stories and novels without worrying about the Jewish heritage or about public relations or about why he shouldn't, after all, really hate the Jews himself.

One result has been that many writers, including some to-day such as Sam Astrakhan and Dannie Abse, are trapped in the ethos they were supposed to be rendering and connecting with that of the culture outside which so conditions it; trapped, too, in triteness and piety and equivocations, or like the author of *Remember Me to God*—in some ways an even glibber book than *Marjorie Morningstar*—trapped in sentimental evasions of one's ambivalence about his Jewishness. Even a talented writer such as Meyer Levin was almost as completely unable to get outside his material in *The Old Bunch* as Louis Zara was in his ethnocentric *Blessed is the Man*—both Chicago novels of the 1930s. Thus Levin's book, held to be a classic social novel in some quarters, suffers badly in this failure from an instinctive comparison of it to Farrell's *Studs Lonigan* trilogy. Charles Angoff's more recent chronicles of Russian Jews in America demonstrate, if anything, that these tendencies can get even worse with time.

Occasionally in the past, writers were able to overcome these disadvantages. Henry Roth did it in *Call it Sleep*, so did Babette Deutsch in her early poetry. Daniel Fuchs's *Homage to Blenholt* and *Low Company* and Charles Reznikoff's *By the Waters of Manhattan*, all seem just to miss being in complete control of their material. And in each case can be sensed the writer's struggle to overcome the powerful tendency of the material to dictate to his imagination and judgment and the special artistic and moral poise that this required of him.

Here, possibly, we have one of the sources of the energy and moral stamina that mark the breakthrough in handling Jewish content as well as American. Malamud's *The Assistant*, Roth's 'Goodbye, Columbus', Markfield's 'The Country of the Crazy Horse', Mrs. Rothchild's 'Home for *Pesach*'—are written as much against the grain of Jewish genre fiction, are as much a raid upon it under the colours of freshness and honesty, as are the raids Bellow has been carrying out upon the American genres as well as this one. Bellow and Malamud tend to succeed by an almost ruthless suppression of any familiar American-Jewish décor in their fiction; the younger writers succeed by making it come alive through using the flow of their own vivid reactions to Jewish characters and milieus. Also, as life has come back into the genre, the piety and the self-hatred (one as morally relaxed a reaction as the other) have gone out. There is the new recognition, as David Riesman puts it, 'that the existential dramas of daily living are coloured rather than created by ethnic and cultural localism'.

The writers we have been looking at attempt to hold up a segment of American-Jewish life and study it at arm's length, and in doing so, they assert in one way or another that, in Riesman's words, 'the Jews are chosen not by history or God but by the writer'. It is hard for a Jewish writer to assert this through his material: it is much easier to remember the six million Jews or the ugly, merciless hustler in the family who turned one's stomach and spirit. Similarly, it is hard not to take the peculiarity and local colour of Jewish life for granted and simply work it in. And it is the awareness of these pit-falls, the sweat and strain to avoid them at the back of the novel or story, that have helped to produce the literary and moral advance. The Jewish writer has finally reached the point where he shares the fate and fortune of the Gentile writer—the necessity of struggling with his material.

What remains, though, is something distinctly Jewish—the preoccupations with sentiment, suffering and righteousness, with morality. One of Delmore Schwartz's stories is entitled 'The Child is the Meaning of this Life' and to the extent that this is true we can generalize with some assurance about the moral imprint that modern American-Jewish writing bears. Products initially of a culture that still remembers itself, in Howe's words 'committed to the exploration of moral order', these writers generally tend to be more interested in content than in form, in a writer's moral reference rather than in his craft, in concreteness of situation, emotion and idea rather than in artistic decorum and sophistication. In so far as the American-Jewish writer remains a child of Jewish culture, his work tends to be conditioned by its attitude toward art. Howe and Greenberg define this attitude as follows in terms of Yiddish literature:

> Beauty was a quality rather than a form . . . The Jews would have been deeply puzzled by the idea that the aesthetic and the moral are distinct realms, for they saw beauty above all in behaviour . . . Not the play of manners but the direct, fearful encounter of moral assumptions was fundamental.

Since Yiddish literature was largely a ghetto literature, it concentrated on demonstrating values that men could live by and remain human under the dehumanizing forces of poverty, isolation and fear. One need only glance at the fiction of Malamud, the poetry of Karl Shapiro, the criticism of Trilling or the dramas of Arthur Miller to see how this tough, realistic inspection of values has carried over. And to the extent that American-Jewish writing touches the American imagination, it does so mainly in this way, and especially at the points where the New England-Puritan strain abides.

However, the main characteristic of this writing to-day is its creative energy rather than its focus, and its tendency is to flow outward to the American world rather than inward and backward to the Jewish. Even in works which have been the literary signs of the large-scale 'Jewish Revival' one senses the stronger attraction. Kazin's *A Walker in the City*, for all its fast attachment to Jewish Brownsville, mainly registers the typical purpose and passion of the imaginative boy, reading his way through the American classics in order to break through the ethnic confinements of his life. Similarly, Trilling's 'Wordsworth and the Rabbis' betrays by the very movement and tone of the essay, the true locus of his affiliations. The early discussion of the Torah is cursory and diffident; and there is a kind of intellectual relief in the prose once Trilling quickly moves on to Wordsworth's thought and to content with which he is thoroughly at home. In the major direction and force of the young Kazin's reading, we can note a second source of this general literary energy: the desire and drive of the Jewish intellectual to rise out of his early, circumscribed culture—his special hunger for a place in the world. Thus to-day he reads Isaac Babel more attentively than Peretz and Aleichem; for in the experiences of this Talmudic student who rode with the Cossacks, he finds a truer image of his own conditions and aspirations. Also in the tensions of Babel's fiction, he finds a radical sign of the tensions that direct his own passage through to the major world. 'America! America!'—the title of one of Schwartz's stories and of one of Kazin's chapters—still expresses the common inner exclamation, the common desire to be in contact with it, to grapple with it in one's work—the attraction and the challenge. So he moves in—boldly, perhaps, or politely but inevitably in some stance of attack, for the main obstacle to overcome is the sense of his own differences and the deepest purpose is the assertion of his right to understand.

The American-Jewish writer, of course, is not alone in these things. At present he happens to be in the most favourable social and cultural position to make his move. The son of a bookish tradition, he is now also economically secure enough to convert business energy more purely into creative and scholarly energy—to become an Arthur Miller rather than an Elmer Rice, a Leon Edel rather than an Isaac Goldberg, an Aaron Copland rather than a George Gershwin. And because he is relatively secure in his personal career (almost all the writers here mentioned either teach or edit in respectable places), in his intellectual grasp of Western culture, and in his English prose and metres, he can begin to be bold. However, Ellison and Baldwin are unmistakable signs that another sub-culture is beginning to produce its secure and venturesome writers. Moreover, in the Puerto Rican slums of America's northern cities, there are, no doubt, the first inspired writers of their English compositions. One notices their talented middleweight is on his way up, the first small business men have opened the groceries and clothes stores, there is even the first movie star. It is very familiar, very heartening. In another twenty years there will be a fine jazz clarinetist and maybe a novelist or two, along with the lawyers and high-school teachers. In the following generation, a son of one of these—securely rooted in both his heritages and aware of the tensions to be channelled—may well be writing a note in these pages about the Puerto-Rican breakthrough in American letters. All of this promises well for its future.

A Nation of Art-collectors

In America everyone buys art—art meaning paintings, drawings, lithographs and reproductions; very few works of art, sculpture to a limited degree and some prints but no engraving. Bankers always did it but now farmers, taxi-drivers and plumbers also do it. Rich men, poor men, women, students, the young and the old—they all do it. And their choice is as diverse as their own characters. Expensive, cheap, advanced, conservative, obvious, hermetic, all find their admirers. So much activity over such a broad field gives the whole scene a frenzied, amorphous quality which is hard to clarify and to understand. In order to do so one must dissect the mass into separate areas and see what appears to be the basic characteristics of the activity; whether it is a healthy scene or whether it is an inflated unreal fantasy.

The traditional collector, the connoisseur of knowledge, of cultivated sensibilities, of passion, is becoming a *rara avis*. He still exists but in much smaller numbers. His field of collecting, as before, is usually a limited period or a limited type of object. His limitations are part of his power and his intensity. His taste is independent, personal and discriminating. It is a quiet activity much less heralded by the public press than the more spectacular flurries. Unfortunately the young do not seem to be joining this group as they did in the 1920s and the 1930s. Even acknowledging the paucity of numbers the connoisseur collector is the real backbone of collecting to-day, as always. He is usually closely allied with a museum, is well known by all the real *cognoscenti* and is respected as the continuing tradition.

The great activity is due to another group; let us call them the buyers. They are in every way the opposite of the connoisseur-collector. They are huge in number and represent vast amounts of money coming from all income levels from the very rich to the lower income brackets. Their taste, if it can be so called, is indiscriminate, shapeless, and spreads over the whole broad field. Their intensity is momentary and evanescent. Consequently they are easily led and easily influenced by fashion, publicity and ballyhoo. They do not seem to want knowledge or to miss the lack of it. For the dealer they make life easy and for the painter they are a life-saving boon. The most that one can hope is that from this group development may possibly take place and that there may come a real connoisseur-collector or a real patron of museums and scholarship.

A new factor in recent years is the development of the tax-exempt foundations. They are not museums or universities but act as a middle ground between the individual and the institutional. The foundations are usually set up by one man in his lifetime or in his will, or by one family, and are governed by a self-perpetuating board of trustees. They do not actually collect, they buy. What they buy is then given to schools, museums, unions and other organizations. Or they buy and then lend to the same types of organizations. Their activity has little influence on the collecting world. What they buy depends on the function of the foundation and on their choice of agent to do the buying. Curiously enough, it is not a conservative point of view but partakes of the diverse points of view of the individual collectors and buyers discussed before.

And what do all these people buy? Shall we begin by saying what they do not buy? There is practically no collecting of art of the past outside of museums (which are outside our investigation) and very few connoisseur-collectors. Even in the latter category there is a tendency toward a real connoisseurship of the nineteenth century. This group also encompass the only serious concern with works of art. They are the only supporters and active collectors of art of the past in paintings and to an even greater degree in drawings.

The great world of high fashion is as limited as always. Now its most favoured period is French Impressionism and post-Impressionism. Everyone—but everyone—can recognize a Renoir, a Cézanne, a van Gogh, and so, like any recognizable symbol, they are irresistible to this rich, careful group. Not much less obvious but slightly less conservative and more declaratory is the painting of the school of Paris during the first third of our century. These simple statements correspond to the rage of the 1920s for the eighteenth-century English portrait. Shades of Lord Duveen, but a less glamorous repetition of the same point of view! The reasons are the same, the buyers are the same, the values are equally inflated. Only the paintings are different, and here one must admit that the present fashion probably is for the greater painting quality. But transpose Renoir for Raeburn, Cézanne for Gainsborough, Gauguin for Reynolds and what do you have? All easily recognizable, all symbols of wealth and the basic consideration of names, names, names. A few, more daring, have sallied into the past, which is only considered as the background for the Olympian height of their favoured period of French Impressionism and post-Impressionism. They may buy a Fragonard, a Greco, a Rubens. A dangerous procedure. They may discover that paintings, and quite good ones, have been painted for some centuries.

The new discovery of a heritage of American art has created a whole world of interest. This heritage is not very old or very long. One had known the colonial painters with respect and historical interest, but the nineteenth century in American art loomed large on the horizon only within recent years. The combination of chauvinism, of the undemanding character of the work, and of a true relation to the American point of view has made it a major factor in collecting to-day. Unfortunately, it presents its difficulties. The nineteenth century in America was not a great fertile field of artistic creation. There were a few fine painters, more good direct anecdotal painters but largely it was a period of completely provincial pedestrian work. To steer through these pitfalls has been impossible for most and only a few early and discriminating collectors ended with great and fine examples. The major part of the work collected has been minor, to say the least, but it has provided a local past for the self-conscious American.

During the past generation, American painting has come alive on a broad and serious level. It has found a ready response in the collecting and buying world and is treated seriously, as it should be, no longer as the stepchild of European art. Its departures are various, its statements are integral and personal. It finds an understanding audience of quick and violent reactions. Its aesthetic premises are broad, its integrity is great and it creates a local scene of real feeling and real understanding which is very active and very rewarding. The much vaunted 'School of New York abstract-expressionism' is certainly a part of the local scene, but only a part. It has found many buyers but few discerning collectors. Supported by probably the best piece of log-rolling done here on the local scene, it has resulted in a tremendous fanfare of publicity, with the concomitant results. It is worth noting that only very recently has a local market for local work grown up in various cities outside New York. One cannot refer to it as provincial work—it is often quite first-class, but to have it recognized and bought on its own home ground is a new experience in the United States.

Well-known or even quite new paintings of England, France and Italy are all highly appreciated and collected. Americans have always been very quick on their uptake and knowledge and support of immediately contemporary European painting. Monet was bought largely in Boston long before the French had started. In fact, all the Impressionists were bought in America, particularly in Chicago, long before their acceptance in Europe or England. The search for the new, the novel, the original, even the outrageous is hectic in its intensity. This is a welcome point of view for the young painter who can, if so discovered, become well known with one exhibition. The publicity is great, his works sell rapidly to a large variety of buyers, from museums and big collectors to the friendly supporting group. However, the demands for continuing novelty are very wearing and often result in an early flurry and a later let-down both in the character of the work and in the size of the market. Withal it is healthy, but its dangers are great and its results sometimes unfortunate. The backbone of the whole activity remains the independent collector or buyer who exerts his own taste according to his own lights. As these lights vary so greatly, it means that the types of art purchased are as varied as possible in point of view and, more important, in quality.

The actual act of buying is much simpler these days than ever before. The surrounding world does not impinge so much. This is partly due to the character of what is collected—certainly no particular knowledge or advice is needed to buy nineteenth-century and contemporary work. It is like buying anything clearly marked, whether it be painting, line or food. The role of the art dealer has diminished. He is now only the merchant and the publicist—very rarely does he act as the expert and adviser. This diminution of function is due partly to the character of the dealers and partly to the lack of necessity of their earlier function in regard to the clarity of what is bought. No longer does the art-historian-expert hold great sway and power. The day of the expertise bound in morocco leather is over. Opinions are considered but only considered. Provenance and publication count largely: but let anything be printed in a book and it is believed beyond question. The art-historian-expert agent has little relation to collecting these days. So little, in fact, that the connexion between the buying and art-historical world is nearly non-existent. The art-historian lives in a group of his own, only inhabited by other art-historians. There are of course exceptions but these are usually in the capacity of advisers on contemporary art by art-historians whose scholastic field is quite far removed. The relation of the collector-buyer to the museum is quite another thing. This relation is made as close as possible by the wise museum man. He works at developing the collector, he does everything to foster his addiction in hope that the museum will benefit either immediately or later. Certain museum men now have the power that a Berenson once had and do not only advise but in certain cases control completely what goes into the collections under their influence. The critics have no power with the collectors or the buyers. They are read, admired, or disliked but in no way sway any purchasing proclivities. They are a help or a hindrance toward publicizing what they write about but generally perform only the function of a journalist. The best critics are the best journalists.

And what do people pay in New York? Almost the same as they pay in London or Paris. The days of great difference in price between the United States and Europe are over. In many cases prices are higher in Europe. The means of transportation are now so easy and so fast that buyers know what Paris and London prices are even before they buy in New York. This is largely due to the activity of English and European auction rooms and the publication of the prices at the sales. In America the auction room suffers from having less to offer and being less a day-by-day market of all kinds of work. It is less a custom for an American to view and attend and buy at sales than it is in either London or Paris.

The same confusion about a real sense of value pervades New York as in all the other great art markets and leads to a lack of comparative sense of the value of various kinds of paintings and objects. Here one finds one quite paradoxical fact which perhaps does not exist in Europe. It would seem that the American buyer prefers to pay a high price. The higher the price the surer he feels of the guarantee of the importance of the object of his choice. This is not only a result of the sense of confusion mentioned above but more deeply of a lack of knowledge about what real profound values are to each separate individual.

Taxes are a consideration in America in relation to collecting. In the United States one's collection is considered part of one's estate and is thus subject to inheritance tax on death. However, as most buying by Americans is done out of income and not out of capital, there has been considerable alleviation in a recent ruling by the tax authorities. This allows a collector to give at any time during his life, to a museum or tax-exempt institution, anything which he wants to give and which the institution will accept, and yet to retain a life interest in the object given and thus to have it on display in his collection for most of the time. This gift is then deductible from one's income tax at the date given and at a valuation set upon it by experts acknowledged as such by the tax authorities. This has been a great boon to the museum and institutional world and has stimulated both buying and giving. Vast sums are given to museums and institutions. These are tax deductible but the poor painter and sculptor are not: new buildings shoot up everywhere but little painting or sculpture is called for as part of that building.

And so, what of collecting in these days in the United States? Of activity and zest there is much; of cultivation there is little and of style there is less. Its values are its gargantuan movement, its continuing exchange of the actual objects, and the real fascination in exerts on the addicts. From it certainly comes a life in the art world that is vigorous, bold and valuable. From it all there will remain for time to come a really enduring statement of a few collectors, buyers and artists which will be the recognized symbol of our time.

Connoisseurship and Conservation

King George V, when opening its new building at Cambridge, called the university library 'a power-house of learning'. The phrase caught the fancy of many people who disliked that industrialized profile (not foreseeing the different kind of hideosity in store for Bodley), and it was widely quoted as an unexpected example of subtle architectural criticism. Whether the monarch really intended a *double entendre* may be doubted. That he was uttering a truism cannot be doubted; yet it is a truism still often ignored.

The dark rumblings of the creative imagination, the intoxicating ferment of the world of ideas, sometimes seem not merely remote from but positively antithetical to the quiet dust of county archives, the antiseptic atmosphere of the British Museum reading-room, or even the polished calm of the National Gallery of Art in Washington, D.C. Anybody, said William Blake, could be a good judge of pictures if he had not been connoisseured out of it. And if Mr. Mark Rothko might find himself ill at ease with Wincklemann or Ruskin, the admirers of Mr. Henry Miller or Mr. Tennessee Williams or Mr. Jack Kerouac would surely, though perhaps quite unjustifiably, maintain their heroes' unconditional freedom of any debt to Dr. Johnson or Matthew Arnold.

Philosophical and scientific ideas are, no doubt, in rather different case. Fresh sparks are still to be struck from Descartes and Newton. Thinkers can no more get away from the shadow of Aristotle or Einstein than economists from Adam Smith and Maynard Keynes, historians from Gibbon, or composers from Beethoven and (however much they may dislike it) Wagner. Nor, the conservators would say, is this merely a matter of printed words or diagrams in a current text-book. 'Even if modern editions', said Dr. R. W. Chapman, 'were adequate in the information they furnish—and notoriously they are not—they do not satisfy that Sense of the Past without which the study of literature and history is unimaginative and formal. That the student should have some access to originals is necessary for practical purposes, and necessary also for his spiritual health.' It is odd that this should still be a contention rather than an axiom to many people to whom it would never occur that an Arundel print could be any substitute for *Primavera* herself in Florence or the Wilton Diptych in London, or *La Grande Jatte* in Chicago.

The importance—indeed, the absolute necessity—of such spiritual protein for the nourishment of ideas, for the humanizing and fertilizing of the imagination, if it has not positively been more deliberately appreciated, has certainly been more vigorously acted upon in the United States than in the rest of the world during the present century. Alexis de Tocqueville, in 1832, was admittedly addressing himself to a single sector of the field when he wrote that

> in fifty years it will be more difficult to collect authentic documents concerning the social conditions of the Americans of the present day than it is to find remains of the administration of France during the Middle Ages; and if the United States were ever to be invaded by barbarians, it would be necessary to have recourse to the history of other nations in order to learn anything of the people that now inhabits them. . . . No methodical system is pursued; no archives are formed; and no documents are brought together when it would be easy to do so.

To-day Tocqueville might have something equally trenchant to say about the scale and volume of American acquisition, especially institutional acquisition, not just in the department of domestic history but in every department of the arts and sciences; from the Wright brothers' 'Kitty Hawk' in the Smithsonian and Cotswold villages transplanted to Michigan, *via The Blue Boy* at San Marino, California, to seventy-nine First Folios of Shakespeare in the Folger Library and the Malahide Papers at Yale. The enthusiasm, the energy, the organization and the money that the United States has expended on soil, seed and manure for the pastures of culture and scholarship have justly excited the wonder and envy, less justly sometimes the resentment, of countries whose already enormously rich endowment had naturally bred a more phlegmatic attitude to additions to it and, until fairly recently, to subtractions from it.

The pace and the scope of America's effort to catch up have often resulted in indiscriminate policies, sometimes in bull-dozer tactics; and these are more apt to be remembered by onlookers than the heightened, if usually belated, awareness of the importance of their own, often neglected, 'heritage of culture' which they owe to the forcible evidences of American enthusiasm. A man in a hurry will buy the bundle while he has the chance and sort out the contents later. The cost of trained sorting is frequently much higher than the price of the bundle. But he can afford it—and the whole bundle has been preserved. Many people to-day are understandably appalled at the increasing mass of bundles, each with its documentation, its catalogue cards, its capacity for breeding Ph.D. theses and notes in the learned journals, each of which in its turn demands another catalogue card and breeds more footnotes. They reflect that there is no record of Keats or Shelley studying in the North Library; they wonder whether Mr. Robert Frost, in Ripton, Vermont, or Mr. Ralph Hodgson, in Minerva, Ohio, writes any the worse for his long distance from the New York Public; they doubt, perhaps, whether St. Paul's and Groton subscribe to the belief enunciated by the most philosophic of Eton masters that 'the shadow of lost knowledge at least protects you from many illusions'.

It is true that in America—a country still frequently described as 'young', though its states were united a century before Germany's or Italy's—many of the inhabitants do suffer from illusions; and only a little less painful than a disillusionment of one's own is the spectacle of the disillusionment of a friend. Yet if some illusions—such as that Mr. Hemingway or Mr. Faulkner will one day write 'the great American novel'—seem inexplicably persistent, an illusion after all begins life as an aspiration or a dream. And a surprising number of American dreams have confounded the sceptics by coming true.

The furiously ambitious projects of the railroad builders, the industrialists, the financiers, the technicians, have had their counterpart in the field of scholarship and the humanities: not less effectively because the projectors were more often than not content to provide the tools with which others would work; and with a certain similarity of method inasmuch as many of them graduated from oil to Shakespeare or steel to Rembrandt, from banking to illuminated manuscripts or farm-machinery to Impressionist painting. The Du Pont chemical fortune lies behind the great museum of American furniture at Winterthur, Maryland. Andrew Mellon's princely benefaction of a National

Gallery was founded on steel and banking. Havemeyer's pictures in the Metropolitan Museum, New York, Folger's Shakespeares in Washington, J. Pierpont Morgan's incomparable library, are all monuments to the application of business resources and business methods to the enrichment of America's cultural life.

Department store millions have flowered into the Institute for Advanced Studies at Princeton and the Lessing Rosenwald collections of early prints and early illustrated books. Henry E. Huntingdon, the railroad tycoon, was determined that the West Coast should have a library of equal academic standing to the older foundations of the Eastern seaboard, fit to be named in the same breath as the Bodleian; and he achieved it. Thanks to the Palmers, the Ryersons, the Bartletts, the Winterbothams and the McCormicks, it was possible for the director of the Art Institute of Chicago, in response to a patronizing supposition that a roomful of Renoirs must have cost the institute a pretty penny, to put the visitor from New York in his place: 'In Chicago,' he said, 'we don't buy Renoirs: we inherit them from our grandmothers.' Of how many English (or for that matter, French) families could that be said?

Readers of Mrs. Saarinen's *The Proud Possessors* or Mr. S. N. Behrman's *Duveen* will be able to cite a certain amount of chapter and verse in support of the prevalent European theory that American collectors are not so much connoisseurs as accumulators. They will recall the remark inaccurately (but aptly) attributed to Mrs. Potter Palmer: 'People in our position are expected to own a Corot.' Even those who are aware of the extensive and liberal patronage extended by private people in the United States to contemporary painters, writers and artists of all sorts are all too prone to equate their motives with those of Lord Chesterfield. It was thought most enlightened of King's College, Cambridge, to make Mr. E. M. Forster a Fellow without imposing any duties on him beyond that of being himself. Yet it has been common practice for years in a score of American universities to make provision on the staff for a resident poet or a resident critic whose function is not to teach but to talk and write.

It has sometimes been suggested that connoisseurship and conservation policies in the United States are in danger of getting over-organized. If this is a valid criticism, the development may be attributable to two causes outside the jurisdiction of Parkinson's Law. The first is a proliferation and over-duplication of institutions themselves, academic and other (natural enough in so vast a country), and growing-pains among the younger ones. The second is the gradual but accelerating decrease in the number of private collectors of major stature. The former ill will cure itself in time. The latter sickness, from which Europe suffers equally, is probably mortal. Its roots are economic and political. In this country nobody (except perhaps the purchaser of the Duke of Westminster's Rubens) can begin to think of collecting on an eighteenth- or nineteenth-century scale. There are no more Ferdinand de Rothschilds, Samuel Courtaulds or Leicester Harmsworths, nor can be in any foreseeable future; while those families who have inherited collections from their forebears have to sell them to pay death duties. In the United States there are, certainly, plenty of men as rich in capital assets as the great collectors of the past. But, as has already been noted, under the present American tax structure the only way they can collect on the grand scale is by giving, or promising to bequeath, most of their acquisitions to an approved institution and writing the cost off their income tax each year as a charitable gift. This system, which is naturally envied by librarians and museum directors in this country, has short-term advantages which are visible to those who would like us to emulate it, and long-term disadvantages which are not. It is a godsend to conservators. But it is the death-knell for major connoisseurship.

The Printed Word

While printing and publishing ranks eighth among United States manufacturing industries, according to 1956 business statistics, a relatively small number of its 853,000 employees is engaged in the preparation and manufacture of books. The book industry consumes considerably less than 1 per cent of the national output of paper. The American spends less than one-fifth of 1 per cent of his national income on books and maps (lumped together, for some curious reason, in government statistics), a third as much as he does on magazines and newspapers. He spends four times as much, roughly, on keeping his radio and television set in repair, about the same amount as on cut flowers, seeds and plants. The majority of the workers in the printing trades produce magazines and newspapers, telephone directories, tickets and time-tables, advertising matter, packages, labels, forms—all that enormous stream of ephemera required to keep a highly industrialized society functioning. Like most American manufacturing industries, especially those dependent upon highly skilled labour organized into tight and powerful unions, the printing industry is increasingly preoccupied with research aimed at automation, the elimination of handwork, higher speeds and lower costs. Many new processes, methods, and materials are being tested or introduced for composition, printing and binding. There is an uneasy realization in the trade that the next few years will probably see changes even greater than those which followed the introduction of machine composition sixty-odd years ago.

The most spectacular recent advances in printing cannot be economically adapted to the small runs customary in the book trade. The block-long battery of presses and binding machines capable of turning out more than 55,000 copies of *Life* per hour, combining colour with black and white, all folded, stapled, even addressed and neatly sorted for the waiting mail cars, would take care of the demand for the most prodigious best-seller in an hour or two. The capital required to build these enormous and complicated machines is so great that they must be kept running almost around the clock if they are to meet schedules and be profitable. The book printing trade, made up of a large number of comparatively small plants, turning out unstandardized products, is neither large enough nor flexible enough to be able to afford these giants. Nevertheless, within that part of the printing industry producing books there is a tendency toward larger plants, with bigger, faster, and more costly equipment; there must be longer runs, with few interruptions for change from one job to another, if these are to pay. Consequently, while it is relatively cheap to print in the United States an edition of 50,000 or more copies, the publisher with a potential market of 500 copies, or even 5,000, finds the going hard. This means that the publisher of scholarly books, of highly specialized works, of *avant garde* literature with a limited appeal must find cheaper printing sources or methods, or he must depend upon subsidy from authors, patrons, or on his own purse to survive. Such publishers may have recourse to printing abroad, or to typewriter composition, to lower costs. The economics of constantly rising costs, and the resultant pressures to reduce them, have brought about a lowering of physical standards. Books in the United States are not, for the most part, as well made as they were twenty years ago.

There is intense competition for the book market between the offset printers, working with a photographically produced flat printing surface, and the letterpress printers, who use a relief surface from type and engravings. Comparatively few books, and those art books for the most part, are printed by the third important method, gravure, which utilizes an intaglio surface. The trend toward increased illustration, especially in children's books and school books, has given the offset printer notable advantages: he need not use expensive, heavily coated art papers when he prints pictures; it is easy for him to design and paste up elaborate lay-outs combining type and illustration; he saves by the elimination of engravings. Although the lithographers, supported by aggressive research and advertising programmes, have captured a considerable part of book printing, the bulk of American book printing is still done by letterpress. Letterpress printers have begun to imitate successfully many of the methods of their rivals, setting up their own publicity and research programmes. They have developed new metal and plastic plates which are durable throughout very long runs and have improved make-ready methods, cutting down markedly the time required to switch from one job to another. The new plates are to a great extent an outgrowth of the methods used in making offset plates.

Composition costs, which are fixed no matter how long the run, represent the smallest part of printing a large edition. They bulk high, however, in the production of small editions, especially if there are elaborate tables, footnotes, indexes, or other material difficult to set. The popularity of offset printing, which does not require the raised surface of metal type, has made possible the introduction of so-called 'cold type', which does not involve the casting of molten metal letters. The cold type methods include the preparation of copy on ordinary typewriters; on special typewriters which can produce the evenly justified lines to which readers are accustomed; and on special typewriter-like machines with a wide range of types based on conventional book faces, including italic and bold face, which the typographer needs for the design of a really efficient, let alone handsome, volume. None of these has yet won wide acceptance, partly because of reader and (more important) author resistance; partly because the more versatile machines are expensive and, in spite of their advertising claims, require skilled operators; partly because the letters with which they are fitted cannot as yet, because of the mechanical limitations of the machines, equal the types from which they were copied.

Another approach, the assembly and photography of individual characters directly upon a printing plate without any intermediate composing machine, has been a research goal for about a century. Vast sums have been spent on photo-composing machines, and every major manufacturer of composing-room equipment has announced or introduced some such machine. Nevertheless, almost all printing to-day still involves the use of actual metal type at some point in its production. The high initial cost of photocomposing machines, the difficulty of making corrections on film, the huge investment in existing plant—whatever the reason, photocomposition has not yet made the Linotype, Monotype, or even foundry type obsolete. Its greatest success has been in advertising and in books which combine small amounts of text with many illustrations.

Changes in binding methods have been fewer and slower than in other phases of book production; the most noticeable one has been the increased use of so-called 'perfect' binding (a classic misnomer), originally only used for paperbacks but now applied to many hard-bound books. It is a cheap method, since it eliminates sewing and relies on adhesives alone to hold together the trimmed sheets of the book. Librarians and others concerned with durability and permanence look upon it with considerable disquiet; printers and publishers, especially of school texts and other materials which rapidly become obsolete, are rather attracted by a book which is almost self-destroying. There have been changes in binding materials in an attempt to find cheaper substitutes for cotton binding cloths. Heavily coated paper, used during wartime scarcities, proved unsatisfactory; plastics, which are rapidly being improved, are winning favour. Printed cloth bindings are popular, especially for juveniles and text-books, many of them inspired by the highly successful covers of the better paperbacks. They eliminate the need for dust-jackets, which can represent a considerable outlay.

Unfortunately, the highest paid (and sometimes most gifted) talent for printing design in the United States is applied not to books but to advertising; moreover, printing budgets for advertising pieces are comparatively high, so that many of the handsomest pieces are seen only during a brief interval between the opening of the morning mail and their consignment to the waste-basket. The book designer in a large firm has little time to spend on any single book, and much of that time must be spent on the constant battle to keep costs down. There are some private presses and collectors' societies which publish handsome books without profit, as well as subscription ventures which make the publication of illustrated *de luxe* books pay; even the trade publishers put out an occasional book, usually heavily illustrated and aimed at the gift market, with which special pains have been taken. A survey of the recent 'Fifty Books of the Year' exhibitions of the American Institute of Graphic Arts, of that organization's exhibitions of children's books and text-books, or of the various regional shows held under local sponsorship will reinforce the belief that, on the whole, current American book design is not very revolutionary nor even very original. The double-spread title-page, sans serif types, and unorthodox margins of the new typography, frequently applied in a heavy-handed and doctrinaire fashion, are being succeeded in popularity by a new set of neo-Victorian and other romantic clichés.

Perhaps the most original work comes from California, where there are a number of individualistic designers, often their own printers; the Golden West also apparently has patrons willing to pay for putting out handsome books in small editions. Illustration is rarely found in trade books, being saved for limited editions, juveniles, and school-books. Generally, the freshest and most stimulating work is found among children's books, the most rational and best conceived design among the text-books and university press publications. School books are usually bought directly by the local school boards, who demand high manufacturing standards; printings of 50,000 or more copies allow a generous budget for design and production. The university presses, relieved of the necessity of making a profit and frequently assisted by subsidy, are still for the most part swayed by the idea that a good book represents a permanent addition to knowledge, and manufacture with that premise in mind; they consistently win a major share of the awards for good design and production. Many of the new lines of quality paperbacks, comparatively highly priced, are notable for the attractiveness of their covers, their intelligent design, and their decent printing.

The most interesting trend in publishing during the last decade has been the growth of the paperback trade, and especially the success of the quality series. One of the serious *lacunae* in the American book trade is the shortage of really first-class bookshops; there are probably fewer than 500 stores in the whole country whose major commodity is books, and almost no city in the whole country with under 100,000 residents can boast a satisfactory bookstore. The others rely primarily upon mail order (one reason for the great success of the book clubs) or the selection of paperbacks at the drugstore, supermarket, or bus station, which make it possible to build a decent, if impermanent, library for very little money. It is estimated that more than 233,000,000 copies were sold in 1957, as against 32,000,000 hard-bound adult trade books. Even though the greater number of the 6,000 titles listed as being in print last year consisted of light fiction, popular uplift, or how-to-do-it-books, there were also in the mass-market series many reprints of the classics, together with serious works on science, philosophy, history, politics, and art. From the higher-priced series, many of them inspired by the example of Penguin but now grown far more esoteric, the devotee of Existentialism or Zen, of Beckett or Genet, of the medieval Latin lyric or the New Criticism can fill his shelves.

These, sold primarily by bookstores, have scored particularly in college towns and other haunts of the egghead. Many books only moderately successful in hard covers at $4 and $5 have gone through several printings, each of about 20,000, in paperback editions. This correlation between price and sales is one which publishers are reluctant to face, however; nor has much been done to increase the sales of regular trade books by actively encouraging the establishment of new book-shops to make books more easily available.

Another notable increase in sales has been achieved by the encyclo-paedia and other subscription-book publishers. Aggressive (one is tempted to say ruthless) selling, constant revision, and the increased use of colour, illustration, and design techniques borrowed from the magazines are among the reasons for a 41 per cent increase in 1954 sales over those of 1947; government estimates show that in 1954 almost 26,000,000 copies of encyclopaedias and other subscription-books were sold for a total of $89,000,000, a sum second only to that paid for school books.

A favourite parlour game among publishers and other bookish people in recent years has been speculation about the effect of television upon book buying and reading. So far there has been little impact upon the book trade; it is the magazines and newspapers, badly hurt by higher costs, lower circulation, and lost advertising revenue, which have joined the film industry on the casualty lists. The publishers, not content with holding their own, have begun to work with teachers, librarians, and like groups in programmes aimed at interesting young people in reading and in building their own libraries.

The recent wave of criticism of the American educational system, a by-product of Sputnik and the cold war, has helped to make con-verts to the old-fashioned virtues, among which reading must be numbered. There is increasing awareness that ideas are important, and that many complex ideas are more effectively transmitted by the printed word than by a thousand pictures. There is also an increased interest in discovering bright children early in their school careers and encouraging them to make the most of their talents; not surprisingly, the ability to read rapidly and intelligently turns out to be one of the most reliable criteria. It seems likely that 1984 will find books still being printed, no matter how efficient the microfilm, the punch card, and the audio-visual device become, and that those books will not be too unlike the ones we read to-day.

Imaginative Historians

The American continent has entered deeply into the imagination of its peoples. The land itself, in its immense scale, with geographical regions differing from one another as Spain from Norway, with the hardship, adventure and experience of discovery that it presented to its multitudinous settlers, has often tempted the imaginative American writer to turn historian. The larger themes of American history, the Revolution, the migrations of peoples, the spread of democracy, the conflicts of sections verging into separate nationhood and leading to civil war—these, and many others, retain a relevance, an immediacy which has attracted writers other than professional historians and which still does much to sustain, even to justify, the interest of Americans in their history. More than this; the historian in his study has also heard the call of the wild, or at least of the market, and in recent years has made it his business to reach out to those readers who are thought more likely to respond to stimulation than to instruction.

Much, therefore, of American historical writing has come to be of a genre which, in flavour characteristically American, is at its best truly imaginative, at its worst sentimentally popular, and in some instances, to use the words of Mr. Alfred Doolittle when told by Higgins that he was either an honest man or a scoundrel, 'a little of both, Henry, like the rest of us, a little of both.' A recurrent criterion for both the purposes and methods of such writing is that of a kind of contemporary significance, or immediacy; a concern with national self-discovery has made much of it in a sense introspective; while the writers differ from one another in style according to their own qualities and that of the public they strive to reach. These works are in large measure a reflection, and in quality a widely varied reflection, of the meaning of history to American readers.

The themes chosen and positions taken often reflect another distinctive attitude, that of engagement. To put it crudely, American historians are always taking sides about the past in ways dictated by their commitments in the present. They have taken sides over Hamilton and Jefferson, over the character and intentions of the framers of the Constitution, over judicial review, over racial questions, and, of course, over the Civil War and Reconstruction. Among contemporaries, Arthur M. Schlesinger Jr.'s early *tour de force*, *The Age of Jackson*, which did much to establish the distinctive historical identity of that epoch, was criticized on the ground that it tried to force on its material an unhistorical parallel between Jacksonian reform and that of the New Deal; and without doubt it owed some of its inspiration to the interest which has, in fact, subsequently led Mr. Schlesinger to attempt a full literary portrait of *The Age of Franklin Roosevelt*. There is little in English historical writing to compare with this tendency. The commitment of the chroniclers of labour, the Hammonds and Coles perhaps comes closest; but the gentle stream of Whig history, dimpled occasionally by differences of opinion about the intentions of George III or the fortunes of the gentry, provides no comparison to the partisan torrents which, in America, have been thrown against the earthworks of opposing social orders. In France, where so much history has been written to maintain the divisive traditions of the past, where the Revolution, the Terror, Napoleon, the Second Empire, monarchy against republic, authority against provincialism have been kept alive, the engagement of American historians might be the more easily grasped.

History thus approached is doing more than living in the imagination. It is being made to fulfil an unhistorical purpose, which may lend vitality to the writing but has also vitiated much of the history. It would be a mistake, however, in discussing the historical imagination, to overlook the importance in America of the concept of relevance. A lay scepticism of the activities of the intellect, something of which American intellectuals are almost morbidly conscious, is always most readily appeased by some form of appeal to principles of utility; this type of appeal is commonly made by professors justifying history courses to sceptical undergraduates. The proposition that history helps us to understand the present, and is therefore useful in shaping decisions, is generally felt to give the subject an air of respectability. (It is noticeable, in this connexion, how many American students like to apply themselves to recent history; they generally prefer to write papers and essays on topics falling within their own or their parents' lifetimes.) And even the more remote past, particularly the American past, is constantly judged in terms of its relevance to the present. If justification by works appears in the narrow criterion of utility, justi-fication by faith is found in the broader criterion of immediacy. It is often in this sense that the past, whether or not it is made to enlist in some specific contemporary cause, has seemed important enough to be worth preserving.

All history, being part of man's knowledge of himself, may be con-sidered as a form of introspection; and a great deal of American histori-cal writing is marked by introspection in a particularly judging form. Through the voluminous writings on revolution, constitution-making, on popular government, slavery, civil war, reconstruction and reform, one may catch glimpses of the present and the past watching each other warily as from opposite boxes at the opera, each suspecting the other of being about to commit a *faux pas*. Americans in the Revolu-tion discovered a common purpose before they discovered a common identity; and since Crèvecoeur's question, 'What is the American, this new man?' history has played a natural part in the quest for the elements of national identity.

After the Revolution, in the course of little more than a century, the Americans discovered and settled a continent, and it was only in the process of doing so that they made a nation—very nearly, in fact, made two nations. It is therefore not difficult to understand why Turner, writing at the end of the settlement period, should have made so vivid an impression. Nor is Turner out of place in the present con-text. Admittedly, as a professional historian, he addressed his paper of 1893 on the Frontier to his academic colleagues. True also that his thesis, which attempted to explain the major factors in American in-stitutional development in terms of the settlement of the frontier of free land and the influence of geographical sections, was exposed to radical criticism; but Turner had achieved something of an imagin-native order, and no doubt he knew it. For he had caught a glimpse of the whole continent, held up in its segments and colours in a unity that comprehended past and present in one picture, in a literary replica of the fashion that seemed so natural to artists before the decay of the Middle Ages. If his viewpoint was arbitrary, the view itself was panoramic. His Frontier paper was an epic in a prose which only a professionally trained historian could read without excitement.

Turner's vision was a particularly gratifying answer to the quest, through history, for an American identity and for American principles. For he purported to explain not only institutions but national character. His view, thus, was at once expansive and introspective; and the fact that he himself was already beginning to worry about the future did not prevent his followers from catching a note of self-congratulation about the past.

The American experience differed in each section; the benefits were not evenly distributed. But distinct from all the rest was the experience of the South; distinct—and giving rise, in defeat, to the most intensely introspective moods of all. The Old South had barely ceased to exist when it began to blossom in legend and in apologia, a mood which was fostered by Northerners uneasy about the terms of their victory. For generations it proved difficult to cut through the undergrowth of myth and sentimentality. Southern life (seen mainly from the viewpoint of the great plantations), the Southern constitutional argument, the course of Southern politics, the growth of a minority consciousness—all these were the subject of innumerable disquisitions, historical, tragical, comical and pastoral. But it was a Carolinian journalist, the late W. J. Cash, who, some twenty years ago, produced the boldest and most persuasive interpretation of the distinctively Southern experience. *The Mind of the South* is not a history of ideas; it is rather an evocation of the mind, a re-creation of the personality, by which Southern ideas came to be worked out, Southern attitudes assumed. He is at his best on the Old South, and this is American imaginative historical writing at its most brilliant.

The work is steeped in an almost sensual appreciation of the interplay of factors natural and human, of the workings of climate on man, of the social order upon the individual, and of the growth of a sectional, and peculiar, psychology, affecting even those who dissented. In spirit the work is impressionistic; but it is an impressionism directed by deep reading, and by the intimacy of personal experience, and controlled by an incisive historical judgment. The long, rhythmical sentences are full of power. Again, this work is essentially introspective; the past which it brings so vividly to life is part of the present; and, finally, it is not so much an examination of historical events as of historical states of mind.

This last point is one of the clues to contemporary developments in the imaginative field, embracing widely differing themes. Professor Handlin's *The Uprooted,* for example, treats of the experience of the immigrants of the later nineteenth century; leaving the more common topic of 'Americanization', it reminds the reader forcibly of the terrific problems of the individual migrant, of the first generation. Not all his stylistic devices are entirely felicitous; that of suggesting highly personal problems by introducing the intimate thoughts of figures who remain merely symbolic shadows does not work without embarrassment. But it is a work which, though grounded in a deep reading of sources, derives its force from a sympathetic imagination.

The leading contemporary influence is that of Professor Richard Hofstadter, who has very largely created his own style. His striking interpretation of the Progressive era, *The Age of Reform,* though of unmistakable originality, has, however, certain characteristics of genre. It is essentially a re-creation of states of mind rather than an exposition of events. But (as also in Professor Vann Woodward's wonderful biography of Tom Watson) it achieves this through a deep and perceptive analysis of the social and economic circumstances in which ideas and attitudes developed. Hofstadter's influence can be seen in a still more recent work, *The Jacksonian Persuasion,* by Marvin Meyers. This book does not set out to say why people voted for Jackson, but to capture the moods of Jackson's very diverse supporters; though more academic than the others mentioned, it is strikingly successful in what is essentially a venture in the same genre.

The works of this order vary enormously in quality, scope and purpose; but they have come to represent a strong, perhaps a dominant strain in the more imaginative historical writing of the United States. It is not far-fetched to say that, though lesser in scale, they belong to the school represented at its most brilliant in Europe by Paul Hazard. It may be called the school of documented impressionism.

This school is comparatively new. Not entirely so, for Turner clearly has certain qualifications for it. As a concept of history, it involves difficult problems of style, which have been satisfactorily solved by only a few. The older writers were generally content to appeal to the intrinsic drama of events, described in a spare but fluent prose. Even so vigorous a hand as Claude Bowers adorned his story with little of simile or metaphor. Behind such men one feels the assurance of a solid education in the classics of the language and, what is more, of a readership of similar qualifications. But in quite recent years this assurance seems to have crumbled away. It has not been sufficiently appreciated that when the historian departs from analysis and narrative to venture on the exciting task of re-creating past experience, of capturing mood and social climate, he needs gifts of an unusual literary order. And when the imaginative historian does not command the sheer literary power of a Hofstadter or a Cash, he tends too often to get his ideas of readability from the adjectival cauldron of *Time* magazine. And this degeneration in stylistic taste is not at all accidentally accompanied by a degeneration in the sense of historical proportion. Past and present, instead of illuminating each other, get mixed up, and the historian, becoming a mere commentator, tends to mistake himself for a seer. Immediacy, so often too freely invoked, is called in to provide an almost glamorous vindication for this departure.

Behind this facile descent into a kind of literary Jacksonian democracy one may suspect a degeneration of basic education in English and American literature. The prose of Addison, Gibbon, Macaulay, of Tom Paine, Hamilton, Madison, Emerson and Thoreau seems either never to have been read or, if read, to have made no impression. The classics have lost their immediacy. This is not to suggest that eloquent, even lyrical prose must necessarily be unsuitable as a medium for history—far from it. What is utterly deplorable is the feverish attempt to communicate seriously held opinions about matters of serious consequence in a vogue copied from the bright but tasteless vivacity of the weekly news magazines; or even the glossier advertisements. Imagery, pressed into this service, loses its force; it is to be noticed that this type of writing tends to use images loosely, without care for their meaning. Their function is to arouse expectation or a sense of glamour rather than to make the author's meaning either more vivid or more precise. Such methods constantly betray their weaknesses in what Dr. Leavis would call a series of tropes.

One may cite as a case in point the extraordinary incongruousness of the new verb 'to mushroom' when used of the growth of (say) the steel industry; but examples are so numerous that selection becomes arbitrary. One of this school, in a book that was widely praised for its stylistic resourcefulness, warns us of the danger of conflict between East and West in 'a hail of atomic weapons'. The feebleness of this image is too obvious to call for anything more than a large blue pencil mark in a school exercise book. But how many exercise books are so marked under the current dispensation of latitudinarian education?—a serious question, in the light of the fact that books packed with this kind of brash exuberance are seldom criticized by reviewers on grounds of style; and indeed are often praised.

The Civil War histories of Mr. Bruce Catton, of which *This Hallowed Ground* may well be the most popular of all recent imaginative history, are not strictly works of documented impressionism, historical introspection, or journalistic enthusiasm. Mr. Catton possesses a masterly gift of narrative and command of complex events: he can march whole armies under the reader's eye while holding his attention and keeping the map clear. His humanity enables him to bring to his work a sense of the suffering of individuals. The more the pity that when he pauses from his enthralling narrative for a moment of solemn reflection his vivid colours quickly melt into a purple that is not royal but merely sentimental. Thus, in a reference to Lincoln's second inaugural (interjected into an account of events in 1861) he can write:

> Nearly four years later, when he was just five weeks away from the casket with the bronze handles, the echoing capitol dome above, the blue-coated soldiers standing with sober and disciplined unease in the flickering purple twilight, Abraham Lincoln tried to sum it up.

The author's thoughts are here so choked with the echoing dome in the purple twilight that the hasty reader might almost imagine Lincoln delivering his second inaugural from the coffin. Elsewhere Mr. Catton speaks of Benjamin Butler 'grinning sardonically with eyes that did not mesh'. No doubt the image is meant to revolt; but the verb 'to mesh' applies to machinery, and is hopelessly incongruous in this context, as well as being even technically inept. Does Mr. Catton think that normal eyes 'mesh'? One hopes not. Mr. Catton has been rightly praised for his brilliant gifts (let any sceptic read his account of the battle of Gettysburg!) But it is not a little disturbing that neither he nor, apparently, his critics seem able to tell the wheat from the chaff.

The vogue of news magazine history reflects two separate trends: a conscious drive to hit the best-seller lists, and an indifference to literary precision in both writers and readers. The older generation give the impression of sharing with an identifiable body of readers the fundamentals of English literature; but the contemporary school of adjective-packers seem to lack this assurance. They give a different impression, rather that of shouting for the attention of the crowds who drift in and out of the drug stores; of competing with television with its perniciously limited demands on the attention. They even lack confidence in the innate power of the words they use, and are driven to bolster their overworked and enfeebled nouns with adjectives until they resemble the victims of ancient medical practitioners, drained of blood and bunched up with pillows.

The best in the imaginative style of historical writing is being done in America today. So is the worst. They rub along side by side, often on the same shelves, without even threatening each other's popularity. It is, after all, a pluralistic society.